AF479009

The Matter Within

NEW CONTEMPORARY ART OF INDIA

Within

Contents

Foreword

A little more than two years ago, the Asian Art Museum of San Francisco approached us about the possibility of creating a complementary contemporary exhibition to *Maharaja: The Splendor of India's Royal Courts*, which would be on tour from the Victoria and Albert Museum in London. Knowing that contemporary art from India is still relatively unknown locally, and that it had not yet received a serious museum examination in the Bay Area, we were excited to collaborate with this excellent institution and to present a carefully curated look at recent art from India. *The Matter Within: New Contemporary Art of India* is the result of that effort and in every way accomplishes what we set out to do, unveiling fresh insights into this growing body of important work.

Over the past few years, as global attention and interest has shifted to the exponentially growing economies and powers of China and India, several contemporary Indian art exhibitions have begun to appear in the West. Contemporary art from China has, of course, already made an important impact in the art world and has been extensively exhibited. Not so with India, and the exhibitions that have appeared have been largely ethnographic in nature, curated around an idea of "Indianness" that serves to isolate and even exoticize art from the region. This challenge of disrupting this paradigm is what we sought to take on as we began to think about this exhibition. We wanted to look deeper.

The Matter Within: New Contemporary Art of India focuses on three different media: sculpture, photography, and video. After extensive research in India as well as Europe and the United States, important locations of the Indian diaspora, YBCA director of visual arts Betti-Sue Hertz decided to focus the exhibition around three themes, as well: embodiment, the imaginary, and the politics of communicative bodies. These ideas seem embedded in the work of many contemporary artists of Indian descent, regardless of where they live. In an art historical context, it seemed important to look at the work through these lenses.

From this focus emerges a picture of contemporary art from India that extends well beyond the geographic and into the world of ideas; this is the core of YBCA's mission as an institution, and it is also fundamental for many of these artists. Our hope is to shift some of the predominant narratives about this work and inspire future exhibitions that also take evocative approaches.

As is always the case, pulling together the resources for an exhibition of this quality is a Herculean task. YBCA is grateful to so many people for their help in making it happen, especially our organizing committee, a small group of passionate supporters. Under the leadership of former board member Priya H. Kamani and with the leadership assistance of Rena Bransten and Peter Bransten, this key group helped raise the funds for the exhibition and this catalogue. We are grateful to all of them for their great work and wonderful energy.

Both Betti-Sue Hertz and I made research trips to India to meet and talk with artists. The enthusiasm with which they greeted us and their support for the ideas behind the show were extraordinary and helped move along the process of producing the exhibition and the catalogue. Special thanks to Sakshi Gallery in Mumbai for organizing a reception and to Indrapramit Roy at Maharaja Sayajirao University in Baroda, one of India's premier art schools, for introducing us to many of the young artists who are revolutionizing contemporary art in India.

YBCA is proud to support the documentation of this important exhibition through this catalogue.

KENNETH J. FOSTER | *Executive Director*

Acknowledgments

An exhibition and accompanying catalogue of this scope would not have been possible without the kind help and support of a great number of people. We are extremely indebted to all of them.

The exhibition *The Matter Within: New Contemporary Art of India* and its accompanying catalogue represent the close collaborations of many gifted colleagues: at Yerba Buena Center for the Arts; in our San Francisco community; and in our extended community in India, Europe, and New York. International projects are particularly challenging, and I owe much to our visionary executive director, Kenneth J. Foster, for so enthusiastically embracing an undertaking of this scale, scope, and depth from the earliest formation of the concepts and ideas. Former board member Priya H. Kamani inspired me to take a deep breath as I embarked on the important and challenging effort to bring contemporary art from India to San Francisco. Her generosity and willingness to introduce me to her friends, colleagues, and family in India was crucial to the success of the exhibition. Board member Raman Frey was also very supportive and every so often gave me that extra boost when I was feeling overwhelmed by the project. I am tremendously grateful to my YBCA colleagues Scott Rowitz, managing director, Charles Ward, senior director of external affairs, and Kathy Budas, senior director of marketing and communications, all of whom bring their enthusiasm and vision to our visual arts programming to ensure its success. I am also especially grateful to Namrata Gupta, director of individual giving, who wholeheartedly supported the project. All of these leaders and their staff provided us with the ardent support we needed to secure funds and promote the exhibition to a large and diverse public. I duly acknowledge the truly talented staff of the visual arts department for their professionalism and insights as well as their willingness to go the extra mile so that every detail and nuance of the exhibition, research, and production were of the highest quality. Many thanks to Thien Lam, visual arts curatorial assistant, whose dedication,

insightful texts, and general administrative, editorial, and research skills were welcome contributions to the completion of this project. Julio César Morales, visual arts adjunct curator, continually provides refreshing perspectives on our curatorial work. I am especially grateful to Amy Owen, our senior exhibitions manager, who, with grace, unflaggingly keeps everything and everybody on track, and to Gabriel Harrison, our wonderful exhibition designer, for helping us realize the best possible exhibition plan. Patrick Gillespie, senior preparator, excellently assists in the management of our installations, leading teams through the production of exhibition components. We are grateful for the fine production of graphics by Amanda Boesen. Thank you to Jon Sueda of Stripe SF for his unending ingenuity in graphic design and identity for the exhibition and, importantly, the design of this exhibition catalogue.

Our former interim registrar Sarah Loudin enthusiastically managed the incoming loan process for this object-laden exhibition with complicated shipments from India, the East Coast of the United States, and Europe, along with Tara Hadibrata, former assistant registrar. Our registrar Anne Marie Purkey Levine and assistant registrar Rebecca Silberman skillfully managed the return of the objects to their owners. Facilities manager Tony Pellegrini and his team were always invaluable in assisting us with our building needs, and Nick Colin, community engagement program manager, and the team of gallery guides provided visitors with many opportunities to better understand the central thesis of the exhibition. I would also like to acknowledge the many interns and volunteers who did research for the project and assisted in various ways: Maria Nicolacopoulou, Samira Rahmatullah, Cho Rao, and Sheetal Varma were invaluable, each willing to contribute their skills and enthusiasm to the project. I am especially grateful to Ms. Rao for personally making contact with so many of her friends and colleagues in India with whom she had worked in the past, and providing us with introductions to artists, writers, and art dealers to ensure the success of the exhibition.

This exhibition came into being, in part, as a response to an invitation by Jason Xu, executive director of the Asian Art Museum of San Francisco, and Forrest McGill, that museum's chief curator, to create an exhibition of contemporary art of India that would be on view at the same time as their presentation of *Maharaja: The Splendor of India's Royal Courts*. It was a pleasure for us to bring our project to fruition to coincide with that important historical exhibition. I am especially grateful to my museum curator colleagues Sonya Rhie Quintanilla and Qamar Adamjee, who specialize in South Asian art, for sharing their expertise and wisdom with me and also guiding me through the literature on Indian art history.

We are very grateful to all of the individuals at the galleries and foundations who assisted us with loans or loaned works to the exhibition, including Vincent Worms and Alex Matson at Kadist Art Foundation, San Francisco; Rebecca Davis and Sadia Rehman at Bose Pacia, New York; Mortimer Chatterjee and Tara Lal at Chatterjee & Lal, Mumbai; Devi Art Foundation, New Delhi; Dominique Fiat, Paris; Frith Street Gallery, London; Peter Nagy and Rajeev Dhawan at Gallery Nature Morte, New Delhi; Sunitha Kumar Emmart and Aarthie Sridhar at GallerySKE, Bangalore; Nicolas Nahab and Valentina Labroue at Galerie Yvon Lambert, Paris; Gen Watanabe at Haunch of Venison, New York; Latitude 28, New Delhi; Adam Jones at LUX, London; Galerie Nathalie Obadia, Paris and Brussels; Sree Goswami at Project 88, Mumbai; and Parul Vadehra at Vadehra Art Gallery, New Delhi. Devika Daulet-Singh's important work in this field at Photoink, New Delhi, inspired me to give photography an important role in *The Matter Within*. We also thank Edward Nahem in New York and Harris Legome in Philadelphia, who loaned works from their personal collections to the exhibition.

During my research trip to India I met with numerous people in the art world and beyond who shared their time and wisdom with me, enriched my experience, and gave me insight into the culture and art of India. I want to especially thank, in New Delhi, Gopika Chowfla for guiding my efforts in that city before my arrival, and the artists Ranbir Kaleka and Rashmi Kaleka, who were very kind to spend their valuable time sharing their enthusiasm for art throughout the city. I am also grateful to the artists Bharti Kher, Amar Kanwar, Ajay Desai, Rishi Singhal, Anita Khemka, Sheba Chhachhi, Sakshi Gupta, and Ravi Agarwal for sharing their vision and insights with me. Brian DeMuro and Puru Das took me to the first contemporary dance festival to take place in New Delhi. It was an honor to meet with Pooja Sood, the executive director of Khoj International Artists' Association, an organization that has been instrumental in giving support and encouragement to many of the artists in this exhibition at earlier points in their careers. In Mumbai, Vaishali Kamani and Saurine Doshi graciously hosted me in their home during my stay. Susan Hapgood, a friend and a curator, generously shared her time and enthusiasm as we toured the city's art galleries. Shireen Gandhy of Chemould Gallery and Matthieu Fosse at his photography gallery were kind enough to provide me with new insights into many wonderful contemporary artists in the region. I also want to thank the artists Jitish Kallat, Reena Kallat, and Brinda Chudasama Miller for sharing their work and perspectives on the local art scene. In Bangalore I was very much guided by GallerySKE and my personal friend Ayisha Abraham to a better understanding of the art scene in that city. I also thank the artists Kiran Subbaiah, Krishnaraj Chonat, Srinivasa Prasad, and Sheela Gowda for sharing their work and thoughts. In New York I learned much from visiting with the artists Chitra Ganesh and Shelly Bahl.

I would like to acknowledge the enormous contributions made by our generous donors, who believed in our ambitious ideas and supported them wholeheartedly.

Following Priya H. Kamani's initial support and belief in this project, Rena Bransten and Peter and Leela De Souza Bransten took up the torch and hosted two events at their homes to encourage others to stand with this effort. We are very grateful to everyone who joined in, including Samira Rahmatullah and Munir Alam, Sanjeev and Kathy Malaney, Rekha Patel-Grosvenor, Raj and Krutika Patel, Girish Satya and Purvi Sangani, Sheila and Ketan Kothari, Rajnikant T. and Helen C. Desai, Christopher Stafford and Eduardo Barbosa, Diana Cohn and Craig Merrilees, Berit Ashla and Aron Cramer, Brooke and Steve Waterhouse, Sabrina Riddle, Petra Schumann and Rob Wullenjohn, Ashish and Namrata Gupta, and Monica and Steve Henderson.

We also thank the Asian Cultural Council for supporting artists who traveled to San Francisco for the installation and to participate in the public programs.

Additionally, I would like to thank the participants in our public programs associated with this exhibition. The art historian Santhi Kavuri-Bauer and the artists Allan DeSouza, Sreshta Rit Premnath, and Anjalika Sagar and Kodwo Eshun of the The Otolith Group participated in Seeing Distance: Lens-Based Practices in Contemporary Indian Art, a component of the symposium titled Making India Visible at Stanford's Center for South Asia. It was a pleasure to collaborate with the Center's director, Thomas Blom Hansen, and associate director, Sangeeta Mediratta, on this program. YBCA hosted an evening of two panel discussions titled Trading Ideas: Emerging Discourses on Asian Contemporary Art, organized in collaboration with the Asian Contemporary Arts Consortium. ACAC's director, Xiaoyu Weng, and I organized the program, which included the following distinguished speakers: Melissa Chiu, Vishakha Desai, Apsara DiQuinzio, Britta Erickson, Santhi Kavuri-Bauer, Joan Kee, Carol Yinghua Lu, Tasneem Zakaria Mehta, and Xie Xiaoze.

Our deep thanks go to our contributing essayists to this publication, Nancy Adajania, Parul Dave Mukherji, and Zehra Jumabhoy, for sharing their knowledge and enthusiasm through their thought-provoking and insightful essays. Their contributions to this publication and to the field of contemporary Indian art in general are making a profound impact on our understanding of the importance of the art of South Asia. I am also indebted to our entry writers who contributed new ideas to the work presented in the exhibition. They are Maya Kóvskaya, Georgina Maddox, Samira Rahmatullah, and Thien Lam.

It is with the deepest gratitude that I thank the talented artists who, despite relentless work schedules, gave time generously and participated enthusiastically in the exhibition. They are Ayisha Abraham; Rina Banerjee; Shaina Anand and Ashok Sukumaran of CAMP; Nikhil Chopra; Anita Dube; Gauri Gill; Shilpa Gupta; Sunil Gupta; Siddhartha Kararwal; Dhruv Malhotra; Anjalika Sagar and Kodwo Eshun of the Otolith Group; Sreshta Rit Premnath; Pushpamala N.; Jeebesh Bagchi, Monica Narula, and Shuddhabrata Sengupta of Raqs Media Collective; Tejal Shah; Sudarshan Shetty; Bharat Sikka; Anup Mathew Thomas; and Jiten Thukral and Sumir Tagra of Thukral & Tagra.

I am so thankful to everyone I've mentioned here for believing in *The Matter Within: New Contemporary Art of India,* oftentimes before anyone knew what its final form would look like. It is an honor and a pleasure to be included in this extensive community of people who care deeply about contemporary art and its important role in understanding culture as well as the individual artists' dreams, experiences, and commentary on the world around them.

BETTI-SUE HERTZ | *Director of Visual Arts*

Fragments of India: With Thought, Feeling, and Emotion

Betti-Sue Hertz

India presents itself as a country with a long and embattled history of political upheavals instigated from within and without; unequal power dynamics among myriad cultures, linguistic groups, and spiritual sectors; and, in recent decades, dramatically accelerated economic growth. Needless to say, these scenarios make for a widely varied citizenry and social landscape in a country that is already vast in terms of its geography and history. We may think we're familiar with India: from what's reported in American news outlets, from the cuisine, from our constant exchange with its burgeoning tech cities, and of course from Bollywood. But there is much about India that escapes the scope of mainstream culture and communications media. Through the works of nineteen artists and artist groups, *The Matter Within: New Contemporary Art of India* gives significant attention to the microcultures, counternarratives, off-site dramas, and transhistorical messages that have been left out of the dominant stories about contemporary India. Many of these artists are making vital contributions to our understanding of life there; others are operating more abstractly, thinking about the country's historical and cultural legacies. All are aesthetically inventive as they probe social, political, and economic conditions, and the effects of these conditions on various populations. Whether they are working with ideas that are highly personal or representative of large populations, they demonstrate a deep awareness of what matters from an Indian perspective. They are navigating complex routes between past and present, fact and fiction, and new and old identities, against a backdrop of tremendous societal flux.

As India assumes an increasingly important role on the world economic stage, the work of its artists becomes ever more widely acknowledged as a vehicle for expressing aspects of its culture that are difficult to convey outside the realm of the aesthetic. This exhibition hopes to further this potential by contributing to a better and deeper understanding of current shifts, their emotional, intellectual, and spiritual effects, and their potential to represent new desires. *The Matter Within* is a fragment made up of voices from various subject positions in relation to India as a place and as an idea. While some of the works in the exhibition are documentary in nature, others blur reality and fiction, and yet others take a more speculative turn, often hinging on a historical record or archive.

The Matter Within includes works in sculpture, photography, and experimental video. These intersect with a triad of conceptual threads—embodiment, the politics of communicative bodies, and the imaginary—that form the central thesis of the exhibition. I first came across each of these concepts in seminal scholarly texts by writers deeply invested in conceptual understandings of the flows of cultural production in and about India. The reference to embodiment is taken from Meenakshi Thapan's feminist sociology. Thapan writes, "Embodiment is experience in our everyday lives as lived and communicative bodies."[1] I find this idea intriguing, as it places embodiment, a concept with deep roots in Indian art, into the context of the everyday lives of women. The "communicative bodies" Thapan references are not symbolic or archetypal, but lived and marked by the challenges of daily life. Political history and social mores put pressure on the bodies of individuals, which are literally shaped by circumstance. Specific identities emerge from those external conditions.

To explore the ways that individual bodies can come to represent subcultures in transition, I also turned to Geeta Kapur's discussion of sensuality and perception in relation to material culture. She writes, "Indian thought is imbued with a deeply sensuous, therefore empirical perception of the given world (the very concept of immanence, basic to the mythic imagination, implies that the meaning of the universe dwells in the phenomenal world and that no transcendent categories need be brought into the picture), and this is quite apart from the fact that even materialism as such is in no way alien to Indian philosophy."[2] For Kapur, even the mythic imagination depends on the things around us that amplify sensory experience.

The third concept figuring in *The Matter Within* is the role played by the imaginary in the manufacturing of identities, often from a negotiation of what is real and what is conjured up mentally to augment gaps in cognitive reconciliation with emotion and the psyche.[3] In contemporary global terms, the gaps and fissures of the imaginary have been mined as creative sites of invention and reclamation for the ownership of the image itself. Initially, I considered three different variants of the term "the imaginary." The first involved ancient religious narratives whose secular corollaries in fables, tales, and pictorial storytelling are told through the lives and adventures of elaborately depicted deities, hybrid human/animal mythological forms, and fantastical beings or characters. As the architecture writer, satirist, and graphic novelist Gautum Bhatia suggests, "It often happens that you write an exaggeration of a real situation, thinking it is so absurd and it would never happen; then you read something similar in the newspaper within a few days. There is a very thin line between the real and the imaginary in India."[4]

"The imaginary" is also a significant term within the lexicon of postcolonial theory and has had a major influence on Indian cultural intellectual thought in both domestic and diasporic scenarios. The sociocultural anthropologist Arjun Appadurai emphasizes the potential and possibility of slippages and misreadings when considering "the other" in situations of unequal power relations, whether through ignorance or as a strategic tool of domination. He writes, "The imagination has become an organized field of social practices, a form of work (in the sense of both labor and culturally organized practice), and a form of negotiation between sites of agency (individuals) and globally defined fields of possibilities."[5] The imaginary surfaces in discussions related to literature (for instance Salman Rushdie's book *Imaginary Homelands: Essays and Criticism 1981–1991*) and politics (Sudipta Kaviraj's 2010 book *The Imaginary Institution of India: Politics and Ideas*) in such a way as to suggest that it is a term so commonly used to describe things Indian that it doesn't require explanation.

The third and most recent definition of "the imaginary" is as a pragmatic term for conceiving and promoting "Future India" in the public sphere. This India of the future conveniently conjures notions of progress and prosperity. It functions as a marketing slogan to convince both striving individuals and foreign governments that a better life is imminent, especially if the populace participates wholeheartedly in capitalism and corporate enterprises. It also promotes India as an emerging global superpower. In all three versions, "the imaginary" serves as shorthand for envisioning a condition, or signaling a form, that is soon to take a more complex version.

Of the works in the exhibition, Rina Banerjee's sculpture may best exemplify the convergence of all of these imaginaries. Banerjee disperses the solidity of the human or animal form so that it becomes a host for the parasites of material culture—specifically objects of trade stemming from colonial times. Cowrie shells trigger memories of African and Indian trade, for example. Tchotchkes from tourist travel attach themselves to a three hundred-year-old turtle shell. In this reading of her work, the remnants of the glory of the past must reconcile themselves with the

---

1.
A larger excerpt from this passage: "We exist through our bodies and the *materiality* of our existence is a certainty. We are embodied socially through our location in a sociocultural and political space. In this sense, we are located in time and space, race, ethnicity and gender, and history and culture, which shape and limit us in different ways. Our embodiment is therefore experience in our everyday lives as lived and communicative bodies. . . . In foregrounding this subjectivity, it is important to refrain from providing anecdotal accounts or personal narratives that do not in some way reflect subjectivity in the social so that it is an engagement with the social that is the bedrock of lived experience." Meenakshi Thapan, *Living the Body: Embodiment, Womanhood, and Identity in Contemporary India* (New Delhi: Sage Publications Pct. Ltd., 2009): 3.

2.
Geeta Kapur, "Partisan Views About the Human Figure" in the exhibition catalogue *Place for People* (Bombay: Jehangir Art Gallery; New Delhi: Rabindra Bhavan, 1981): n.p.

3.
My understanding of the imaginary in the postcolonial sense is that it requires a spatial or temporal distance from the subject under consideration. Of the artists in the exhibition, it seems to me that those who are not living in India are more engaged with this concept, as they have a less literal and embodied critique of the misunderstandings of India that were propagated by the British during their rule.

4.
"Line Between Real and Imaginary Is Thin, Says Satirist Gautam Bhatia," *Daily News & Analysis*, April 11, 2010, http://www.dnaindia.com/opinion/interview_line-between-real-and-imaginary-india-is-thin-says-satirist-gautam-bhatia_1369877.

5.
A longer excerpt from the Appadurai discussion of the imaginary: "The image, the imagined, the imaginary—these are all terms that direct us to something critical and new in global cultural processes: the imagination as social practice. No longer mere fantasy (opium for the masses whose real work is elsewhere), no longer simple escape (from a world defined principally by more concrete purposes and structures), no longer elite pastime (thus not relevant to the lives of ordinary people), and no longer mere contemplation (irrelevant for new forms of desire and subjectivity), the imagination has become an organized field of social practices, a form of work (in the sense of both labor and culturally organized practice), and a form of negotiation between sites of agency (individuals) and globally defined fields of possibilities." Arjun Appadurai, *Modernity at Large: Cultural Dimensions of Globalization* (Minneapolis: University of Minnesota Press, 1996): 31.

fluidity of culture and the impossibility of containing culture within a boundary—either the boundary of the human form or the geographical boundary of a nation. Banerjee's work also engages a desire to construct a productive intervention for negotiating reality through the imagination, which finds its way into the use value of artistic production.

In her sculptures Banerjee conjures up images of humans as well as other sentient beings. Her study of classical Indian art is evident in her references to deities in the Hindu pantheon as well as her interest in elaborate scenarios from Indian epic tales. Her masterful 2011 sculptural installation representing Durga—a deity of feminine creative, independent, and compassionate forcefulness—at rest, tired from her constant battles, weaves together these two powerful references. Through assemblage, the work collapses symbols from ancient and colonial sources into the contemporary. Its title, *She drew a premature prick, in a fluster of transgressions, abject by birth she knew not what else to do with this untouchable reach, unknowable body as she was an ancient savage towed into his modern present,* 2011 (see p. 31), adapts Victorian grammar and phrasing as a purposeful statement regarding the effects of the British colonial presence in India. The sourced objects and materials include epoxy American buffalo horns, silver and silk trim from a Banarasi Indian wedding sari, and a replica of a Victorian doll head, all of which carry the weight of historical traces from earlier times. Banerjee's interpretation of Durga is a reflection on the modern woman, with her overburdened and overstressed life. The artist's concerns resonate with Thapan's discourse on issues of embodiment and lived experience for contemporary Indian women.

Thapan's assertion also mirrors the thoughts of the art historian Vidya Dehejia, who wrote, "My interest in human embodiment is also in relation to the expression of inner feelings, selfhood, and identity, viewing none of these as isolated single issues but rather as multiple constituents of human embodiment. . . . The mind, imagination, emotions, and memory play as much a role in the construction and experience of the human body as do the social expectations and the male and female gaze. . . . And embodiment thereby becomes both experience and body, agency and physical corporeality, life and matter."[6] In art, lived experience is transformed into coherent objects; it is a unique genre of communication and materialization.

In her many works related to non-essentialist embodiment, the artist Tejal Shah focuses attention on the social construction of gender identity. Her series *Women Like Us* (2010) (see p. 83) exemplifies the "communicative body" as a strategy for upending conventional notions of femininity and beauty. Her portraits of masculine women, a project that began with and then expanded beyond women wrestlers in provincial cities, is a testament to the fluidity of gender and gender identification. Though Shah's project focuses on external appearances, it is assumed that appearance, dress, and demeanor are markers for a corresponding internal sphere of thoughts and emotions. Her wrestlers and Banerjee's Durga have more in common than may be apparent on the surface. Just as Banerjee shows Durga in a new light, offering an alternative to conventional narratives about women, Shah presents a counterimage to the onslaught of media representations promoting hyperfeminized identities.

Even the briefest study of classical Indian figurative sculpture reveals the great value of the body in Indian art as a site of subtle and substantial changes in form, as a marker of cultural shifts and collisions. In art the figure is often deployed as a symbolic visual regime for the representation of states of consciousness, often through specific known narratives that illuminate spiritual aspirations toward the divine. While *The Matter Within* does not specifically address these traditions, this art history certainly informed the curatorial direction of the project. For example, Dehejia's contemporary reading of the premodern arts of India references *rasa,* the Indian theory of aesthetics, which emphasizes varieties of thought, feeling, and emotion, and notes the centrality of the well-formed human body in historical inscriptions and literary sources. "Over the centuries, the sensuous bodily form, female and male, human and divine, has been a dominant feature in the vast and varied canvas of the Indian artistic tradition. The human figure—complete, elegant, adorned, and eye-catching—was, indeed, the leitmotif."[7] Her discussions of the body in traditional Indian art led me to consider the field of sculpture as a carrier of legacies and breaks in social and metaphorical spheres of reference for enlightenment. Although the forms may vary widely, the human figure continues to play a vital role in contemporary art. Artists are configur-

6.
Vidya Dehejia, *The Body Adorned: Dissolving Boundaries Between Sacred and Profane in India's Art* (New York: Columbia University Press, 2009): 6.

7.
Ibid., 1.

ing new imagery and physical forms in dialogue with current shifts in the urban sphere. Materiality and its attendant qualities of cultural specificity are being used to express fresh perspectives on India, ranging from new ways of working with materials and form within naturalistic modes of representation to fantastical inventions that access the absurd and the grotesque. Even postminimal works rely on materials that carry emotional impact within reductive form.

In the late 1980s, Anita Dube, an early protagonist of feminist art in India, was a member of the Indian Radical Painters and Sculptors Association, a group of political artists based in Baroda. At that time Dube articulated a new direction for politically progressive art. She argued that instead of rejecting Western forms outright, artists should seek out radical expressions within those paradigms while responding to the local context.[8] Dube's recent sculptures insist on the erotics of politics as a form of resistance to mainstream power structures. A conceptual artist working at the intersection of ritual and individual experience, she fuses the collective memory of materials with language. The sensuality of her work, as both pleasure and pain, is paired with single words, phrases, or poetic texts. In the exhibition, four-foot-high candles in the shape of the four-letter words "love" and "void" express the illusion of solidity (see pp. 34–35). Meant to be lit throughout the exhibition (which was not possible at our venue), the intent is that they should slowly burn down into pools of melted wax, concretizing the transitory nature of things (and, by extension, life itself) through the dissolution of form.

In another work by Dube, the word "wound" is cut out of a sheetrock wall, creating a view to the other side (see p. 33). Here, figuration is again indicated through the parallel system of language and a play with embodiment via both physical absence and physical presence. In a 2000 interview Dube noted, "The object-sculpture is a reverential thing for me, however subversive its contents. The tension of this opposition is something I enjoy. The Bhakti tradition has created a place for gods in our daily lives and people sing to them and bathe, clothe, and feed them as if they were alive. I have a similar relationship with my sculptures—a human, intimate one—and I am also interested in them having the effulgent quality of the gods, which is transformative, nourishing, and spiritually included. And then there is this marvelous contamination via a profane intermixing with the real world."[9]

Sudarshan Shetty's sculptures insist on human and animal sculptural form as an embodiment of the living and breathing body through their relationship to the material culture of local Mumbai history, Hindu religion, and symbols of globalism. Shetty's outlook is relational, as he believes that there is an intrinsic interdependency between our desire to collect objects and the production of visual art, and that in both activities we are attempting to manage the inevitability of our mortality, even though it is futile to resist death itself. It is this dialectical drama that motivates us to engage with and make sense of the objects that surround us. His untitled life-size statue of himself made of gold-covered fiberglass—standing not upright but leaning atop a pedestal of steel sheeting—greeted visitors to *The Matter Within* (see p. 45). He originally created it for his 2010 solo exhibition *this too shall pass* at the Dr. Bhau Daji Lad Museum (formerly the Victoria and Albert Museum) in Mumbai.[10] There, the statue was placed directly in front of a marble statue of Prince Albert, managing to both block and overshadow the museum's (former) namesake. The work is interactive; audience members are made to understand that they can help the statue stand up straight by putting money in the coin box attached to the pedestal.[11] The work taps collective memories of many toppled statues, from Vladimir Lenin to Saddam Hussein.

Banerjee, Dube, and Shetty all approach the body as a site for activating the senses, a symptom of being alive, and a seductive opportunity to engage in political and social critique. Their work, while worlds apart from the revered ancient sculpture of India, does share some characteristics with those finely tuned forms. For each of these artists, the body is a container of history, a carrier of desires, and an embodiment of the pressures placed upon it by external forces.[12] Bodies represented in both sacred and secular traditions—imagined beings and consciousnesses realized through molding and carving—are starting points for new morphings, resuscitations, and contemporary constructions. The effects of materiality and its attendant qualities as well as cultural specificity in terms of how materials are used and put together begin to define: ways of being in society; ways of creating new imagery and physical forms for the future, from the absurd

14

8.
"Dube suggests that there is no way to negate the influence of the West given India's longstanding colonial contact with it. The embrace of the West was an articulation of dissent, a means by which the artists of Kerala could trouble the extant versions of a pristine Indian culture unfettered by the encroachment of colonialism. Unlike Kapur's earlier embrace of modernity as a viable option for the articulation of a unique postcolonial identity, Dube shifts its categorical deployment by appealing to the polyvalence of modernity. Modernity, for Dube, is striated through the particulars of its manifestations and in this way she upholds the notion that 'the experience of modernity is local.' The locality was clearly Kerala; yet its visual articulation was manifest through a critical embrace—rather than a wholesale rejection—of the Western modern. Dube's proposal to complicate modernist paradigms of the West (instead of jettisoning them altogether) stands in distinct opposition to the ongoing discursive debates over the last two decades in India." Kathleen Lynne Wyma, *The Discourse and Practice of Radicalism in Contemporary Indian Art 1960–1990*, PhD dissertation (Vancouver: University of British Columbia, 2007): 134.

9.
From Phillipe Vergne's interview with Anita Dube in the exhibition catalogue *Anita Dube* (New York: Bose Pacia, 2005). Originally published in 2000 in *Art Asia Pacific* no. 26.

10.
This museum of fine and decorative arts, now a municipal museum, opened in 1872 at the height of the colonial period as an outpost of the Victoria and Albert Museum in London.

11.
It takes about 55 pounds of weight to straighten the figure to a fully upright position. The statue and coin box are connected by a mechanical pulley system.

12.
As a point of contrast, and to further support my assertion regarding the connection between ancient sculpture and current artistic practices, I include here Geeta Kapur's analysis of the 6th-century Maheshamurti at Elephanta Island, off the coast of Mumbai (also from "Partisan Views About the Human Figure"): "Maheshamurti at Elephanta, on the other hand, is the most magnificent of all icons as also a symbol to contain the cosmic upheaval of creation and destruction. . . . What is remarkable is that even in hieratic art the sensuous grasp of the body-form is never withheld. The way the ideality of the icon is realized in the very body is exemplified most beautifully in a Chola bronze: stressed contours flow into a smooth and continuous body-surface, and the limbs arrange themselves in a posture of classical majesty. This is prescribed perfection in that it follows the word of the *shastras*, and yet it appears as if the icon were a pristine conception formed by the touch of Eros. Now Eros, a life generating force, defies not only death but any effort to abstract spiritual meanings; thus however esoteric the iconography of Indian images, the best of them are fully inducted into the life-process. In this sense they overturn the hieratic injunctions while yet maintaining their rigor."

to the grotesque; and ways of intervening into layers of tradition to create new imaginaries free from reality-based forms.

Embodying past personages often allows artists to create works that inhabit different worlds and historical periods simultaneously. The Otolith Group's film *Otolith III* (2009) (see p. 111) is based on an unrealized speculative film, *The Alien* (1967) by the renowned filmmaker Satyajit Ray. Ray's only science fiction film project was to be produced in Hollywood, but the effort ultimately failed. The script was based on the short story "Banku Babu's Friend," which Ray wrote in 1962 about a boy who discovers a magical alien in a spaceship that lands in a pond near his village in rural Bengal, and the story unfolds as the villagers begin to worship it. The other main characters are an Indian businessman, a journalist from Calcutta, and an American engineer. *Otolith III*, through montage edits and shifts between documentary and cinematic registers, swerves in and out of sequenced time imaginaries in an interplay between itself and the Ray script. The imaginary is a construction of film as a potentiality that can only be completed posthumously through a series of questions and conjectures. *Otolith III* hinges on the concept of a prequel, and is therefore in a permanent state of liminality. Partly composed of fragments of several of Ray's realized films, it is a kind of archive of scenes that could be replacements for those that were never realized, and it becomes a platform for contemplating the dimensions of speculative thinking. The Otolith Group's project is a reclamation of the dualities of the impossibility/possibility of creation/re-creation. It also takes into account the differences between Indian cinema and Hollywood, as a symbolic gesture toward the doubt of mimicry.[13]

In her film *I Saw a God Dance* (2011) (see pp. 103–105), Ayisha Abraham utilizes the documentary form and infuses it with local lore, an archive of film clips, and contemporary interviews to mediate her subject: the innovative classical dancer Ram Gopal. Ram Gopal captured dreams in his movements. He created exotic characters that would delight. He imagined himself as god-like, and his audiences largely believed in his magic making. His lifelong process of fantasy and identity construction included an extensive stay in London, where he became ever more entangled in colonial legacies. He was also a homosexual and of mixed Indian and Burmese heritage, and today is all but forgotten. Abraham's project recovers the dancer's contribution to the modernization of Indian classical dance while questioning the historical gaps that can result from prejudice and oversight. Abraham was greatly inspired by footage shot by Tom D'Aguiar, an avid amateur filmmaker who captured Gopal's dancing in home movies. Abraham's video is ethnographic in approach and in spirit. Her subjectivity makes contact with that of her artist-innovator subject, breathing new life into his personage.

Nikhil Chopra's fictions present invented characters who are amalgamations of himself, his grandfather (a gentleman painter of Kashmir landscapes), other Victorian personae, and larger histories, simultaneously bringing to life experiences of the 19th, 20th, and 21st centuries (see pp. 61–63). He performs his historical and contemporary identities via the device of theater without walls. His staged performances, which he carries out in European cities—on the streets, along waterways, and in parks—refuse to separate the invented and imaginary from real, everyday life. Like The Otolith Group and Ayisha Abraham, Chopra converges his own inventions and assisted recollections of past personages with our current imaginings of heroic personalities.

In *The Matter Within,* artists working within the paradigms of the photographic canon and responding to the conventions and innovations of that medium—as well as the history of photography specifically in India—distill and represent social and environmental conditions of all kinds. They operate within the reality-based spheres of the informal street shoot and the formal portrait. The physical world provides a sense of place for the persona, the character, the body, offsetting the figure from its surroundings while allowing it to remain central to meaning formation. What is communicated through photography is the collaboration and convergence of the desires and agendas of the artist and the social dynamics of India—a subset of India's vast cultural geography concentrated into a specific figural, spatial, and historical territory.

Anita Dube eloquently praises Gauri Gill's photographs of western Rajasthan (see pp. 65–67), taken over a twelve-year period, as describing the sheer power of the landscape to shape the lives of the nomads and migrants who dwell within it: "There is something unhinged in the

13.
The Otolith Group's film is modeled on Chris Marker's *Sans Soleil* (1983). Sunil Gupta's photo-story *Sun City* (2010), included in the *Matter Within,* adheres even more closely to the structure of another Marker film, *La Jetée* (1962). Both The Otolith Group and Gupta adapt Marker's experimental filmic form to Indian subjects and new (Indian) narratives.

dire poverty and marginality of these people; in the wound of their gaze; in their mimetic excesses; in the inhospitable landscape; in the vicissitudes of survival, that is in sync with what Barthes calls the 'madness' within photography, its unhinged character. Landscape, animals, and human beings—everything is in a huddle here, intertwined and interdependent, such that their spirit of survival shines through."[14] The desert shapes the lives of its inhabitants in specific and localized ways that are almost inexplicable.

Anup Mathew Thomas has created a body of work that takes literally Dube's earlier text from the 1980s. These works validate the inclusion of local aesthetics and traditions as a rich field of references available to contemporary artists working in the Indian context. His awareness of the subtleties of contemporary politics in the state of Kerala may be unreadable to outsiders, but these matters are of great importance to local residents. In his *Metropolitan* series from 2006, he photographs Christian clergy standing in front of their churches, wearing their finest robes (pp. 89–91). Representing various denominations—Catholic, Orthodox, Episcopalian—they are metaphorically propped up against the backdrop of the unstated statistic that only 3 percent of India's population even practices Christianity. In this way Thomas represents a specialized and localized power that nonetheless is a minority within the larger religious landscape of the country.

Dhruv Malhotra's *Sleepers* (2008–present) (see pp. 73–75) are photographs taken of New Delhi's streets and public architecture at night, showing bodies in repose, presumably unconscious, sustaining an obvious inward focus as they lay passively available to the photographer. We cannot help feeling curious. Who are they? Why are they sleeping outside? Something of their identities is revealed from their location in the city: a roadside spot, a park, or a work site. The pictures underscore how photography enables the body to represent ideas that are larger than the persons represented.

On the whole, *The Matter Within* offers intimate views of often-neglected subjects, rather than a totalizing, holistic view of India as a place or an idea. The concepts and topics on view demonstrate the artists' commitment to presenting images that are left out, absent, ignored, or suppressed by the mainstream media. They provide a window—into a specific person or group of people, local sites, or concepts of experience and the body—that decisively rejects a belief in the inclusiveness of widely circulating nationalist narratives.

A perfect example: Shilpa Gupta's *Untitled (Sword)* (2009) (see p. 37). It is a hand-hewn, eight-foot-long sword with its tip broken off, jutting horizontally out from the wall to cut through the gallery space. The small broken-off piece is attached to the sword by thin sewing thread and hangs down, almost touching the ground. This work compacts historical meaning through the poetic force of symbol. It is specifically intended to trigger memories and heated emotions surrounding Partition, the 1947 event in which nearly 350 years of colonial rule in India ended with a controversial compromise to divide the British-ruled region into two countries: India and Pakistan. Gupta's sculpture is about the grief, despair, anger, and helplessness that still remain in the thoughts, feelings, and emotions of many living in India and Pakistan. Decades after the official reshaping of territories and political allegiances, this one dramatic and powerful event of severing remains a deep, lingering wound for many. Proponents of "Future India" may want to construct a third generation of "the imaginary" based on economic growth. But it is only through acknowledging the legacies of the past, as Gupta does, that true, democratic transformation can take place. Capitalism's economic rewards are still far out of reach for most of the people represented in *The Matter Within*. I wonder if it is because Partition may still be too recent of a memory.

14.
Anita Dube, "The Desert Mirror," *ART India* (May 2010), http://gaurigill.com/huge_document.php?pd=Anita_Dube_Notes_on_Gauri_Gill_Notes_from_the_Desert.pdf.

The "New" Indian Sculpture

ZEHRA JUMABHOY

But in doing all of this, the very term we had thought we were saving—sculpture—has begun to be somewhat obscured.[1]

Round and round they go, like magic lantern displays from the distant past: the glinting eyes of a cat, a floating yellow fish, and a copulating couple drifting in and out of each other's arms. This motley crew jumps onto walls like storybook illustrations come alive. Welcome to Nalini Malani's *The Sacred and the Profane* (1998). In this work, rotating Mylar cylinders painted with images gleaned from Moghul miniatures, Kalighat *patuas,* and Old Master drawings cast colored shadows in a "video-shadow play," as Malani calls her creation, that borrows elements from painting (the clever brushwork on the cylinders), animation (the eerily active cartoonish characters), and sculpture (the swirling transparent sheets). As the images encircle the viewer, the boundaries between disciplines meet and merge.[2]

Malani was one of the first successful proponents of installation art in India. Much like her fluid visuals, her tale is enmeshed with those of others. This essay is an attempt to tell their story.

In the 2003 book *Indian Art: An Overview,* the Baroda-based art historian Ratan Parimoo winds up his account of modern Indian sculpture precisely where Malani and her colleagues began theirs—the dawn of Indian installation art in the 1990s: "In the present period, several sculptors have turned to installation as a natural extension of their attempt to give a broader social context to their work."[3] At first, Parimoo's proposal that the development of installation was a "natural" progression from sculpture seems justified. After all, the 3D, embodied experience of Malani's shadow play draws upon the same impulse that Parimoo notices in offerings of the 1970s and 1980s: a "move away from . . . sculpture placed on pedestals."[4] One of the names Parimoo drops to support his claim is Ravinder Reddy, acknowledged for his big-headed fiberglass fabrications. *Krishnaveni I* (1997) is a massive bronze-hued head of a woman, sans body. She resembles stone deities found in places of worship or sold (in tinier form) in bazaars. With her plaited black hair, she contemporizes the ritualistic while she ritualizes pop culture. The Sanskrit term *Krishnaveni* is the name of a famous Telugu actress. But it also connotes the immense Krishna River, whose holy waters are venerated by Hindus. *Veni* means "braid of hair," hence, Reddy's brassy beauty is Mother Nature and movie star rolled into one. If we are unsure whether to worship her sacred attributes or her profane ones, Krishnaveni isn't the only figure to generate such confusion.

1.
Rosalind Krauss, "Sculpture in the Expanded Field," *October,* vol. 8 (1979): 41.

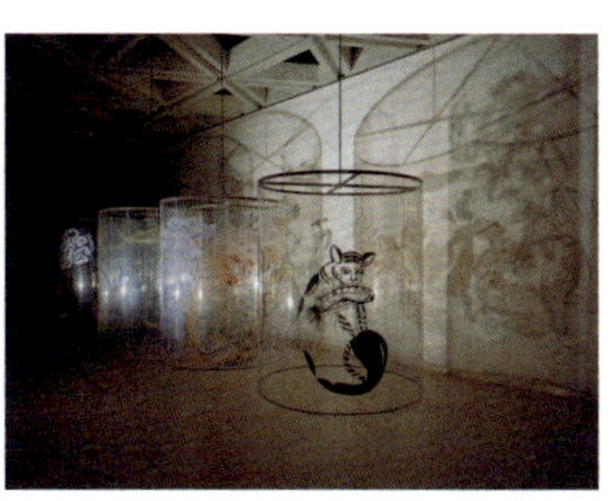

Nalini Malani
The Sacred & the Profane, 1998
Shadow play - four acrylic reverse painted Mylar cylinders
59 x 48 in.
Installation view at Art Gallery of Western Australia, Perth
Collection: Art Gallery of Western Australia, Perth

2.
Alex Potts says: "Post-modern fashion has rendered largely redundant the categorical distinctions between different forms of art." See Alex Potts, *The Sculptural Imagination* (New Haven and London: Yale University Press, 2000): 4. Although Potts focuses on Europe and America, his analysis of sculpture and installation is relevant in an Indian context too.

3.
Ratan Parimoo, "Modern Indian Sculpture" in *Indian Art: An Overview,* ed. Gayatri Sinha (New Delhi: Rupa & Co., 2003): 185.

4.
Ibid.

At the Prince of Wales Museum in Mumbai reposes an ancient sculpture of Lord Shiva, dancing his dance of destruction in ornately carved metal. Rumor has it that while the statue is on display ostensibly for its spectacular craftsmanship, it is also worshiped every morning by the museum's Hindu staff, and that this daily *puja* is one of the stipulations of the donor's bequest. Is it art or icon? Can it be both? According to the art historian Walter Benjamin, the age of mechanical reproduction marked a switch from the "cult value" of an object (tied to its "aura" and "parasitical dependence on ritual") to its "exhibition value." But in India, where roadside shrines and noisy religious processions coexist with snarling traffic and heady skyscrapers, such a crisp, clean transition has not transpired. The sacred often nestles within the secular. An object's exhibition value may facilitate, rather than displace, its dependence on ritual.[5]

The New York–based, Calcutta-born artist Rina Banerjee mixes sex and saintliness in her feathery-fabric assemblages and their tongue-twisting titles. Look at: *She drew a premature prick, in a fluster of transgressions, abject by birth she knew not what else to do with this untouchable reach, unknowable body as she was an ancient savage towed into his modern present* (2011) (see p. 31). Whew. The reclining figure has the face of a Victorian doll, the body of a mannequin (the size of an adolescent girl), and the trappings of a desi fashion plate, decked out in a traditional wedding sari and gold jewelry. Is she an underage bride, a sacrificial victim (her posture alludes to that of a young widow committing *sati*), or a vengeful goddess? Banerjee explains, "I am trying to cure Durga of her urge for war, to pacify her."[6] The "ancient savage" of the title recalls the Hindu goddess Kali (the angry avatar of Durga) dancing on the body of her spouse, Shiva, he of the phallic lingam or "prick." Even if a slightly suspicious version of the exotic Orient is being propagated in Banerjee's use of provocative fuss and feathers, there's no doubt that different realms—feminist fairytale, touristic fantasy, and religious totem—cohabitate within her installation. In tune with Reddy's sculptures, Banerjee's doll also displays how the sacred is inscribed in the secular.

Parimoo's reference to Reddy's giant deities alerts us to another connection between installation art and modern Indian sculpture: the step-by-step construction of the anti-monument. While Reddy's females fiddle with monumentality, they manage to maintain their grandeur. A group of younger artists, on the other hand, erect tributes that are tough to take at face value. *The Matter Within* includes numerous examples of such spoofs. There is Sudarshan Shetty's *Untitled* (2010) (see p. 45), a metal mockup of the artist that looks ready to topple over. Fitted with a coin box at its base, it demands money from visitors, and as we dutifully slug coins into this gaudy self-portrait we can't help wondering what we are commemorating: an image of the artist as hero, or as showman? Shetty, visitors are informed, will not stand upright until his coffers are full. Elsewhere is Siddhartha Kararwal's whitewashed *Hangover Man* (2011) (see p. 39), a 3D rendition of a life-size Sayajirao Gaekwad III, the Maharaja of Baroda, riding a snow-white steed. The memorial is constructed out of cheap cotton T-shirts. Has the mustachioed royal been out on the tiles?

Given these examples, Parimoo's assertion that the transition from sculpture in the 1980s to installation in the 1990s was a simple "extension" appears disingenuous. There is too much his peaceful prognosis does not account for. Almost all the artworks Parimoo references, Reddy's included, enjoy a fairly harmonious relationship with sociopolitical structures: recollect Meera Mukherjee's folk art–inspired bronzes and Dhruva Mistry's public sculptures of semi-mythological beasts. This does not hold true for installation's early heavyweights, who forged art out of outrage.

Rosalind Krauss asserts that installation (or, as she put it, "sculpture in the expanded field") denotes a historical rupture with previous artistic forms.[7] Undoubtedly, the traumatic events of the 1990s ripped open India's social fabric. In 1992, Babri Masjid, the 16th-century Moghul mosque in Ayodhya, was destroyed by the Hindu Right, who claimed it was standing on the birthplace of the god Ram. The demolition led to waves of sectarian violence in Mumbai, Gujarat, and Delhi. For many Indians, recurring Hindu-Muslim riots represent the failure of the secular state, spelling the sad demise of Mahatma Gandhi's dream of a nation founded on more than just religious commonalities.[8] Early Indian installation art was a product of this sentiment. Painters such as Malani and Vivan Sundaram as well as the art historian Anita Dube consciously turned to site-specificity to fight fundamentalism.

5.
Walter Benjamin, "The Work of Art in the Age of Mechanical Reproduction," Zeitschrift für Sozialforchung, 1936, "*Illuminations* (London: Pimlico, 1999): 219. The sacred has never been fully disentangled from the aesthetic in India. Think of the lithographs of the 19th-century artist Raja Ravi Varma, whose images of buxom goddesses adorned with sequins and lace occupy many a middle-class living room. These decked-out prints serve a dual function: They are domestic deities to be worshipped and glittery, decorative wall hangings to impress visitors. The coexistence of the "cultic" with the "exhibition" value of Ravi Varma's prints is one of the reasons why art historians such as Christopher Pinney feel that Benjamin's thesis—that reproduction eradicates the aura of an object—is not relevant in India. The more lithographs Ravi Varma made, the more popular religious iconography became in the construction of household shrines. (Benjamin of course might not have been predicting the tendencies of reproduction for all cultural contexts.) Bollywood actors and politicians alike continue to use religious symbols to formulate their public personae.

6.
From an interview with Rina Banerjee at the YBCA website, http://www.ybca.org/matter-within, accessed December 2011.

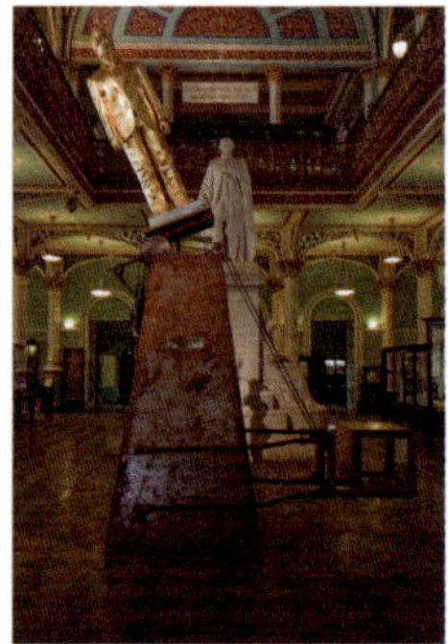

SUDARSHAN SHETTY
Untitled, from the series *this too shall pass*, 2010
Gold leaf on fiberglass, mild steel, coin box, etched brass
Variable dimensions
Installation view at Dr. Bhau Daji Lad Museum
Photo: Anil Rane

7.
While I agree with this idea of rupture in some senses, Krauss seems to be overly motivated by the "historical rupture of form." In other words, her explanation remains formalist and is largely unconcerned with specific social contexts. I would argue that it is impossible to look at such a "rupture" in India without reference to specific political realities.

8.
This founding myth of India also serves to differentiate it from Pakistan, which Indians generally view as being formed on the basis of religion.

If the Hindu Right argues for the equation of Indian-ness with a "pure" Hindu past, both Dube and Malani ridicule such essentialist definitions of identity. Just as Malani's shadow plays borrow iconography from East and West, both Hindu and Muslim art historical sources (see p. 33), Dube's textual artworks also underscore the porosity of boundaries. Tellingly, her *Wound* (2007) is a word hacked out of white drywall. While she uses a conventional sculptural technique—carving—to manufacture *Wound,* the result is an articulation of lack. The letters demarcate an emptiness that allows viewers to peek through both sides of the divide (or should I say Partition?).[9] Thus, much like the slashed canvases of the founder of Spatialism, Lucio Fontana, they cut borders between interior and exterior, Self and Other.[10] This painstaking rending of space causes a rupture within the medium of sculpture itself: *Wound* exists in the very place that sculpture has vacated.[11]

PARTY POLITICS

Street life (however riot-ridden) certainly provides inspiration for Indian installations. Nevertheless it remains their biggest competitor.[12] To the uninitiated, India's metropolises resemble a particularly shocking variety of art: contradictory, brilliantly and hectically colored, and, more often than not, just bizarre. As one flabbergasted American artist (who prefers to remain anonymous) put it as he walked along the traffic-congested streets of Mumbai for the first time in 2009, "Man, this place is an installation! How can I compete with this city?"

Unsurprisingly, then, installation art had difficulty establishing itself in India in the 1990s. Not only did it have to fend off international derision, but it faced similar slurs at home. For many mainstream Indian artists, installations were just a ridiculous foreign import—a sign of superficial, globalized times—that refused to address local realities. One such vitriolic voice belonged to the well-connected painter Anjolie Ela Menon. The fact that Menon herself eventually changed tack, keenly incorporating elements of sculpture into her regular lexicon of painted images (crows, checkered floors, and moony women) is neither here nor there.

In 1999 the art historian Roobina Karode issued a defense of the genre. The street, Karode proposed, should not be viewed as a rival but as a savior. "Installation art in India stands to gain . . . if artists adjust their lens to looking more around them rather than looking elsewhere," she advised.[13] For the Delhi-based art historian Geeta Kapur, installation art's pariah status was the best thing about it, as it enabled this new form to address the sociopolitical conditions of the New India.[14] After all, they came into being virtually simultaneously. As even the most curmudgeonly Marxist historian would acknowledge, Finance Minister Manmohan Singh's economic policies in 1991 marked a watershed. Until "Manmohanomics"—as Singh's policies are known—India had followed a Nehruvian Socialist approach for most of its independent history, meaning that the government maintained a series of protectionist policies and exerted strict control over its private sector, foreign trade, and direct foreign investment. High levels of debt eventually forced politicians to rethink their positions. By signing up for loans from the World Bank and the International Monetary Fund, Manmohanomics ushered in foreign investment and trade. Meanwhile, the state reduced its involvement in the market. The New India had arrived.[15]

Obviously, opinions about this neoliberal dawn differ widely. While enthusiasts (invariably big business and the burgeoning middle class) see globalization as a cause for celebration, detractors maintain that it is Western imperialism in disguise. Global capital, naysayers insist, is homogenizing culture and deepening social inequalities. Unsurprisingly, the left-leaning Kapur does not view the spread of global capitalism with unmitigated joy.[16] So, for her, the fact that installation art played largely outside the white cube in the 1990s gave it an extra edge. It could conscientiously make sociopolitical statements, especially ones that took issue with the market. The artist collective Open Circle, founded in 1998, fell snugly into this agenda. At one time it included the installation artists Shilpa Gupta, Sharmila Samant, Tushar Joag, and Archana Hande in its ranks, all of whom were concerned with revealing "the cultural homogenization and marginalization of otherness, both in India and in the global perspective."[17] In 2002 Gupta satirized the third-world human organ trade with *Your Kidney Supermarket* at Oxford Bookstore in Mumbai. For the

---

9. Perhaps Dube's wounded wall refers to another violent separation: the formation of Pakistan in 1947. The eve of India's independence coincided with this fissure, commonly referred to as Partition, causing mass migrations, carnage, and wars between the two countries.

10. Given her art historical background, Dube might be drawing upon the famous *Wounds* series by the sculptor Somnath Hore (1921–2006), who worked from the 1970s onward and is considered one of the pioneers of modern Indian art. His white-on-white *Wounds* paper-pulp print works were pivotal in bridging painting, printmaking, and sculpture in India.

11. Dube's *Wound* is a visual iteration of Derrida's concept of the *parergon*: "Neither work (*ergon*) nor outside the work [*hors d'oeuvre*], neither inside or outside, neither above nor below, it disconcerts any opposition but does not remain indeterminate and it *gives* rise to the work." See Jacques Derrida, *The Truth in Painting*, trans. G. Bennington and I. McLeod (Chicago: University of Chicago Press, 1987).

12. "Much of my work comes from my experience of the city. If you live in Bombay, you are always walking the edge," says Sudarshan Shetty in a YBCA interview for *The Matter Within*, http://www.ybca.org/matter-within, accessed December 2011.

13. Roobina Karode, "Installation Art in the 1990s" in *Indian Art: An Overview*, ed. Gayatri Sinha (New Delhi: Rupa & Co, 2003): 229.

14. Kapur remains the doyenne of Indian art history. Seen as the only really intellectual, incorruptible voice, her slightly idealistic theories about installation are quoted as gospel by a younger generation of critics.

15. These measures have usually been read as signs of India's globalization or economic liberalization. While the terms are not necessarily synonymous, they have generally been treated thus by enthusiasts and critics alike. So, for the purposes of this essay, I will maintain the conflation.

16. Kapur says, "What is being globalized therefore is American-style capitalism and its implicit worldview." See Geeta Kapur, *When Was Modernism* (New Delhi: Tulika Books, 2000): 339.

17. This is from the mission statement provided for *The Empire Strikes Back: Indian Art Today* (London: Random House, 2010). The collective finally dissolved in 2008, but many of its erstwhile members continue to make art that points fingers at the social, political, and economic ills of globalization. Shilpa Gupta was the first to leave the collective. While *The Matter Within* contains a later work by Gupta, her early activist stance is vital to her oeuvre in general.

show, she transformed the store into a pretty confectionery. Pastel posters in the window advertised "edible sugar kidneys," and delicate faux kidneys, tinted candy-pink and green and sweetly packaged in plastic, were displayed inside. An interactive section allowed "customers" to order online: no more "unpleasant hospitals" or "reciprocal love" required, according to the screens. Gupta's choice of venue targeted a less elite audience than the usual gallery-goer. (In 2002 there were few Mumbai galleries spacious enough to have accommodated such a venture anyway.)

Thanks to initiatives like Gupta's, installation art in India has always been seen as inherently anti-establishment, having, as Kapur famously put it, "a vanguard status." Certainly when Kapur was validating early installations, their Socialist stance was perfectly consistent, since they often operated in the not-for-profit realm. If there were few commercial galleries that could accommodate them, there were even fewer collectors interested in buying them. (The latter were too preoccupied amassing larger-than-life photorealistic paintings.) So when Kapur lauded their "radical interventions in the ideologically regressive one-world system," no one could fault her logic or installation art's edgy integrity.[18]

By 2005, the Indian art world had changed. Ironically, the growing demand outside India for contemporary Indian installations sped the process along. As "revolutionary" practitioners from the subcontinent, its proponents found themselves feted by international institutions. In fact, the more condescending they were about the homogenization of globalization, the better they did on the global stage. As the art critic Girish Shahane noted, "victimhood sells" and "easily readable political art is in demand on the biennale circuit (a circuit which, despite claims on behalf of its anti-commercial status, has increasingly functioned for Indian artists as a gateway to representation by international private galleries)."[19] Soon enough, the outsider stance of installation art endowed it with a superior status in Indian galleries. Kapur's call to arms rapidly mutated into a rhetorical trope, used by catalogue writers to bestow a whiff of street cred on decadent sculptures. Post-2005 installations—generally vast, flashy confabulations—concurrently mocked and milked the money game.[20]

THE BIGGER THE BETTER

Despite its difficult birth outside the white cube, the more Indian installation practice matured and grew, the more it craved the gallery's shelter. In the 1990s and very early 2000s, there were few galleries capable of holding large-scale displays, as they had neither the space nor the resources. But the gallery scene changed in Mumbai, New Delhi, and Bangalore around 2005, triggered by what avid gallery-goers christened the "Bodhi effect." Bodhi Art was a small Singapore gallery, established in 2004, showing nondescript Indian art. The plush new spaces it established in Mumbai (Bodhi Art Kalaghoda in 2006 and then BodhiSpace in 2007) and Delhi (2005) raised the stakes of the game, providing the impetus in these cities for newer galleries to form and older ones to polish up their acts.[21] In Mumbai, the warehouse-like premises of Gallery Maskara opened for business in 2008, and the tiny Chemould Art Gallery morphed into the giant Chemould Prescott Road. Meanwhile, in Bangalore, GallerySKE concentrated its energies on mega-size sculptures such as the glittery, rust-ridden creations of the young Sakshi Gupta as well as the subtler talent of the Bangalore-born, New York–based Sreshta Rit Premnath.

What does all this commercial busy-ness have to do with installations? The answer is simple: Bigger galleries accommodated, and solicited, bigger artworks. We mustn't forget that India (however new and improved) has few competent public museums to boast about. The National Galleries of Modern Art in Mumbai and New Delhi are not especially proactive in this regard. While the public-private enterprise that is the Kolkata Museum of Modern Art (KMoMA) has been on the cards since 2007, it has yet to be built. Museums dedicated to Victoriana, like the Dr. Bhau Daji Lad Mumbai City Museum, were not always enamored of contemporary art.[22] Predictably, then, the art market has been vested with a great deal of power to shape. Swanky galleries and the sudden interest of Western collectors (Charles Saatchi, François Pinault, and Frank Cohen among them) as well as a continuous stream of international survey shows combined to create a particular type of art: eye-catching installations.

18.
Geeta Kapur, *When Was Modernism*, 253.

19.
Girish Shahane, "Between Aesthetics and Politics," *ART India*, art and politics issue, 2009.

20.
This shift from perishable, rustic installations to market-savvy ones was also noticeable in the Western art world, as both Claire Bishop and Andrew Causey point out in their books on installation art. The physical circumstances of the shift, though, were obviously unique in India. While massive installations like Anish Kapoor's can be accommodated in Western institutions such as the Tate's Turbine Hall in London, India has no such spaces. So, even at their biggest, installations in India could not afford to scale the same heights. Nevertheless, Alex Potts hits the nail on the head when he says, "The troublesome facticity of the sculptural object has largely disappeared from view, and in the process lost much of its potential for . . . resistance to image-based consumerism." See Alex Potts, *The Sculptural Imagination*, 4.

21.
Bodhi Art was the first casualty of the art market crash. By 2009 it had closed up shop completely, but by that time it had made a lasting impact on the commercial gallery scene in India and had raised the profile of Indian art internationally.

22.
The BDL's first such exhibition was Nikhil Chopra's performance *Yog Raj Chitrakar, Memory Drawing X, Part 2*, which took place in 2010.

23.
Taken from my interview with the artist for *The Empire Strikes Back: Indian Art Today* (London: Random House, 2010).

24.
He was dubbed the "Damien Hirst of Delhi" by Randeep Ranesh in *The Guardian*, February 20, 2007.

25.
Much of T&T's humor relies on the audience understanding their gleeful digs at this cultural stereotype of the hard-drinking manliness of the North Indian male. Mumbaikars such as myself are always wary of the hard liquor served at New Delhi parties. T&T's deliberately effete getup, not what you'd expect from two Punjabi artists raking in the chips, is another fond jibe at these hearty-healthy chauvinists.

26.
Deeksha Nath, "Language of an Idealized Revolt: Sculptural Installations from the 1990s to the Present" in *Art and Visual Culture on India (1857–2007)*, ed. Gayatri Sinha (Mumbai: Marg Publications, 2009): 251.

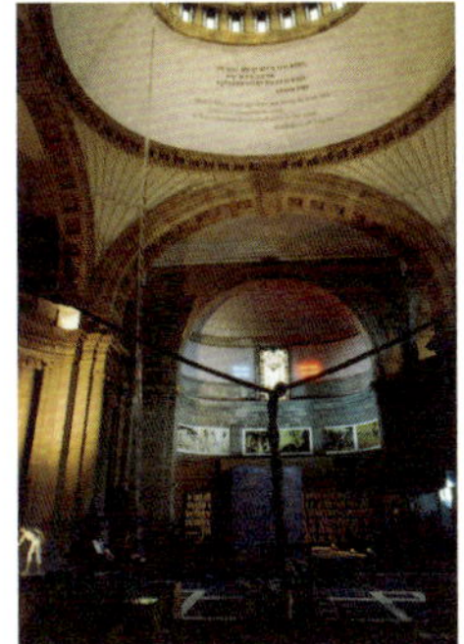

VIVAN SUNDARAM
History Project, 1998
Mixed Media.
Installation view at the Victoria Memorial Museum, Kolkata.
Courtesy the artist.

27.
Ibid., 252.

28.
The Durbar Hall is the part of a palace where Indian kings held their formal and informal conferences. The durbar (court) was also where the British Raj conducted their ceremonies.

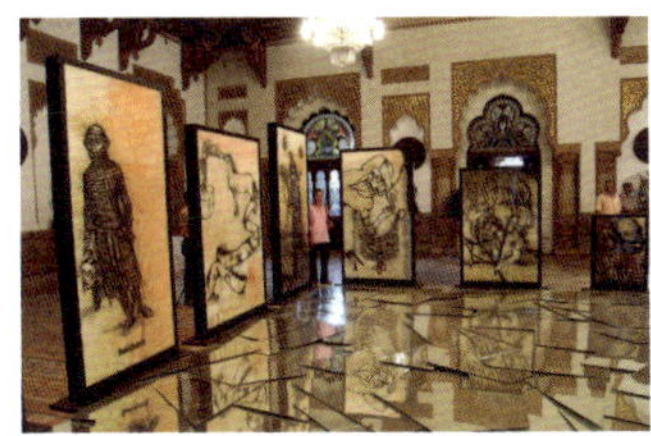

ANJU DODIYA
Installation view of *Throne of Frost* at Laxmi Vilas Palace Baroda, 2007
Courtesy Bodhi Art
© Anju Dodiya
Photo: Prakash Rao and Pablo Bartholomew

Mavericks like Sudarshan Shetty were producing mammoth structures long before the boom, but even this diehard practitioner was wary of a new danger in 2008, "I was making large works even when it was not viable in terms of the market. Survival seemed difficult then, but in some ways it was also easier. The availability of a market brings about the necessity of avoiding falling prey to its stereotypical patterns."[23] For *1 KG War* (2007) the (in)famous New Delhi-based artist Subodh Gupta temporarily eschewed his use of stainless steel (associated by the Indian middle class with prosperity) for actual gold.[24] Gupta's one-kilogram, 24-carat gold nugget speaks about America's vested interests in the war on terror, alternatively seducing and chastising. (It is debatable which sentiment prevailed when it was snapped up at auction.) The artist-designer duo Jiten Thukral and Sumir Tagra also spoof (and pander to) conspicuous consumption. Based in Gurgaon, a burgeoning suburb of New Delhi famous for its mega-malls, T&T (as they prefer to be called) take potshots at the macho Punjabi male.[25] *Now in Your Neighborhood* (2008) (see pp. 50–51) declares that size matters. In this work, pale pink fiberglass bottles form an enormous dinosaur. Since each bottle has a special logo, this pastel beastie is packed with the promise of possession.

In spite of all this, commerce continues to be a topic strategically avoided in the literature about installation art. In her 2009 essay "Language of an Idealized Revolt," the art writer Deeksha Nath stressed that installations are inherently suited to articulating "a critical account of established social structures."[26] Her essay spans low-key works such as Sheela Gowda's tangled red thread in *And Tell Him of My Pain* (1998/2001/2007) and Vivan Sundaram's *History Project* (1998) as well as more glamorous endeavors such as Krishnaraj Chonat's *Ideal Living* (2004). This last re-creates an ultra-plush drawing room, complete with pearl-studded chandelier, rug, and plant. While Nath would have us believe that her examples furnish viewers with "a space for active sociopolitical engagement," it seems foolish to ignore the contextual changes between the earliest examples she cites and the later ones.[27]

Sundaram's *History Project* traversed the down-at-the-heels interiors of Kolkata's Victoria Memorial Museum to make its point. It was constructed in 1921 by Lord Curzon to commemorate the late Queen Victoria, but its insides are no longer as imposing as its facade. As if to underscore the passing of imperial grandeur, Sundaram filled its Durbar Hall with railway tracks, gunny sacks, prints, and the favorite books of Bengal's literati, drawing attention to how the very engines of empire—education, trade, and the railways—were finally used against it by Bengal's intelligentsia.[28] The decaying Memorial Museum, then, once a testament to colonial greatness, is now a testament to decay. I can't help contrasting *History Project* with another meditation on wealth: Anju Dodiya's *Throne of Frost* (2007). This was also staged within a Durbar Hall, but in this case the painting-installations occupied Baroda's opulent Lakshmi Vilas Palace. Double-sided panels displayed glowing paintings of courtly figures on one side and embroidered brocade on the other. They were arranged around a rectangle of shattered mirrors so that spectators could not see the paintings from up close but had to gaze at them vicariously via their reflections. The unapproachable beauty of Dodiya's figuration—elaborately attired ladies, dangling diamonds and pearls—discussed the dangers of vanity and the allure of affluence in a setting redolent of both. It is debatable whether this riff on excess in the heady days of the art-market boom desired to critique commerce, but it certainly facilitated it. *Throne of Frost* was sponsored by Bodhi Art, which flew in "special" guests for a one-night party. Wouldn't it be silly to insist that it was as subversive as Sundaram's rickety rumination on loss?

To be fair, the producers of mega-size sculptures are invariably less naive than their champions. T&T's *Artificial Strawberry Flavor-1* (2008) (see p. 49) basks in the sudden boost in the global status of Indian art. The artists have stuffed a clean white cabinet with empty red fiberglass bottles of varying sizes that are, as the title informs us, completely fake. The bottles are not actually filled with the syrupy, synthetic liquid dear to the hearts of middle-class Indians. They are simulations of an already artificial product. No natural goodness here, T&T admits, straightforwardly. On the bottles are pictures of ordinary youngsters from New Delhi, all of whom we presume aspire to a better life. Art is a commodity, and the gallery is an expensive shop, selling dreams. Sudarshan Shetty, too, shows his awareness of art's precarious position in an untitled work of 2010, made at the height of our most recent global economic hard times. The piece is an ornately carved, uncomfortable looking wooden throne dripping with blood-like gooey red liquid. A neon sign across it spells "stab." Is the global recession about to bite over-the-top art on the backside?

THE OLD ORDER CHANGETH

In January 2011, the curator Arshiya Lokhandwala offered another kind of reality check with *Against All Odds: A Contemporary Response to the Historiography of Archiving, Collecting, and Museums in India*. The exhibition took over the peeling Lalit Kala Akademi in New Delhi, staging a sculpture-heavy critique of the government's attitude toward contemporary art. Twenty artists dealt with ideas of the museum, the archive . . . and inane government regulations. Most elusive in meaning was Subodh Gupta's *Untitled* (2011), which looked like an assemblage of furniture from a low-level bureaucrat's office. Dirty pieces of string and rusty metal chains bound tacky chairs to a splintering wooden cabinet, out of which piles of paperwork seemed about to topple. Electrical wires, concealed with brown Scotch tape, seemed to grow outward from the precariously poised structure, threatening to trip people up. Approach with caution, Gupta seemed to advise. As evening came on the day I visited, security guards walked around the exhibition, summarily switching off the lights. No announcements were made about the institute closing for the night, so nonplussed visitors had to find their way out of the labyrinthine building (both literally and metaphorically) in the dark. Although Lokhandwala had not instigated this performance, it underscored one of the points of the show: Government institutions in India couldn't care less about the niceties of display. Just as the Lalit Kala—a "government gallery" that at one time took its educational role very seriously—is now anxious to get rid of guests, the government-run National Gallery of Modern Art in Mumbai works hard not to have any visitors at all; managed from New Delhi, it is invariably "between shows."

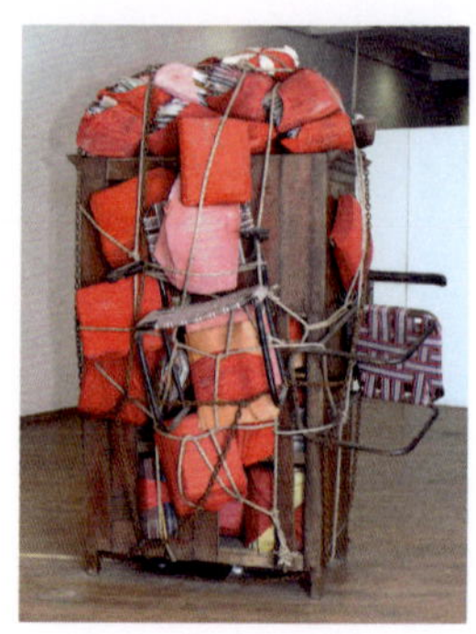

SUBODH GUPTA
Untitled, 2011
Installation view from *Against All Odds*,
curated by Arshiya Lokhandwala
in January 2011,
Lalit Kala Akademi
Courtesy Arshiya
Lokhandwala

And yet, jokes aside, never before has there been such a need for infrastructure in the Indian art world. Since the economic downturn of the last few years, Indian art is no longer considered a sure bet for investors. In order to raise morale and create a new breed of collectors, galleries and dealers need to prove they are not part of a fly-by-night phenomenon. And for this task, museums and academic institutions are essential. After all, what better way to confirm a scene's long-term sustainability than by pointing out its rich past? By carving out a *history* for contemporary Indian art, museums and academic institutions are vital to establishing its longevity.

Since art infrastructure is not a government priority, it is fortunate that private museums have stepped into the breach. The most prominent of these is the collector Anupam Poddar's Devi Art Foundation in New Delhi, which has been up and running since 2008. Poddar's collection of what he calls "bad-boy sculptures" has provided a support system for unwieldy installations; think of Sudarshan Shetty's skeletal steel dinosaur, which regularly shocked guests by having mechanical intercourse with a shiny Jaguar sports car in Poddar's living room. Devi provides a much-needed boost to the scene in these trying times.

Oddly enough, though, it isn't contemporary museums—private or public—that have held the most groundbreaking shows of new Indian sculpture in the past year. Given that so much early installation art in India was conceived in opposition to institutional structures—take Sundaram's dance around "museumization" with *History Project*—it is appropriate that the most interesting displays are being fashioned for museums that are neither contemporary nor fine-art focused. In Paris, the Musée Guimet has held a series of exhibitions of contemporary South Asian sculpture, centering on its permanent collection of ancient Asian artifacts such as coins, vases, and intricately carved idols. Rina Banerjee got her chance to intervene in this scenario with her solo exhibition *Chimeras of India and the West*. Upon entering the ordinarily oppressive library, visitors encountered an incongruous object: a plush wooden armchair upholstered in pale pink brocade, with a gossamer protrusion resembling an elephant's trunk projecting from the center of the backrest. A reference to Lord Ganesha (the mischievous, elephant-headed Hindu god of obstacles), Banerjee's throne is a reminder of imperialism's ominous intentions back when collections like the Guimet's were amassed in the 19th century. "The library is a place where knowledge is kept and controlled and representations of the other are formulated," explained Banerjee to *Artforum* magazine.[29]

29.
See http://www.artforum.com/words/
id=28485, accessed December 2011.

Closer to home, the past is also a battleground for the present. Before it appeared in *The Matter Within,* Sudarshan Shetty's untitled golden replica of himself stood next to the marble mockup of Prince Albert that adorns the entrance of the Dr. Bhau Daji Lad Mumbai City Museum (see p. 45). Smothered in the faux trappings of wealth (gold leaf), this fiberglass Shetty was unable to stand upright. A notice nearby informed viewers that they needed to slot offerings into the coin box so that the weight of the money would correct the posture of the simulated Shetty. Was the artist gesturing to how one version of Western imperialism, the British Raj, is being replaced by another, global capitalism? Or was he just trying to upstage pale Prince Albert? There is one thing we know for sure: Shetty's statue remained lopsided, but its glittery surfaces stole the show anyway. As it did so, it brought contemporary sculpture face to face with its colonial past.

Rina Banerjee

Rina Banerjee's sculptures, installations, and paintings reflect a fantastical world of our most prodigious imaginings and grotesque fears. They are representative of a history and identity both personal and regional; Banerjee was born in Kolkata, raised in the United Kingdom and Cleveland, and now lives and works in New York. She is resistant to the notion of a globalized world where individual cultures have become indistinct. Instead, she embraces exactly those points at which cultures and identities collide as the most rich and fruitful occasions of human encounter.

Banerjee is mesmerized by the colonial past and the multifaceted, diasporic present. Her sculptures are often suspended as if floating in air, conjuring a dreamlike milieu conducive to transformational discovery and possibility. Her works in *The Matter Within* are characteristically baroque. Unlike Nalini Malani's 1996 *Mutants* series, in which mutilated, imploding limbs and flesh serve as allegories for abjection, Banerjee's mutant-like sculptures with their multitude of protrusions and tentacles engender a curious and exotic beauty. They are almost frighteningly extraterrestrial, yet at the same time inviting and seductive—a personification in many ways of the Other in the colonial and postcolonial mindset. In her representation of this Other, Banerjee borrows from the rich aesthetic traditions of Rajput and colonial India. Her use of decorative parasols, feathers, tassels, and horns invokes the visual spectacle of the durbar—an elaborate court affair often accompanied by a royal procession, carried out by Indian kings and eventually their British rulers from the 18th century until Independence. The purpose of the durbar was to affirm political power in the eyes of one's subjects, on the basis of religious and cultural authority. Banerjee channels this public display of intricate ornamentation to establish a similar kind of mysterious yet compelling weightiness in her creations.

She also reclaims and reconstructs the Other to challenge our understanding of sociopolitical constructs such as borders and nationalism, and to open our eyes to the commonalities spurred by the movement of people across continents. As Geeta Kapur suggests in her 1994 essay "A New Inter Nationalism," "Indigenous materials, elusive gestures, and the body are much foregrounded [by third-world artists in the 1990s] . . . as a means of navigating the void that lies at the heart of such geopolitical geometries as local/global." To this point, Banerjee's use of the cowrie bead—native to both India and Africa—is significant both for its reference to migration across borders and the commonalities of the two regions over centuries, as well as for its reference to a historic moment when the cowrie bead was actual currency. In many ways, this one object represents the essence of Banerjee's work, which she describes as exploring "specific colonial moments that reinvent place and identity as complex diasporic experiences."

Unlike the cowrie bead, Banerjee's ostrich egg and touristic trinkets are each specific to one particular part of the world, exemplifying her fascination with items that typify unique places. For centuries global travelers carried home exotic items that came to represent, anywhere else in the world, a specific culture. The ostrich egg, curiously large and unseen anywhere but Africa, was an item of great intrigue for Europeans and Asians of the colonial era. Today, miniatures of famous landmarks and other plastic souvenirs, displayed on Banerjee's sculpture featuring a tortoise shell as the Earth's surface, play a similar role as ambassadors of particular times, places, and cultures. Her inclusion of brown glass bottles—reminiscent of the sea trade during colonial times—is another reference to diasporic experience. Once used to carry fluids and other substances that otherwise could not be contained, the bottles now refer to the impossibility of containing the spread of culture across the world through the movement of people. With their numerous allusions to voyage and discovery, Banerjee's sculptures invoke a world that is constantly changing and re-creating itself as it confronts new experiences and reconciles conflicting forces of cultural and social practice.

···SR

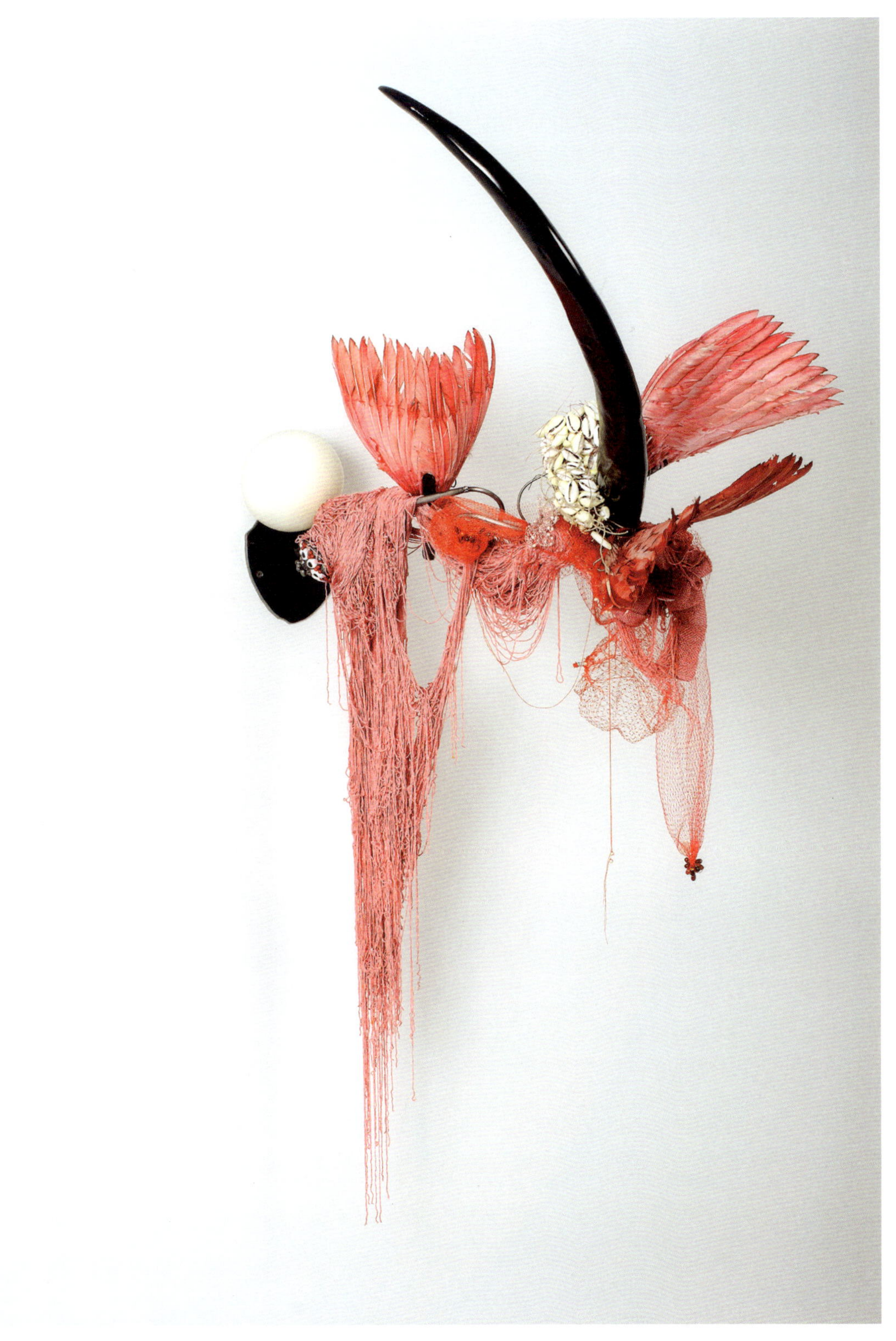

Tender was her wound, pink and playful was her mood, 2011

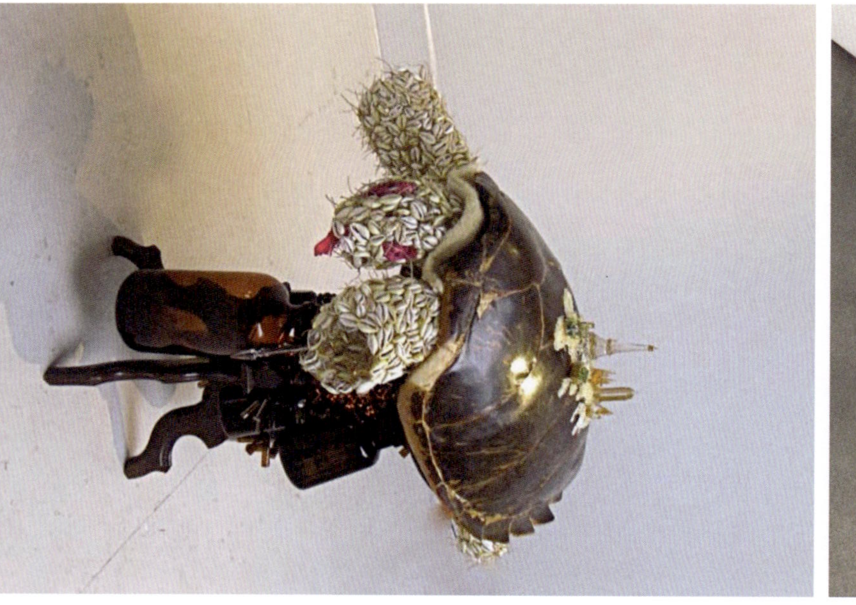

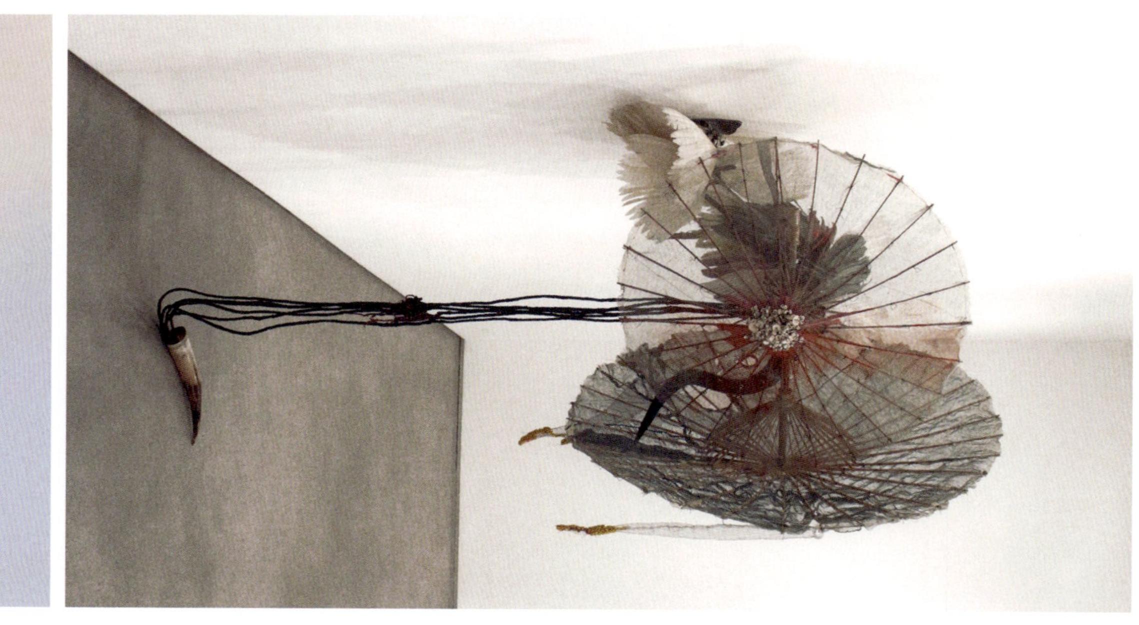

TOP | "a heart of two anchors take one bird and take one butcher, from ear to ear, its a familiar end she was with grin while meat and medicine poured, played yet with the poverty of country was a new friend so she withdrew her smile to clear one anchor that was not her faith the other was my mothers brother, enchanted china, giggled with Africa and strayed to stay in whips of lamb leather, feathers Stained, shells that raised the last anchor human hate," 2011
BOTTOM | Lotions and potions like rivers where in quick motion, as well as essential oils and culture's notions, where these cultures would once be locked in harbor or empires court now took ride on the global, opened themselves up to mysterious and foreign incantations, 2011

She drew a premature prick, in a fluster of transgressions, abject by birth she knew not what else to do with this untouchable reach, unknowable body as she was an ancient savage towed into his modern present, 2011

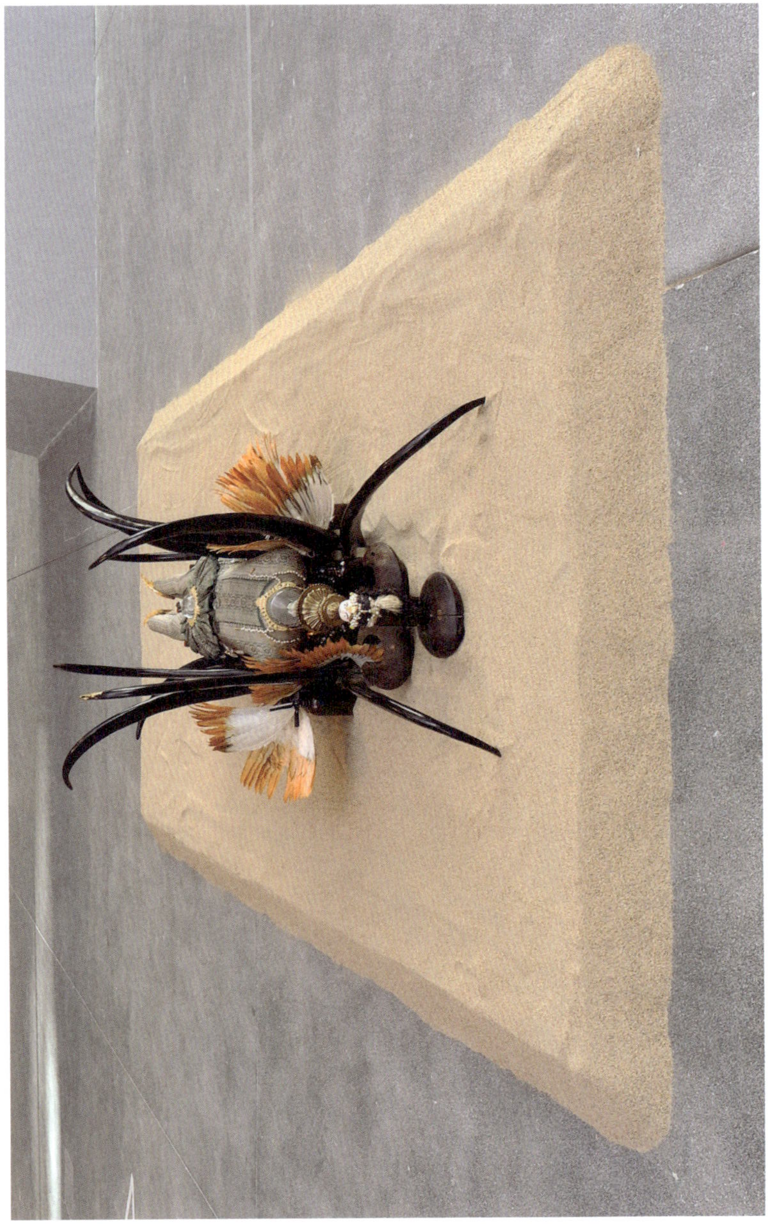

ANITA DUBE

Trained as an art historian, Anita Dube brings a vigorous theoretical sensibility and sociopolitical consciousness to her art practice. She uses a variety of materials, from found-object readymades to industrial and craft materials, and even teeth and bones. Her works have a distinctive tactile sensuality, and they express ideas related to mythology, existential experience, history, and social memory, homing in on the nexus between material culture and intersubjective metaphor. Her approach is both visceral and phenomenological, and her works carry traces of human labor and affect, culture and consciousness. Indeed, she explicitly rejects the Enlightenment binary between emotions and ideas, and her process is driven by ideas that she believes manifest their emotive weight and conceptual content through the creative process of construction. Dube associates her materials with emotional states, and treats her works as a zone of pedagogical dialogue in which ideas and emotions are crystallized into conceptually grounded form.

In her text-based pieces, everyday materials and objects function as vessels for her conceptual content. One major body of such works, from 2007, is a set of words beginning with the letter W: *Wound, Waste, War, Wisdom,* and *Woman.* Striving to make her materials conceptually and emotionally manifest the words they incarnate, Dube cuts the word "wound" into drywall with a saw. This is not a surface wound, she explains, but an injury that passes through the architecture of the body. Through the wound one can see into spaces beyond, and it is impossible to ignore the raw edge. The work is fragile, susceptible, permanently open, unhealable. *War* is made from neon to highlight the sensationalization of violence, while *Waste* takes the form of a huge metal garbage can. The word-sculpture *Wisdom* is constructed from the spines of books whose hard covers have been removed. Dube places the book spines in an acrylic container packed with salt, suggesting that wisdom can be produced, as she puts it, by "pickling knowledge gathered from books with the salt of life."

Dube's first candle sculpture was part of this series. She sculpted giant, almost human-scale candles into the word *Woman* and first displayed them with the wicks lit.

In contrast to the well-known performance works in which she assembles words out of pieces of meat, burning candles enable the word itself to enact its own semantic content in a performative manner. In the candle works the lineage to the Ordinary Language Philosophers, especially J. L. Austin with his Speech Act Theory, is most clear. The word burns, produces heat, and destroys itself, morphing from form to formlessness. For Dube, the possibility of incinerating a word work implies a potential liberation from the accepted meaning embodied in the word. She pushes us to contemplate what words can mean if nothing is truly permanent or absolute. Fire becomes an element of destruction, purification, transformation.

The architectural text-sculptures that followed *Love* and *Void* (both 2007-8), are even larger than *Woman.* They are both performative and interactive, for it is use (by the artist, exhibition venue, or collector) that determines what becomes of them. Collectors of various editions are free to use the work as they see fit. What will people do with the work, the artist wonders? Burn it down to nothing? Bring it to life sporadically, briefly, to perform its flickering metamorphosis for an audience? Keep it in a stasis of cold, lifeless waiting? Even then, the materials are still as volatile as the words they form. They can melt from external heat (one did while it was in storage), and thus they are inherently poised on the brink of potential formlessness.

A sensitivity to the emotive power of materials permeates Dube's oeuvre. A number of works are made from ceramic eyes of the sort typically used in Hindu temples: sometimes affixed to hands, sometimes affixed to the corners where the walls meet the ceiling, sometimes spilling across walls like rivers or a flood of migrating bodies. Many works are covered with "skins" made from materials such as velvet, bandages, or military camouflage. She frequently uses found roots and branches from fallen or felled trees, coating them with human-made materials and incorporating them into tableaux that include text, found images, and mythological iconography to meditate on the intersection of nature and culture.

···MK

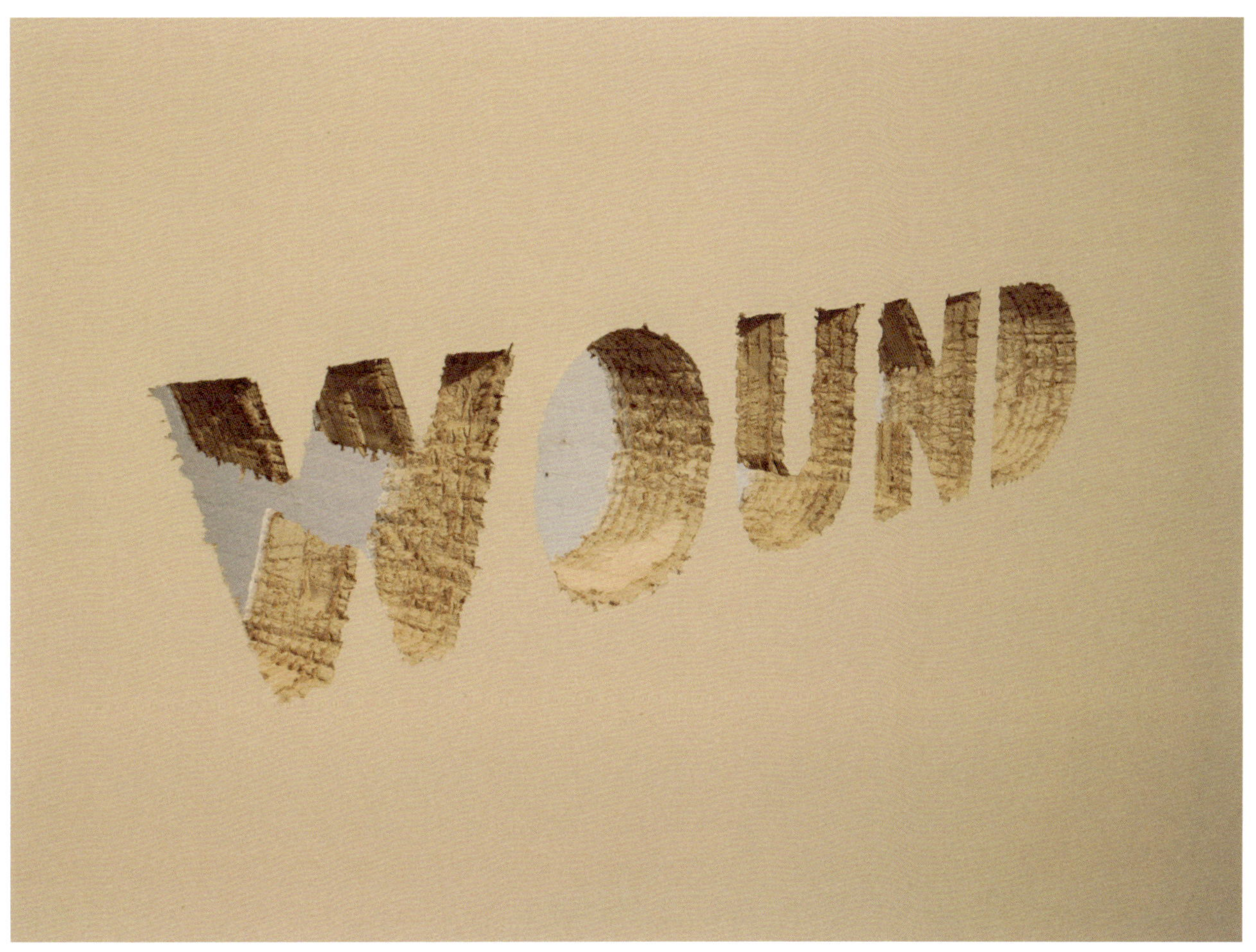

Wound, 2007

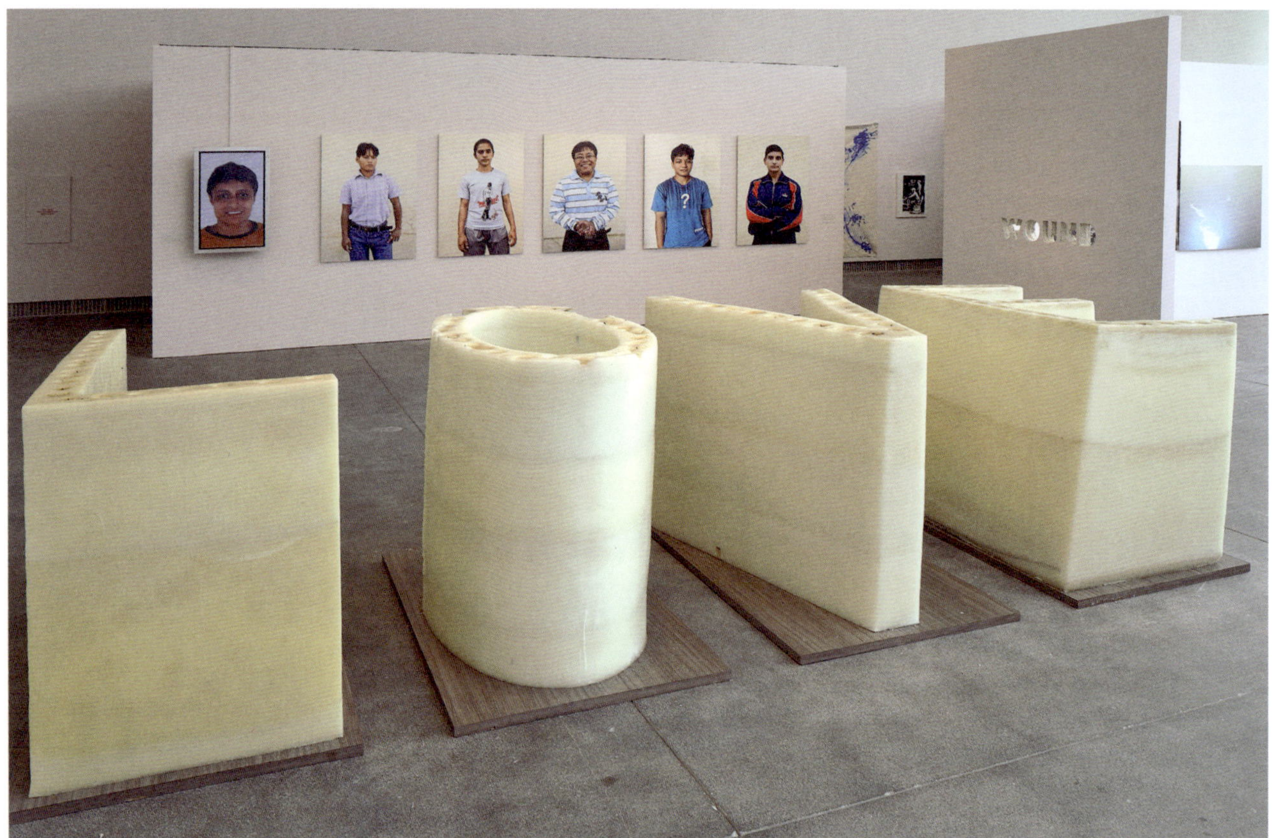

Love, 2007–8

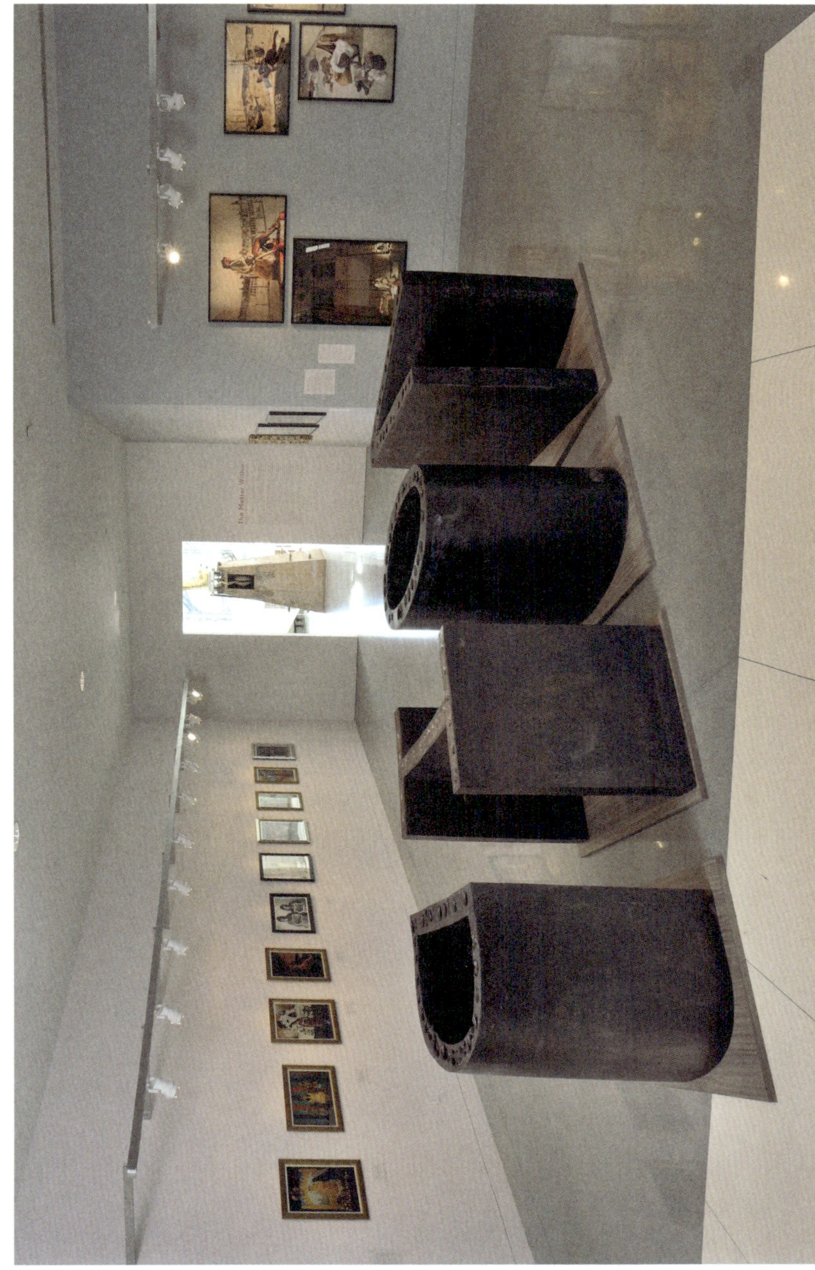

Void, 2007–8

Shilpa Gupta

Shilpa Gupta's highly political work investigates such pressing concerns as globalization, commerce, war, religion, and cultural and historical violence. She explores the aftermath of destructive and conflicting ideologies and creeds, and draws attention to the resulting fear and anxiety that pervade contemporary life.

Gupta's range of mediums extends from video and online projects to sculpture and performance. Her early new-media work stressed the importance of interactivity, for instance *Blessed-bandwidth.net* (2003), an online game in which users chose a religion to incarnate and received a blessing, and *Untitled (Shadow)* (2006–7), where viewers' shadows are incorporated into a video projection. The artist has also solicited viewer participation in non-media works such as *Blame* (2004), in which she handed out bottles of fake blood on trains and on the street. Directions printed on the bottles encouraged the recipients to attempt to classify the contents by race and religion.

The sharing of takeaways is a recurring theme. Gupta has given away pieces of paper incised with the word "memory" and balloons printed with the words "I want to live with no fear." In addition to offering up the possibility of art as a non-commodity, the use of commonplace items puts art into a familiar context. By calling upon languages that are recognizable to mass audiences—for instance bottles and soap in her object-based work and advertising and media in her video work—Gupta aims to engage viewers within a non-intimidating scenario, encouraging them to actively participate.

This wish to place art in a mundane situation is also her reason for taking it out of the gallery setting and into the street, as with *There Is No Explosive in This* (2007), in which visitors are invited to take bags printed with the words of the title and carry them around in the public sphere. This blurring of boundaries between art and life occurs again in Gupta's works that obscure the geographic, cultural, or ideological barriers that usually separate people. In her sculptural work, actual boundaries—walls, gates, barricade tape—figure prominently. These are the borders that divide communities, delimiting both physical and theoretical territory.

A boundary of particular interest to Gupta is the one between India and Pakistan. Partition has been the subject of many of her works, including *In Our Times* (2008), in which she sings the 1947 speeches of Jawaharlal Nehru (the first Prime Minister of India, post-independence) and Muhammad Ali Jinnah (the first president of Pakistan). The speeches were originally delivered three days apart and are strikingly similar in their promises of peace and happiness. She has also executed works that examine boundaries in other locales of conflict such as Quebec, Israel, and Palestine.

Gupta's piece that was featured in this exhibition, *Untitled (Sword)* (2009), alludes to Partition. It is an immense, rusted piece of metal extending eight feet out from the wall, slicing the air and effectively dividing the space in front of it into two sections. It is a static sculpture, yet also interactive—like many other works by Gupta—in the sense that its hulking form juts out aggressively, confronting viewers and demanding that they engage in a physical negotiation with it. Its placement at chest height directly challenges and threatens those who pass. The artist states, "I am interested in the relationship between the object and the viewer, and like to create zones where this can get compressed and therefore magnified."

Similar to the contemporaneous *Untitled (Skewers),* which consists of sharp blades hanging from the ceiling, and the untitled work in which a metal gate attached to a wall swings back and forth, breaking the surfaces on either side of it, *Untitled (Sword)* suggests cruelty, specifically the violence of Partition. Here, the vast contrast between the massive body of the weapon and its miniscule tip, cleaved off and hanging below, signifies a brutality that is difficult to eradicate, ingrained as it is in history as well as in the memories of Indians and Pakistanis.

---TL

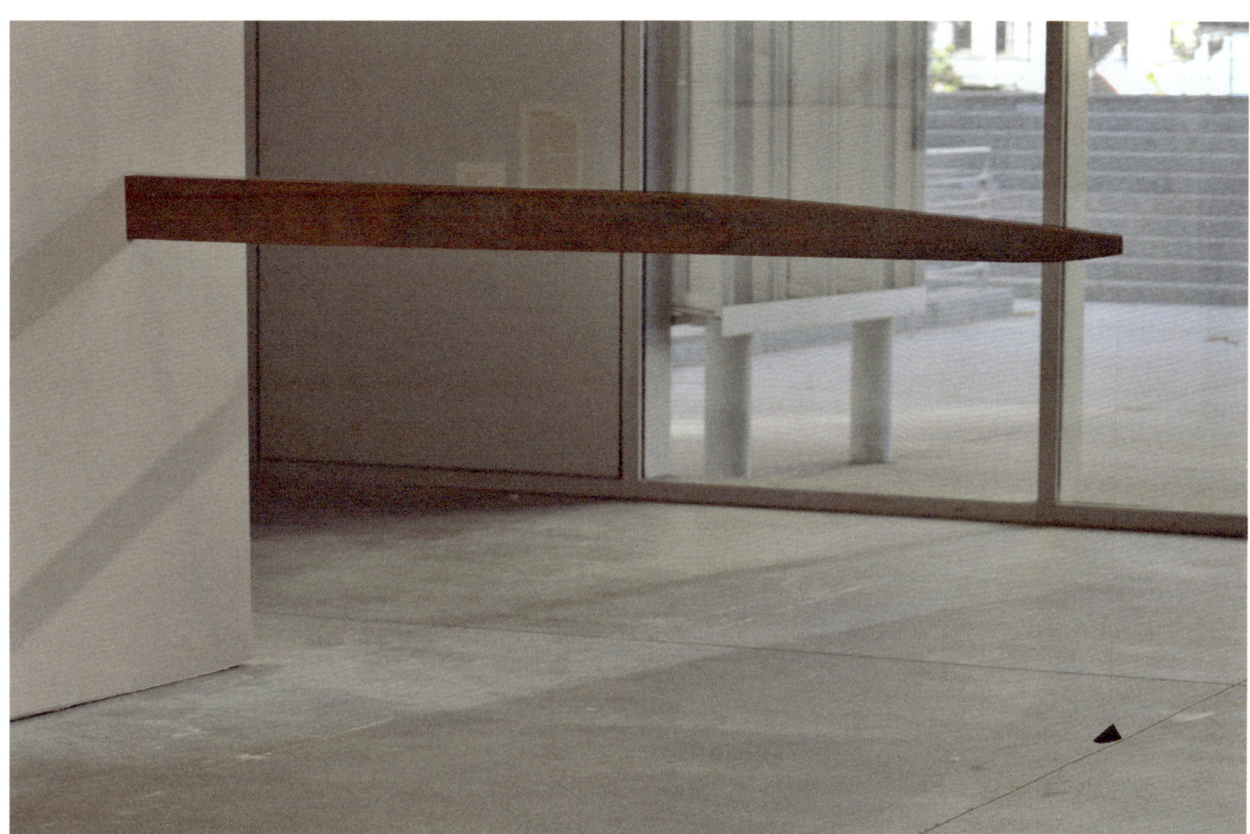

Untitled (Sword), 2009

SIDDHARTHA KARARWAL

Siddhartha Kararwal's expressive and eclectic visual arts practice is centered on how materials can manifest myths. He employs natural materials such as iron, copper, and clay as well as everyday consumer goods: plastic bags, foam sheets, and T-shirts. The physicality of his sculpture compels the viewer to consider his or her own corporeality in relation to the dominating presence of the work.

Kararwal's life-size sculpture *Hangover Man* (2011) was installed on a pedestal in *The Matter Within* to mimic a statue in a public square. It is a re-creation, made of secondhand white T-shirts, of a monument in Baroda, India, of Sayajirao Gaekwad III, founder of Maharaja Sayajirao University, on horseback. The original is situated in the city center, on a traffic island near the university, and it is an important landmark as well as a tourist attraction. In addition to founding the university, which has historically been one of the most important schools of the arts in India, Sayajirao was a noted and enlightened patron of classical music and dance. He was the maharaja of the state of Baroda from 1875 through 1939, a period squarely within the almost ninety-year period of British rule in India.

Kararwal studied fine art at the university, and the statue was part of his everyday comings and goings during those years. Thus, while the work is certainly accessible to all audiences, it was generated out of a local history that has particular resonance within the artist's own life. It refers to a local personage who was of historical importance specifically during the colonial era. These are all themes that run throughout Kararwal's oeuvre.

Hangover Man also references the current global circulation of capital and commodities. The T-shirts are specifically ones that were donated to under-resourced Indian communities by an American charity, but ended up making their way onto the open market. This is often the case with such donated goods sent to India from abroad. One small detail stands out in the sea of rumpled white cloth: an American flag, which looks in scale and material like an oversize label found inside a piece of clothing. It's a funny "Made in America" reference, given the backstory of the piece, but it could also be a more serious allusion to Mahatma Gandhi's focus on textile production and his own spinning and weaving projects, which were an act of dissent against colonial rule.

Through this agglomeration of items of dubious provenance, Kararwal comments on—and, specifically, problematizes—lost eras of glory and royalty. He playfully exposes the gap between official and unofficial economies as a symptom of the NGO culture of philanthropy from the United States to India and the exploitative global economies that propel cheap mass-produced clothing and other textiles from countries like India to the U.S. The enlightened maharaja, then, is made of white T-shirts that circulated on the black market, recycled from a richer and more powerful country, and perhaps originating in India or a country nearby. The ghostly horse and rider are somehow both eerie and comical at the same time. There is a bit of Don Quixote in this rag-doll monarch. Is he charging the windmills of the unstable global economy?

Popularly known as the *Kala Ghoda,* or *Black Horse,* the original, life-size bronze statue of Sayajirao was created by a British artist and funded by the maharaja's subjects and admirers in commemoration of his silver jubilee in 1907 as a token of their loyalty and appreciation. He had ascended to the throne in 1875, when he was still a boy, and soon became known for his confidence and progressive ideas. There are also many tales of his unconventional ways. One such story tells of how he did not bow in the customary manner to the King-Emperor George V. Instead of saluting him three times and walking backward, as was the custom, Sayajirao saluted once, then turned his back and walked away. By reinterpreting a famous statue of an irreverent leader in a manner that deconstructs and destabilizes conventional respect for royalty, Kararwal echoes—and in a sense reenacts—this famous story of the ruler's own behavior when he was alive.

···GM

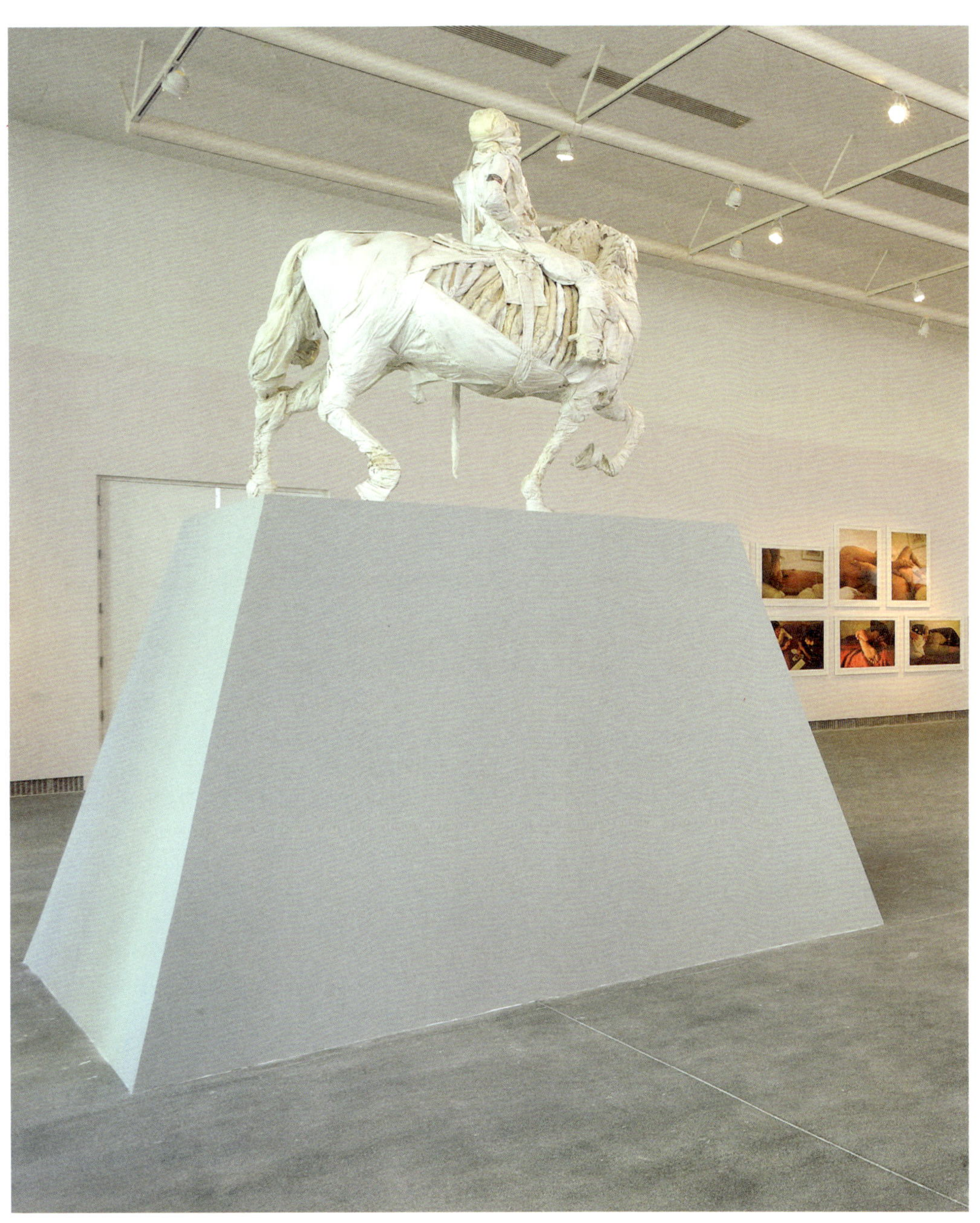

Hangover Man, 2011

SRESHTA RIT PREMNATH

Sreshta Rit Premnath's works are often almost like puzzles, requiring close reading and engagement with specific histories, especially in the arenas of cinema, media, and history. Prennath grew up in Bangalore and has lived and worked in New York for some years now. Throughout his life he has been exposed to all sorts of cultural production from the United States, especially Hollywood movies. His bicultural perspective has fed his analytical approach to art making and his attraction to topics that resonate differently in different cultural contexts. He is particularly interested in lost histories, and in people who labor for the benefit of others.

In *The Matter Within,* Premnath presented a body of work that was inspired by the 2010 bankruptcy and near-collapse of Metro-Goldwyn-Mayer, once one of the most powerful movie studios in Hollywood. MGM's fall from prominence represents the cyclical nature of imperial might, and thus a promising case study in the context of Premnath's larger interest in the legacies of colonialism in the postcolonial age. The work focuses attention not on any particular film but on MGM's iconic roaring lion, which as part of the company's insignia symbolizes its prowess and ambition.

Using a live lion as a symbol of Hollywood proved to be quite popular. Over the years, one MGM lion was replaced by another. Premnath's fascination with the lion inspired him to go to great lengths to track down the biographical details of the actual first one. He researched its life and death and created numerous artworks about it, including a video of his visit to its burial site.

He discovered a photograph of the lion's skin in a local history museum in McPherson, Kansas. To create *Mask* (2011), Premnath stacked up multiple iterations of this image and then singed the edges to create a ragged edge. This work interrupts the naturalness of the photograph, disturbing its referentiality while adding a physical dimension that vaguely recalls a lion's mane in its patterning and layering. It denies the symbol its unifying power by breaking it down for closer consideration.

Hide (01) and *Hide (05)* (both 2010) are triptychs. Each has as its centerpiece a paint-blot-on-canvas work, flanked by two historical black-and-white photographs. The photographs depict "shoots" in both senses of the word: one with a rifle and one with a movie camera. At right in *Hide (01),* two hunters enclosed in a cage contraption take aim at an unseen target. At right in *Hide (05),* a director and a cameraman train their eyes and equipment on an unseen subject. We cannot see what any of them are shooting, but we cannot help imagining that it is the lion on the left in each triptych.

From a distance, the pattern of the central inkblot work could be interpreted as resolving into the shape of a lion's skin mounted on the wall—a reference to the trophy hides one often sees in old ranch lodges or military establishments. The ink blots also make various art historical and social-historical references, for instance to the French postwar artist Yves Klein and his series *Anthropométries,* in which women dipped their nude bodies in paint and then applied themselves directly to large canvases of approximately this same size. Or the classic Rorschach test in which a psychological patient is invited to identify something representational in an abstract inkblot. It is significant as well that Premnath's blots are in blue and green Chroma key colors, the same ones used for video "green screens" to be replaced later with other (representational) imagery.

In his 1957 book *Mythologies,* the theorist Roland Barthes uses examples of artifacts of mass culture—films, ads, cars, children's toys—to explain the relationship between language and power. For him, the creation of mythologies is related to a semiotic system that condenses meaning into distinct signifiers. The signifier unites, in seamless association, an idea and the object that evokes the idea. Premnath embarks upon a similar process in this project by exposing the gap between the semiotics behind the image of the MGM lion and the actual lion. Importantly for Barthes, the iconic image unites everything associated with it under one signifying umbrella. For Premnath, this strategy of unification through symbolism is not only overarching but also a facade—a sham, a cover—for the hegemonic influence of American popular culture. He deconstructs the MGM lion and its evocation of regal power, readying it for further dissection.

···**GM**

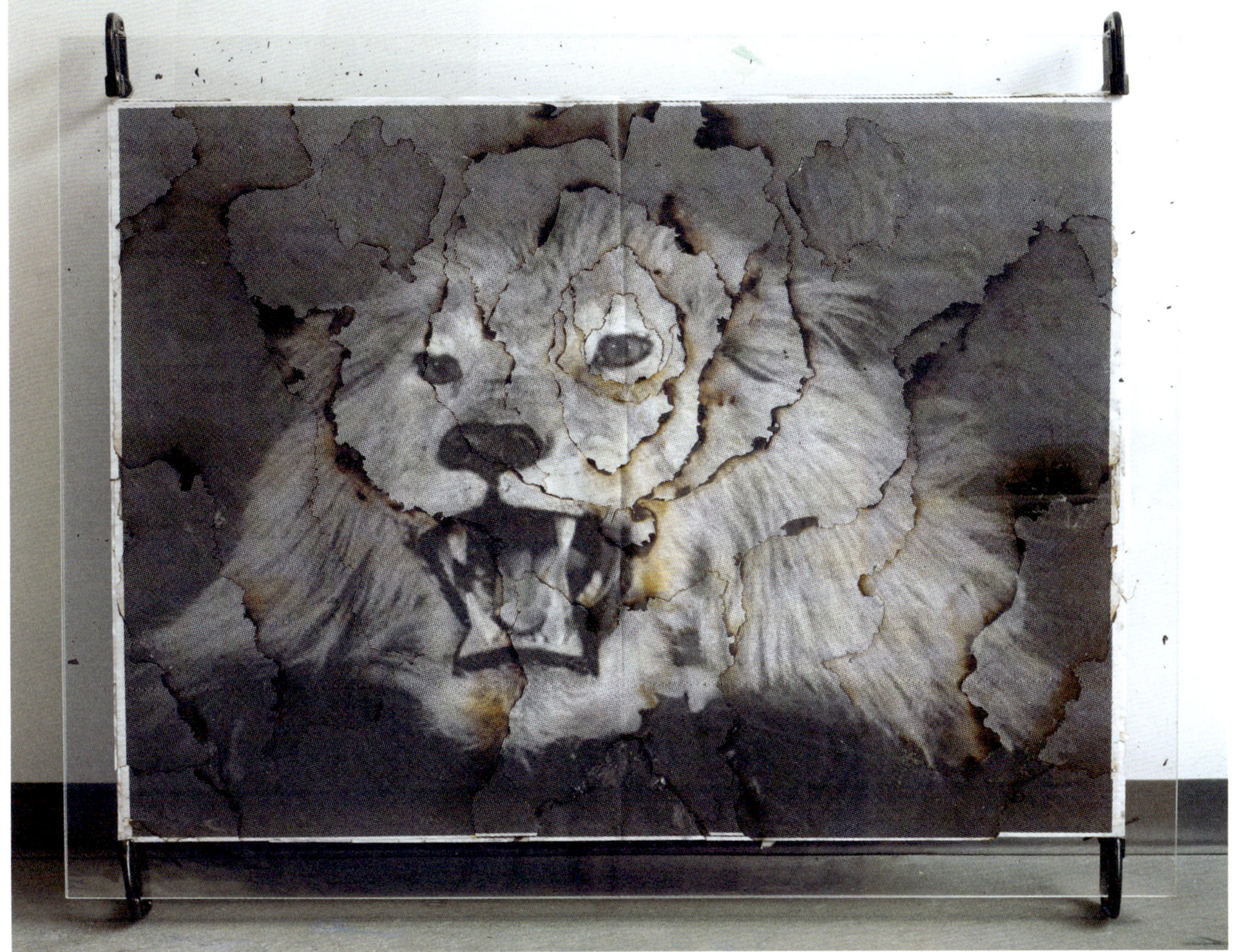

Mask, 2011

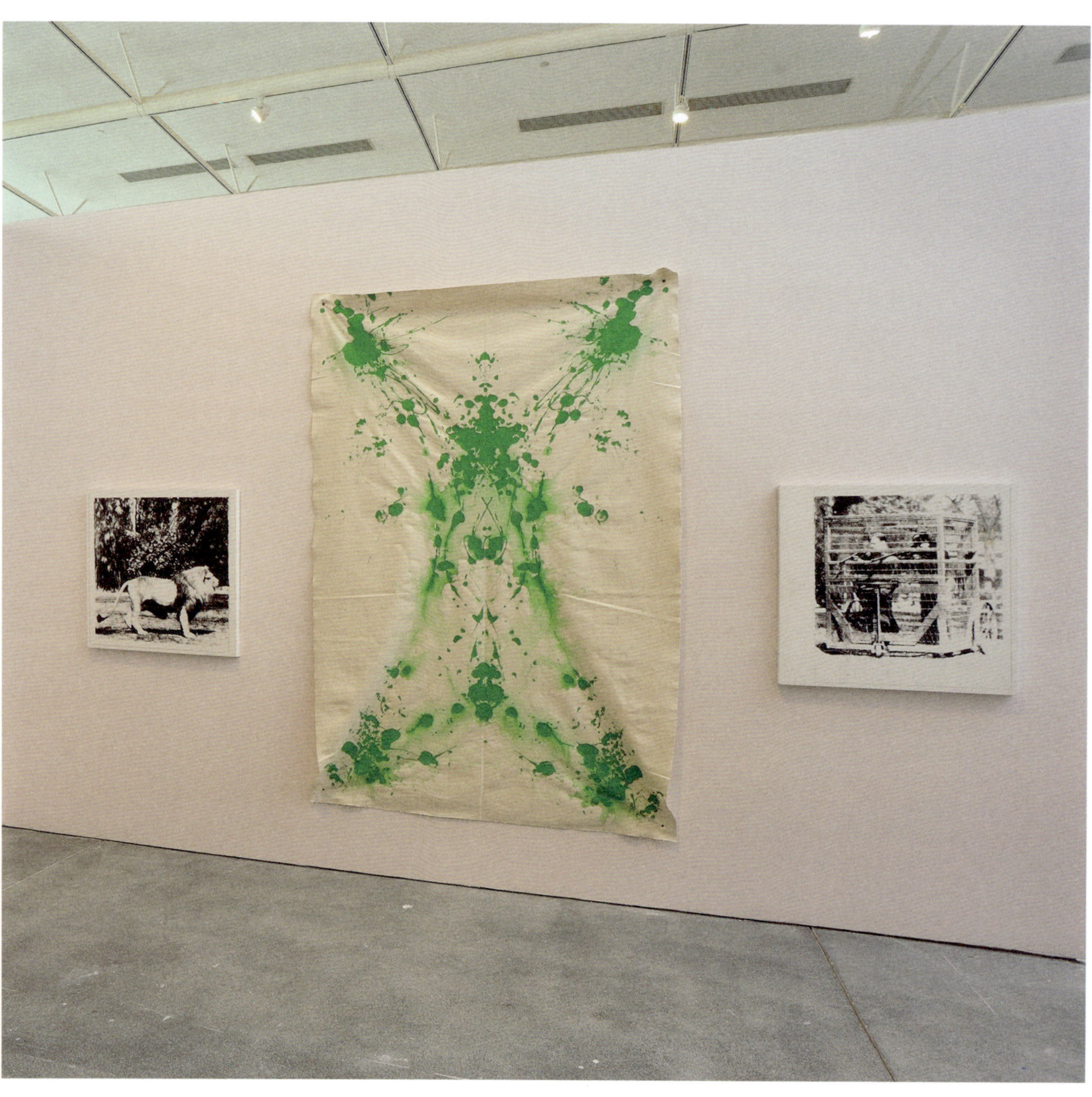

Hide (01), 2010

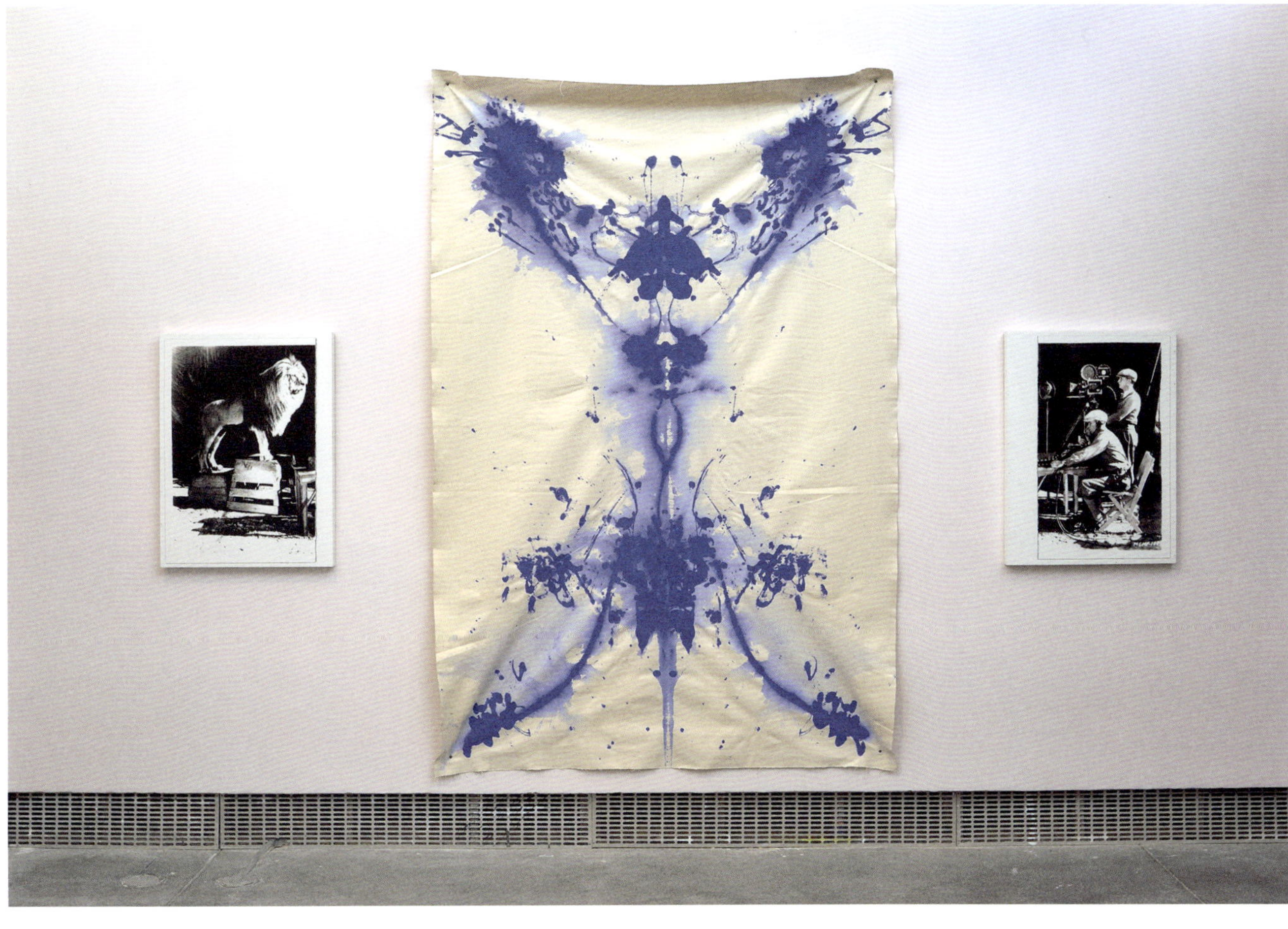

Hide (oS), 2010

SUDARSHAN SHETTY

Sudarshan Shetty's work is encrypted with layers of messages. It is easy to ascribe an obsession with death to the Mumbai-based artist, since he is constantly questioning mortality through his art. But Shetty claims that death is not his true subject. He is more concerned, he says, with the consumer market, commodity culture, and how the objects with which we surround ourselves come to represent our mortality. The emotive range of Shetty's work varies from somber to playful, whether he is photographing a bathtub filled with scissors, a pit orchestra of boat-shaped mechanized cellos that play atonal music, or a metal sculpture of two water buffalo skeletons that appear to be mating. The images evoke death and violence, but also humor.

One work featured in *The Matter Within* was an untitled sculpture from the series *this too shall pass*. Made in 2010, it is a self-portrait made of fiberglass covered in gold leaf. This statue does not stand upright but rather leans at an angle, and gradually moves into an upright position as an accompanying donation box fills up with coins inserted by visitors to the exhibition. The work is directly inspired by statues of political leaders of the type installed in city squares, and it references, in particular, ones that have been torn down by groups of discontented citizens, for instance Vladimir Lenin statues in many cities around the world, and the one of Saddam Hussein that was pulled from its pedestal in Baghdad's Firdos Square by American military troops.

Shetty's sculpture is of course a reflection on democracy and the power of the people to overthrow a despotic leader. That is why the participation of viewers is crucial. The act of putting coins into the donation box becomes akin to casting a vote. On a more abstract level, the work comments on the role of the museum in ensuring a long life for art, and of a value system that insists that art is permanent and must be preserved in perpetuity. Shetty believes that an object must change its meaning as time goes by—and in fact that an object can only achieve permanence if its author incorporates the idea of change into the original concept. This work also points humorously to the artist's own mortality. A tiny plaque on the pedestal bears his name, date of birth (1961), and an imaginary date of death (2010), which not coincidentally is the date of the work's creation. Shetty is not really commenting on the romantic ideology of the "death of the artist" so much as his intention to separate the persona of the maker of this object from the object itself.

Even the chosen material, fiberglass, plays an important role. Initially Shetty considered making the statue out of bronze, but settled on fiberglass covered in gold leaf to more explicitly introduce the idea of artifice. Artifice is also the explicit subject of another untitled work from 2010, this one from the *Stab* series, which incorporates an old chair sourced from Chor Bazaar, a fake-antique furniture market in Mumbai. The word "Stab," written in neon on the seat, mimics a scar dripping blood and provokes both intrigue and revulsion on the part of the viewer. By referencing artificiality, Shetty dips into the collective memory bank that is fed to all of us through the dissemination of global news. He taps these memories in order to awaken our senses to life, as a spiritual order that tempers our consumption of popular images.

···**GM**

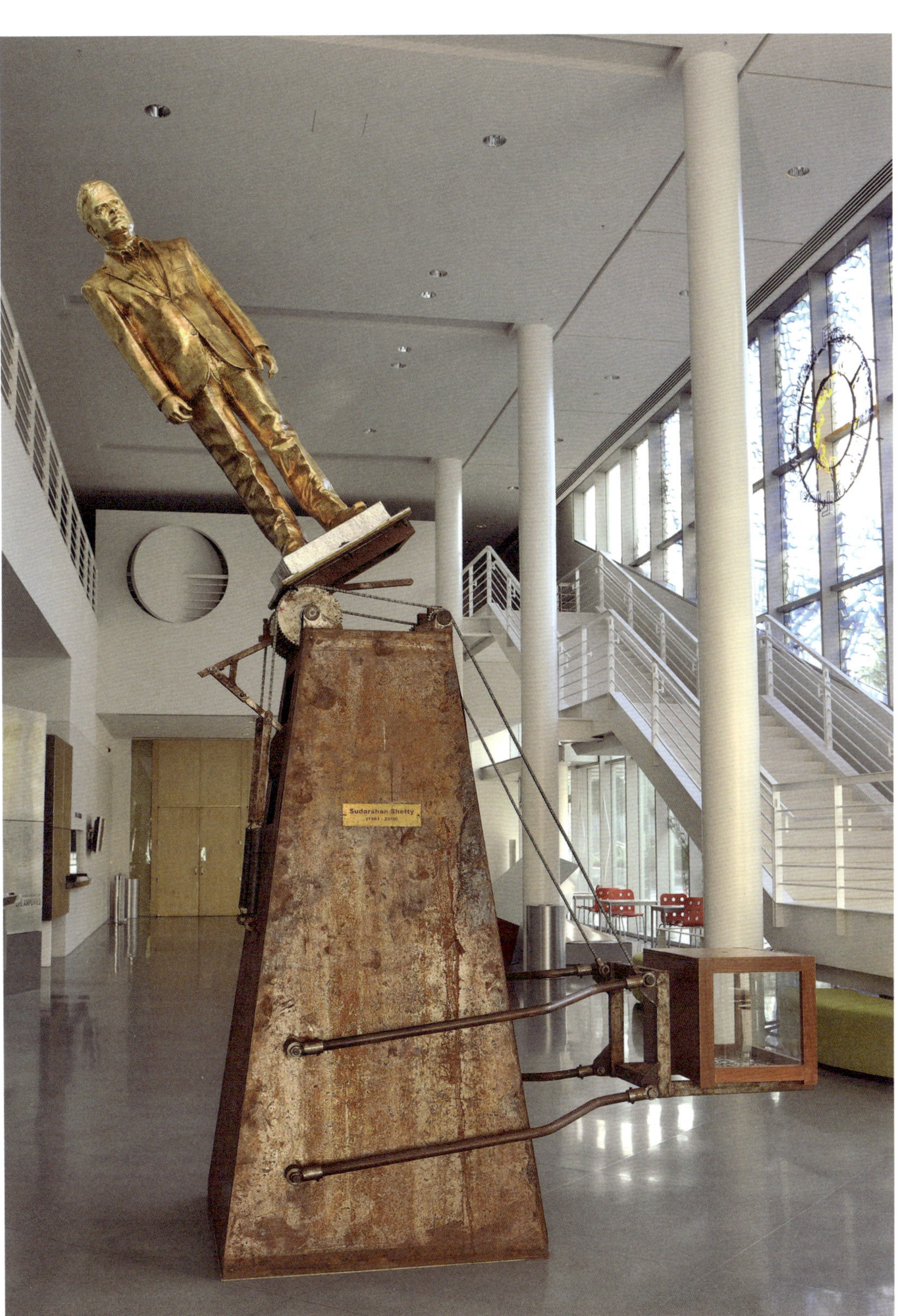

Untitled, from the series *this too shall pass*, 2010

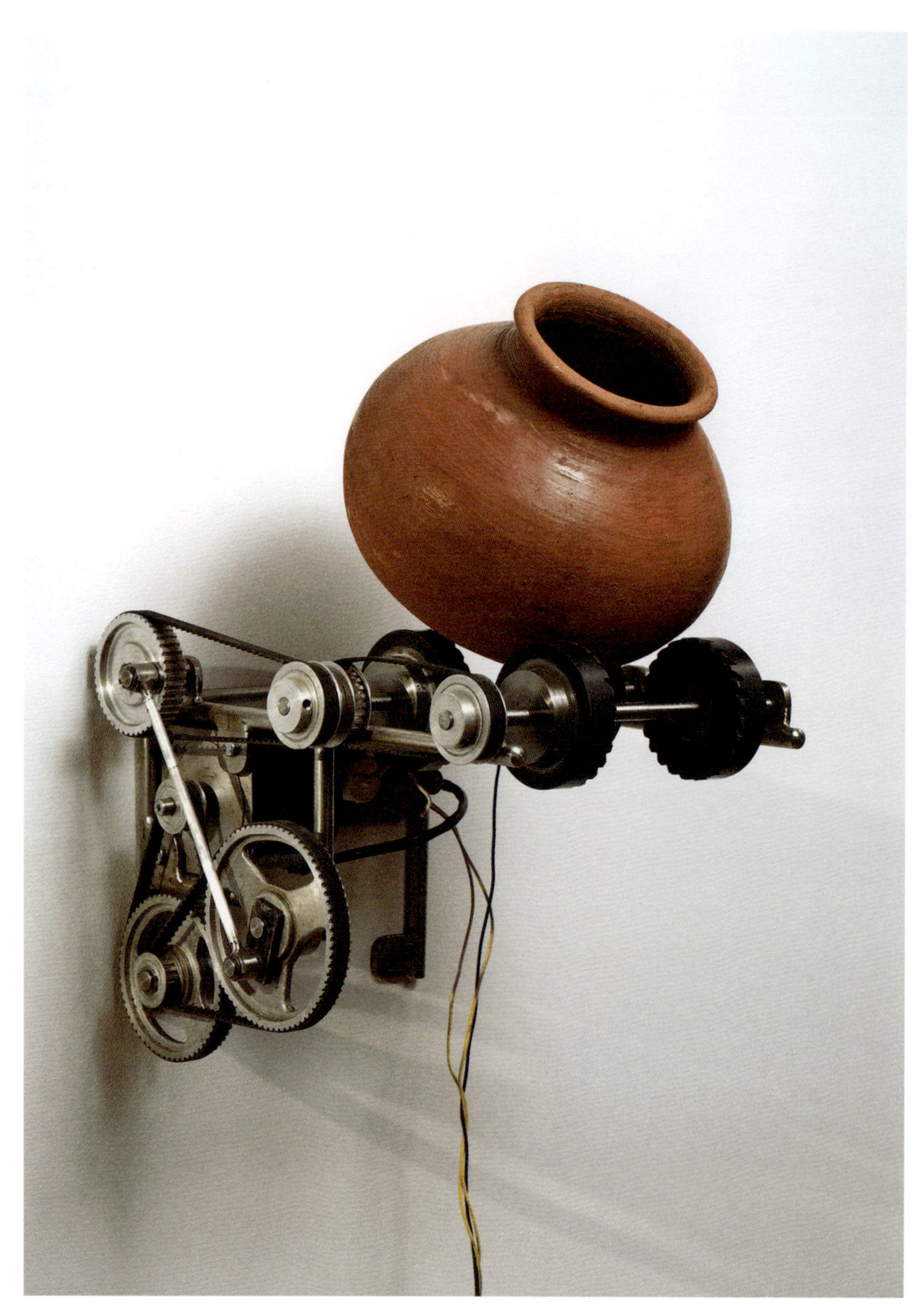

Untitled, from the series *Saving Skin*, 2008

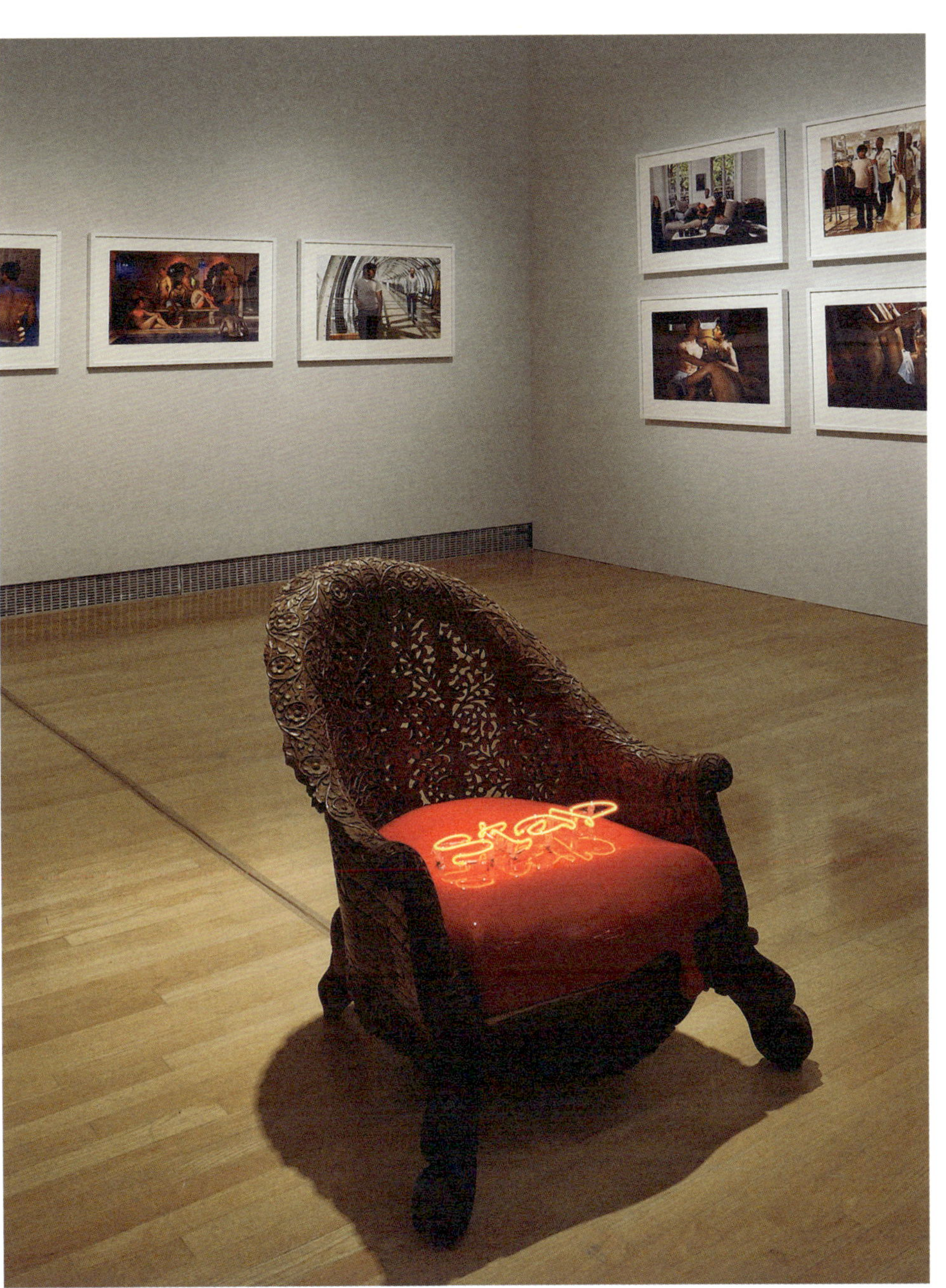

Untitled, from the series *Stab*, 2010

THUKRAL & TAGRA

Thukral & Tagra arrived on the Indian art scene with a bang in 2005 and have come to embody the spirit and voice of the country's youth. They are aware and unabashed; fashion- and design-forward; masters of technology and media; and critical participants in the mass commercialization of their society. They fundamentally challenge the divides between popular culture, fine art, and politics in a style that is consistently irreverent. Their pioneering work crosses the boundaries between graphic and interior design, painting, video, sculpture, and installation, and effortlessly straddles the worlds of art, fashion, architecture, and advertising.

With an ironic 1960s flower-power aesthetic, they address serious social issues, ranging from domestic violence and religious conflict to HIV awareness, and in the process prove an age-old saying: All that glitters is not gold. What audiences initially encounter is glamour and glitz, but a closer look unveils deeper and more somber lessons. The unusual marriage of pop art and social messaging in Thukral & Tagra's work not only distinguishes them among contemporary artists, but also makes them phenomenally influential among young people. The imaginary is a concept often explored and represented by artists. But the ways in which these artists present it resonate particularly well with the youth of India, a population that is rapidly reshaping its identity in the midst of intense multicultural immersion. In Thukral & Tagra's work, the imaginary is realized in two ways: in the escapist form of their fantastical, Technicolor world, and in the aspirational forms of striving Indian youth.

The recesses of their personal index— dreams, memories, and ambitions from their Punjabi heritage and the experience of growing up in a rapidly modernizing India—are key inspirations for Thukral & Tagra, as is the hypercommercialization of modern society. Historically, Indian culture has eschewed waste. Living in a closed economy where production was strictly controlled by the government, Indian consumers were unaccustomed to the concept of brand choice, and by necessity and economy always reused everything, from plastic bags and containers to paper. Today, with the opening up and ensuing boom of the Indian economy, reusability has been replaced with disposability.

Thukral & Tagra's two sculptures in *The Matter Within* offer a critical examination of the supremacy of name brands, and of both the promise and the potential hazard of excessive consumption brought about by the Indian capitalist renaissance. *Now in Your Neighborhood* (2008), comprised of fiberglass casts of hundreds of empty bottles of syrup, takes a comical jab at commercialism, likening it to the giant, unstoppable force of a dinosaur threatening to consume everything in its path. The use of serial repetition in this colossal structure drives home another, more cerebral, point about consumption as not just an activity, but more like a habit or lifestyle. As Arjun Appadurai points out in his 1996 book *Modernity at Large,* "The commodity culture of consumer capitalism can be situated in a wider anthropology of the relationship between consumption and repetition." He further suggests that consumption is centered around "techniques of the body," and that "those practices of consumption that are closest to the body . . . acquire uniformity through habituation: food, dress, hairstyling . . . [making it] extremely difficult to maintain an anarchic consumption regime." For instance eating and sleeping, and rituals of personal hygiene, are all habitual activities and patterns of consumption that are closest to our bodies and assume a regulated form out of biological necessity; without order, the biological system would break down. Thukral & Tagra's repeated bottles allude to the threat of modern-day homogeneity suffocating an ancient and vibrant culture, but that same repetition also lends a kind of harmonious uniformity to the piece, challenging us to look deeper into biological tendencies toward patterns of consumption.

Artificial Strawberry Flavor—1 (2008) reveals another side of capitalism: its seductive effect on dreamy-eyed Punjabi lads desperate to become India's biggest export. With their faces glued to the sides of fiberglass bottles, they themselves become a product to be shipped abroad. Thukral & Tagra are fascinated by the phenomenon of the emigration and eventual repatriation of Punjabis in India, and its effect on Indian families, architecture, dress, and cuisine. In today's globalized India, a whole new aesthetic is being developed that not only influences Thukral & Tagra's work but provides a platform for its continued growth and evolution.

···SR

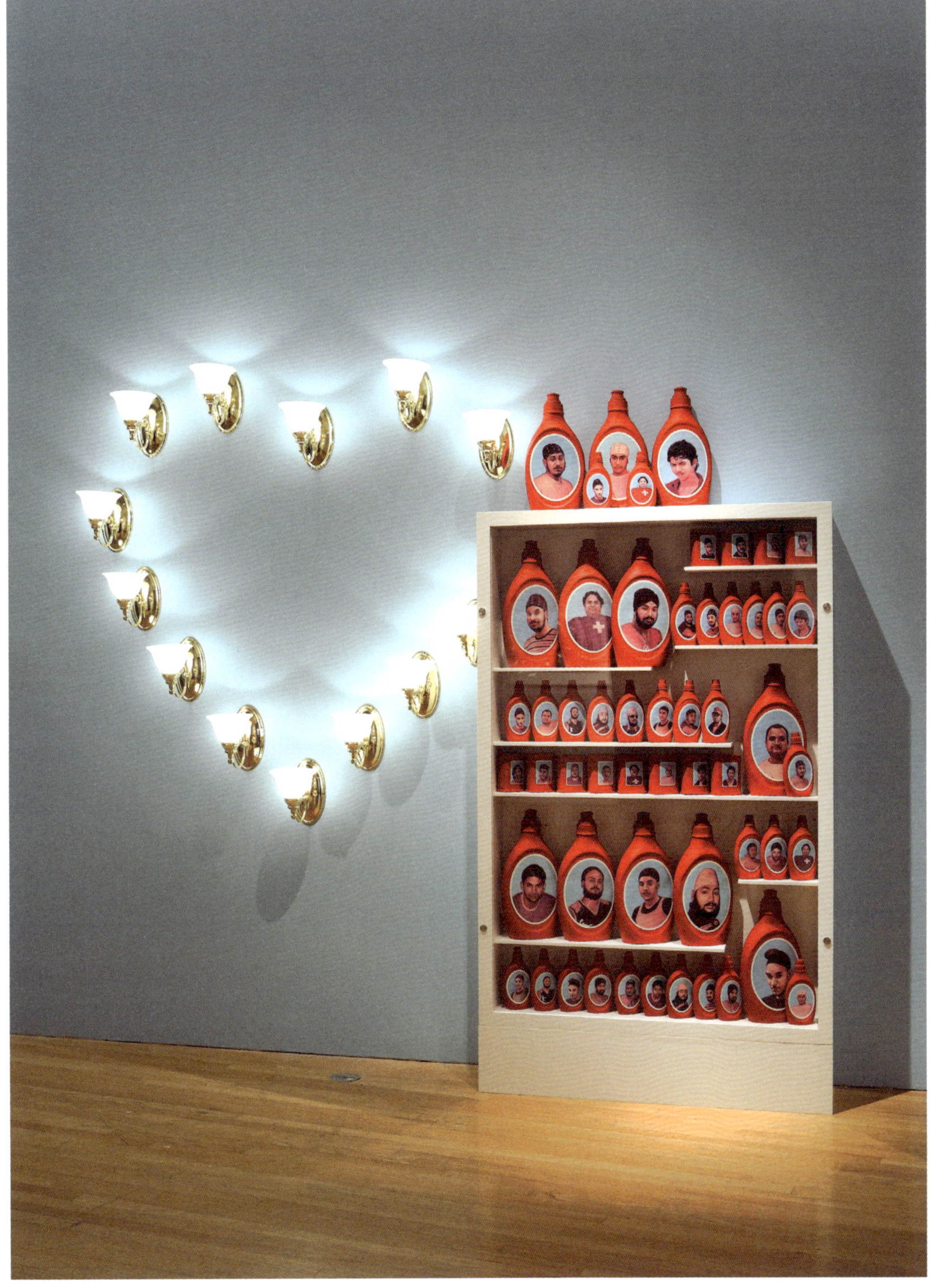

Artificial Strawberry Flavor—1, 2008

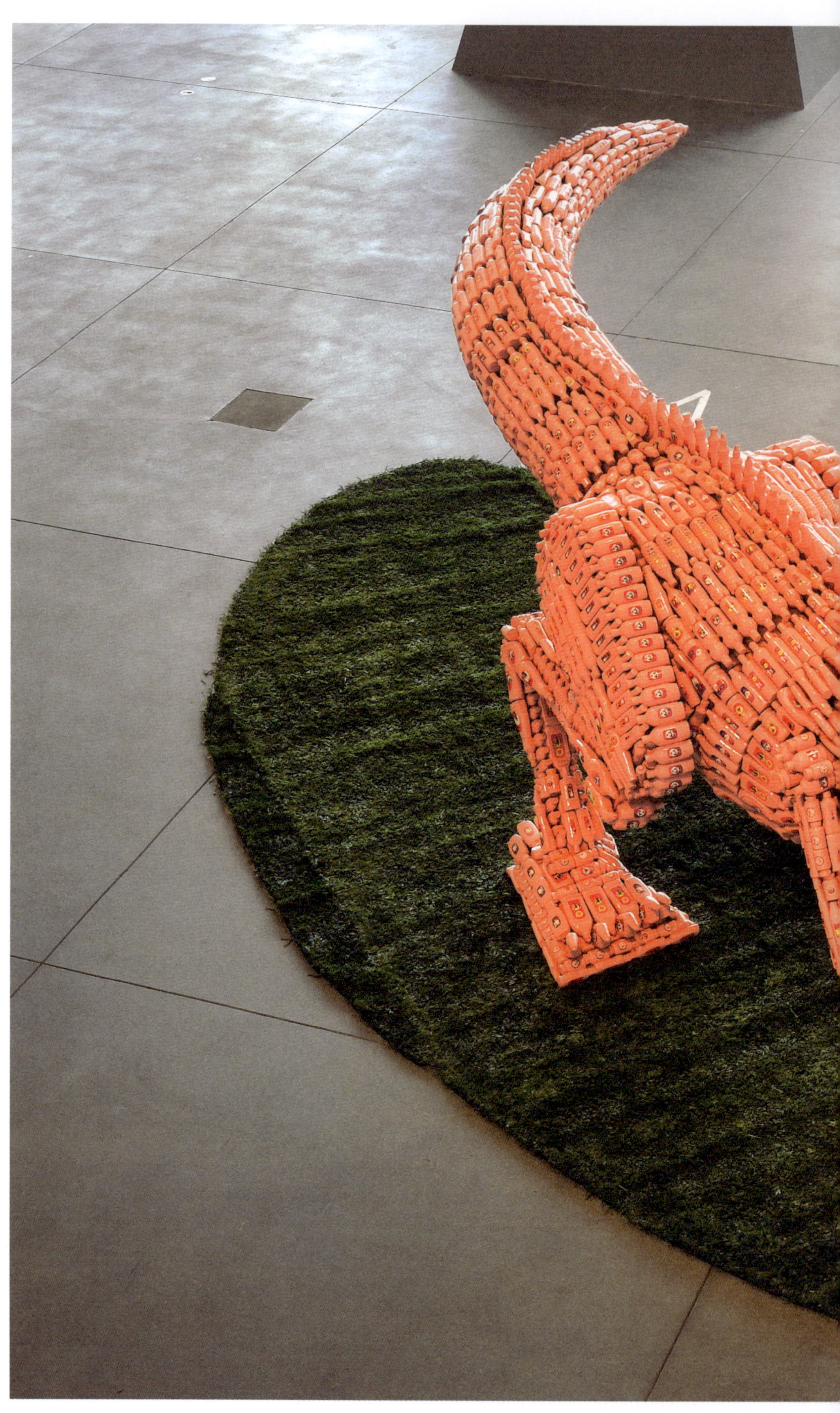

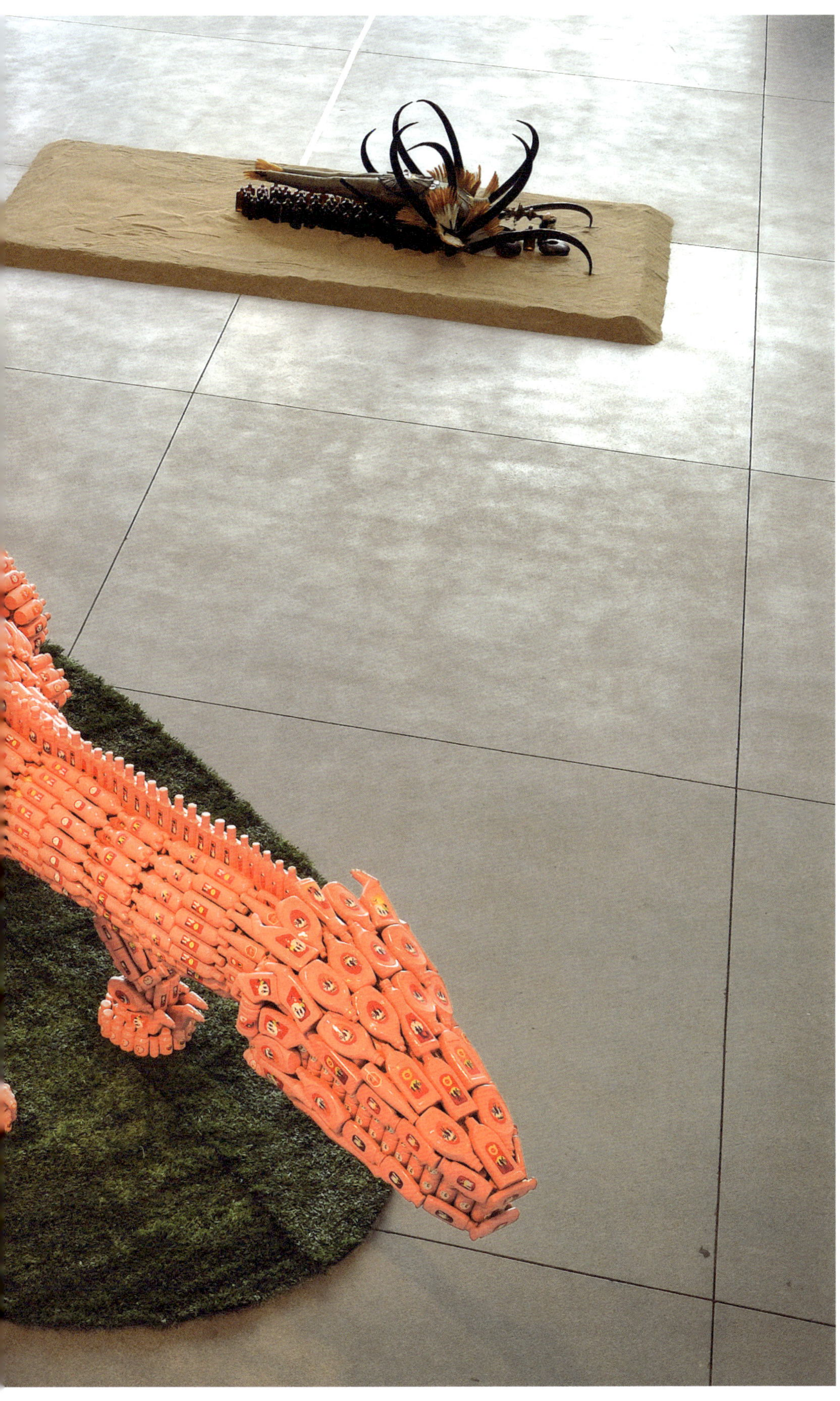

Now in Your Neighborhood, 2008

The Photographic Present: The Here and the Now of Contemporary Indian Art

Parul Dave Mukherji

1.
As cited in Graham Coulter-Smith, ed., *The Visual-Narrative Matrix: Interdisciplinary Collision and Collusions* (Southampton: Southampton Institute, 2000): 1.

2.
Terry Smith, Okwui Enwezor, and Nancy Condee, eds., *Antinomies of Art and Culture: Modernity, Postmodernity, Contemporaneity* (Durham, North Carolina and London: Duke University Press, 2008): 9.

Representation mingles with what it represents.

—JACQUES DERRIDA[1]

The contemporary consists precisely in the acceleration, ubiquity, and constancy of radical disjuncture of perception, of mismatching ways of seeing and valuing the same world, in the actual coincidence of asynchronous temporalities, in the jostling contingency of various cultural and social multiplicities, all thrown together.

—TERRY SMITH[2]

My teenage daughter recently insisted that I watch with her some video clips on YouTube. I had just been sitting down to write (this essay, as a matter of fact) and, noticing my impatience, she pointed out that given my interest in globalization and art theory, the clips might offer some useful lessons. Turning skeptically to the screen, I saw an image come alive of a young British teenager singing a song from a Bollywood film. I stared as if hypnotized at the singer, who performed with poise and confidence. Ordinarily her British-accented Hindi would have provoked laughter, and yet here it only added to the cross-cultural magic she was weaving. It was hardly surprising to learn that such songs performed by non-Indians are the latest trend, and a craze particularly among South Asian males, in India and around the world.

What a sharp contrast from the familiar scenario of an Indian call center employee who cultivates an American accent to serve clients from abroad! The same technology of simulation and videography that allows for mimicry and impersonation also leaves room for the dynamics of dissimulation and masquerade. And caught in their unpredictable constellation is desire.

The mimicry—the manner in which the Hindi words rolled from the lips of someone who probably did not even know their meaning—and the enactment of romance through the juxtaposition of film clips from the original Bollywood film with shots of the British singer captured, for me, not only the contemporary moment but also the central theme of *The Matter Within*. It demonstrated a new rhetoric of embodiment, and the aesthetics (if not the politics) of communicative bodies. The latter is readily observable in today's public protests against corruption that are widely disseminated by the media, such as those triggered by the Gandhian political activist Anna Hazare. Globalization has indeed created a kind of networking in which a reverse swing of mimicry is possible; the East does not always take the West as its role model. It is creating new forms of desire in which India has begun to feature quite prominently as a destination. The video clip also made me realize how photography and the moving image have become a dominant matrix that has shaped contemporary art practice in India.

The title of *The Matter Within* sets up a spatial and conceptual landscape implying an inside and an outside. In terms of photographic practice, where does one situate these inner and outer levels? Perhaps the inner lies in the particular medium-specific capabilities of a camera, and the outer refers to the camera's entanglement with the world "out there." In a certain sense, photography is built to attend to matters outside. Directed at the world, it enacts an indexical capturing of events and thus can compellingly partake of the political. The camera can freeze images of protesting bodies, for instance the mobs holding flags and banners and grabbing news headlines today in India. It can turn dissent into a performative act that can go viral in our media-driven world. And it can directly participate in the politics of communicative bodies. From the July 2011 Slut Walk, which was organized in New Delhi to protest sexual harassment, to the nationwide agitation against corruption spearheaded by Hazare, photographic images circulated in the media have turned public spaces into a vibrant theater of democracy. Globalized networking enables the relay of protest movements across disparate geographies. The New Delhi Slut Walk is a case in point, as it was inspired by the Toronto Slut Walk three months earlier, which went viral through Facebook, newspaper coverage, and telephone calls. In the same way, Hazare's anti-corruption protest in India briefly ignited the imaginations of social radicals in Pakistan and Indonesia. Photographic images play a key role in defining imagination itself as a social practice. With the mobility of images, their ripple effects transcend national boundaries.

The concerns of *The Matter Within* are related to current world geopolitics, which are afflicted by a global economic crisis in the wake of eastward movement of capital. The new realignment of power relations has driven some social theorists to coin another "post" term— "post-globalization"—to describe the rise of the Chinese and Indian economies.[3] In the post-globalization scenario, where national boundaries and flows of capital are loosened, allowing for greater mobility of goods and people and making the local confront the global in unprecedented ways, the title of this show may seem ambivalent. For example, the "village" in "global village" arouses a new sense of intimacy and virtual togetherness induced by fast-moving media images on the highways of information technology. "The matter within" invokes on the one hand the insularity that characterizes the art worlds in Europe and America as they awaken to art worlds that have existed outside the ambit of the West since modernization. It can also be interpreted through the figure of the diasporic Indian artist, acknowledging his or her new visibility in the West in the wake of India's newly buoyant economy.[4]

I believe the central question in understanding the contemporary moment in art practice in India involves the ubiquity of photography. Its sheer pervasiveness tends to shape collective memory of social and cultural experiences to the extent that photographs can even effectively take the place of experiences. Those who lived through the 2002 riots in Gujarat after the burning of the Sabarmati Express Train will vividly remember the photograph of the victim pleading for his life that circulated widely in the media and acquired an iconic status signifying communal violence. Photographs are tied to contemporary reality through indexicality, and hence they powerfully shape collective memory, which can then be excavated by the contemporary artist and transformed into a powerful frame of reference.

THE CAREER OF PHOTOGRAPHY IN THE ART WORLD OF INDIA

Photography arrived in India in the 1840s, two decades after its invention in Europe.[5] From the early history of daguerreotypes in the home-grown studios of members of royalty to metropolitan commercial studios, photography evolved into the realms of documentary and journalism, advertising, and finally the art world. Its belated acceptance as an art form happened partly for the same reasons as in the West; as late as 1913, Abanindranath Tagore, one of the most vocal of the cultural nationalists, condemned it as a materialistic medium that only captured the surface of reality. In his words, photography was a form of camouflage and more of "a hindrance than a help to artistic expression."[6] Also there was the fact that photographic equipment was for a long time relatively more expensive in India than in the West, which inhibited its adoption by modern artists, whereas in Europe the camera was integral to modernist movements such as Surrealism

---

3. Eric Helleiner, "Post-Globalization: Is the Financial Liberalization Trend Likely to Be Reversed?" in *States Against Markets: The Limits of Globalization*, eds. Robert Boyer and Daniel Drache (Oxford: Blackwell, 1996).

4. Anish Kapoor's acceptance of a recent invitation to present a retrospective in New Delhi's National Gallery of Modern Art may not be fortuitous but indicates the growing perception of India's economic rise.

5. For more background, see Pratapaditya Pal and Vidya Dehejia, *From Merchants to Emperors: British Artists and India, 1757–1930* (Ithaca: Cornell University Press, 1986): 182.

6. Abanindranath Tagore, *Some Notes on Artistic Anatomy and Shadangas or the Six Limbs of Painting* (Kolkata: Indian Society of Oriental Art, 1968): 14.

and Constructivism.[7] And even after photography had become popular and widespread, during the heyday of cultural nationalism around the 1920s, it was looked down upon as a Western technique.

Not until the 1990s, when the new media made its appearance in India, did photography fully capture the artistic attention of Indian contemporary artists. As installation art became more and more popular, such works increasingly incorporated photographs and texts.[8] One of the pioneering practitioners of installation art, Vivan Sundaram, created works that incorporated photography as documentary material when he used newspaper photographs of the victims of the Hindu Muslim riots that broke out in Mumbai in 1992 to build a poetics of mourning.[9]

The explosion of affordable digital camera technology also made it suddenly easy for artists to use these devices to record performances, and thus the camera became integral to a second contemporary art form. It is no exaggeration to suggest that it was via performance that photography made its presence truly felt within "high" art in India. Artists foregrounding their own bodies via the camera ushered in an exciting new form of self-reflexivity and interrogation of one's own identity.

ARTIST AS ETHNOGRAPHER

In India, unlike in the West, engagement with the figurative remained unbroken. What marked postmodern figuration in India after the 1990s was the new technological mediation that underpinned its imagination. The emergence of the Baroda Narrative painters during the 1980s prefigured the break with traditional norms of figurative painting. Turning away from heavy engagement with India's classical past, they focused on urban realities, and urban popular visual culture—the world of posters, advertisements, cinema hoardings, crude drawings on highway trucks and auto rickshaws, and, of course, photographic images. Translated into paintings, these tendencies gave rise for instance to photorealism, as in the works of Shibu Natesan and T. V. Santhosh. The Baroda school perhaps reached its consummate expression in the work of Bhupen Khakahr, and his installation *Pan Beedi Shop* at Documenta IX in 1992. In this work he re-created a cigarette stand, a ubiquitous feature of Indian street corners.

To understand the rise of the new figurative painting in Baroda, it is important to see it in terms of an intercultural dialogue between these painters and British Pop art. Khakhar's interest in Pop was inspired by the British artist Jim Donovan, who visited Baroda in the early 1960s on a Commonwealth scholarship and expressed an almost ethnographic interest in the local scenes.[10] By the 1980s, interest in local people and places was firmly in place and led other Baroda-based artists, such as Jyoti Bhatt and Raghav Kaneria, to make photographic sojourns to picturesque villages in the Indian states of Gujarat and Rajasthan to create a new kind of visual archive of their inhabitants. Photography came to be embraced by these "high" artists as a suitable medium in an ambience that was favorably oriented toward popular visual culture.

Village India had been a powerful imaginary for early Indian modernists. Even if Cubism, Expressionism, and other Euro-American modernist movements supplied a stylistic vocabulary for their work, Indianness asserted itself through their subject matter, which often centered on native bodies—usually seminude tribal Santhal women, assumed to be authentic Indians.[11] Thus, when Indian artists such as Bhatt and Kaneria entered the villages with camera in hand, it was difficult to escape the spell of the anthropological gaze.[12] This pull toward the anthropological gaze is also part of a more general postcolonial condition that most contemporary Indian artists find themselves caught in; any engagement with the past, or with current rural reality, necessarily interjects a particular kind of distance between artist and subject.

Photography, and its tenuous links with the anthropological gaze, is a rich means of expression for several artists in *The Matter Within*. For instance when performance meets photography in the work of Pushpamala N., the real subject of the pictures becomes, in a sense, the artist's critical scrutiny of this anthropological inheritance. Her project *Native Women of South India: Manners and Customs* (2000–2004) strongly evokes the figure of a British anthropologist, which makes her collaboration with Claire Arni, a British photographer, particularly interesting. For

---

7.
I am indebted to Shukla Sawant for pointing this out. I also draw from her article "Photo-Fact-Photo-Fiction Constructing the Art World" in the forthcoming *20th Century Indian Art* edited by Partha Mitter, Parul Dave Mukherji, and Rakhee Balaram, to be published by Skira.

8.
Prior to 1990, there were some artists who experimented with photography, for instance Krishen Khanna and Jyoti Bhatt (based in New Delhi and Baroda, respectively). But these may be viewed as sporadic ventures, largely marginal to the artists' primary practice of painting. Nasreen Mohamedi and Latika Katt also worked with photography during the 1980s at times, as an autonomous adjunct to their practices (as a painter and a sculptor, respectively).

9.
Sundaram's *Memorial* (1993) in New Delhi is a case in point.

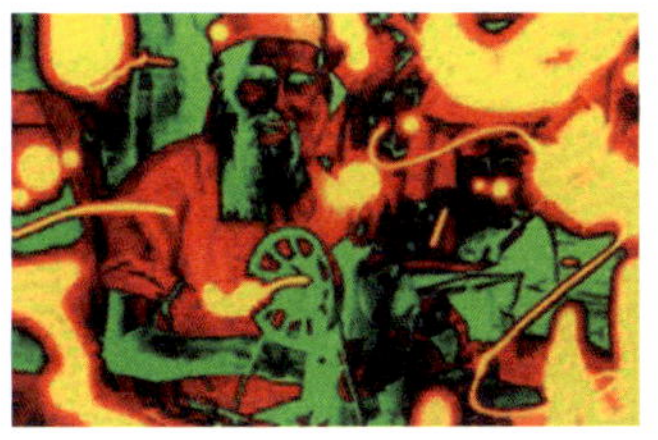

T.V. SANTHOSH
Stitching An Undefined Border, 2007
Oil on canvas
48 x 72 in.
Courtesy the Saatchi Gallery, London
© T.V. Santhosh

10.
Nilima Sheikh, *Contemporary Art in Baroda*, ed. Gulammohammed Sheikh (New Delhi. Tulika, 1997): 126.

11.
The Santhal tribe is also called Adivasi in Sanskrit. They are considered the region's original inhabitants, comparable to the Australian aborigines. Today they live in parts of Bihar, Bengal, and Madhya Pradesh in the central and eastern regions of India.

12.
It was equally difficult for Sunil Janah, a photographer who was part of the Communist Party of India, to distance himself from the lens of anthropology. This was most evident in his photographs of tribal Santhal women from Bengal and Orissa. His photographs are part of the P. C. Joshi Archive at Jawaharlal Nehru University.

Pushpamala N., the only way to undo the logic of the anthropological gaze is by inhabiting the space of a native: staging a confrontation with the colonial gaze, and excessively submitting to it. In this carefully fashioned mise-en-scène she juxtaposes documentation and masquerade, deconstructing one with the help of the other and thus playing with the distance between the self and the other, the historical and the contemporary, reality and fiction.

Gauri Gill's *Notes from the Desert* (1999–2010) (see pp. 65–67) at first glance looks like an anthropological project: a visual record by a contemporary photographer who, in the process of documenting a community, feels compelled to live within it in order to observe it better. A cultural nomad herself, having lived in India and on the East and West coasts of the United States, Gill had already produced a photographic record of the Indian diaspora in a 2002 series titled *The Americans*. How to situate, then, this foray into the villages of Rajasthan? As opposed to Pushpamala N., who in one photograph ironically posed as a tribal Toda woman against the anthropometric grid used by colonial officers to measure the natives, Gill photographs Bacchu Khan, a native Rajasthani man, dressed almost formally and standing in front of an upright *charpoy*, or tribal bed. The distinction is clear: Whereas Pushpamala N.'s masquerade is a parody of the colonial gaze, Gill acknowledges her Rajasthani male subject as a human presence, whose wish to be represented with dignity is accommodated in his ceremonial posture. However, despite her caution with the use of the anthropological lens, Gill's status as an urban artist living in the metropolitan West at times betrays a bit of contemporary nostalgia for community life, for instance in her photograph *Jogi Panchayat near Dungargarh* (1999).

Incongruity and masquerade powerfully inform Nikhil Chopra's series *Yog Raj Chitrakar: Memory Drawing* (2010) (see pp. 61–63). The photographic stills capture live performances through which a fictional character of the artist's creation enters into the everyday, performing daily activities such as washing, eating, shaving, and dressing. His character, named Yog Raj Chitrakar, is strongly reminiscent of India's pioneering proto-modernist Raja Ravi Varma, who was the first Indian painter to indigenize Victorian oil painting by using the medium to depict scenes from the classical epics of India such as *Ramayana* and *Mahabharata*. "Chitrakar" is a nomenclature usually reserved for a village artist, so it is a misnomer for the persona created by Chopra, which is semi-fictitious and semi-autobiographical—partly based on his grandfather, who studied at Goldsmiths College, and partly imagined through the genre of imperial portraiture that inspired many a maharaja in colonial India to commission a portrait that mimicked the work of the Western masters. Mimicry for Chopra becomes a ploy not only to bring to life a contemporary flâneur, but also to create a deliberate disjunction between time and place, as we follow the journey of the anachronistic painter Chitrakar across different geographies and identities. Each geography takes the form of a backdrop against which the artist poses, for instance when he masquerades as a woman in front of New York's skyline. Cross-dressing is only one aspect of Chopra's performance-based plays on incongruity.

Tejal Shah's *Women Like Us* (2010) is a series of digital photographs in which her camera zooms in on portrait subjects who might be male or female (see p. 83). They meet the gaze of the artist—and by extension the viewer—with uncanny directness, seemingly in answer to our stark questioning of their identity. In these photographs, the "natural" or "cultural" is no longer a given but a confabulation that is engendered through the physiognomic fashioning of the self. Shah also stages a collaboration with Varsha Nair in the series *Encounter(s)* (2006) (see pp. 81–82), a theatrical interaction between their two bodies through clothing that stretches uncannily, joining them even across the barrier of a wrought-iron gate.

Poised between the extremes of the nature-culture divide, Bharat Sikka's photographs from 2010 strike a different note. These poetic pictures show the traces left by a bird in flight, a fluttering butterfly, or a dead pigeon; they also allude to a world of statues of gods and generals. What photography represents for Sikka is a wide range of representational possibilities spanning the world of nature and the world of culture. In his mind the latter is twice removed from nature, meaning that a photograph of a statue is a representation of a representation. Sometimes one engulfs the other, as in the smoky landscape of *Untitled (dusty street with lone figures)* (2010) (see p. 87) or *The Kite*, a picture of a broken kite caught in a hazy thicket of trees. He seems to equate the fragility of nature with that of human conviviality; a suggestion of impending doom and ecological frailty hovers around the edges of the work.

TALES OF THE CITY

Although they come from two different generations of photographers, Sunil Gupta and Dhruv Malhotra both view the urban landscape and the human condition as inextricable from detritus, disease, and deprivation. What undergirds their different takes on urban reality is the manner in which each situates himself in relation to matters "outside," in the world. Gupta traverses the realms of the private and the public by portraying intimate moments between gay men. The scenes range from fantasies of sexual orgies to isolated, casual encounters between strangers. Clearly making a distinction between indoors—often showing nude bodies in dramatic lighting—and outdoors—clothed people in natural light—Gupta captures their different dynamics in the way the bodies relate to one another. Any voyeuristic sense of the gaze, the usual distinction between the self and the other, is dissolved by the way the photographer inserts himself within each scene.

Another body of work by Malhotra, his nocturnal photography, pushes voyeurism to an extreme (see pp. 73–75). Moving furtively through the parts of the city that grind to a halt at night, he captures a different rhythm of urban life: inert, sleeping bodies in parks, under bridges, on sidewalks. Going beyond making a statement about poverty, the inability of some people to afford roofs over their heads, his nocturnes capture the poetics of place through dramatic lighting. The prosaic and the everyday assume an air of the uncanny. The ghostly, eerie ambience of these public places almost cradles the bodies of the men who labor by day and are now in repose. Expressing a kind of solidarity in their collective condition, together they are in a dreamlike state, oblivious to the photographer's presence.

The popularity of the documentary form among many photographers in India today expresses the contemporary desire to engage with everyday life—not only to represent it, but to experience it. As these artists refashion themselves as ethnographers traveling the world with their cameras, research becomes an essential part of their practice. Even their modes of presentation often involve the classification systems of a researcher, as for example in the case of Anup Mathew Thomas, whose *Metropolitan* series (2006) (see pp. 89–90) is a catalogue of bishops in front of a variety of edifices. What at first glance appears to be a bland and prosaic interest in the everyday is actually informed by arduous research. In this series, whether Thomas is revisiting a forgotten archive or grasping the present moment, he readily assumes the role of an ethnographer, traveling not so much across time as across places, in search of a narrative strand linking people in different locations. Confronted with *Metropolitan*, we find ourselves doubting the reality of what we see, as the seriality of so many people posing as individuals in photographic portraits has the effect of removing their uniqueness. The elaborate paraphernalia of ecclesiastical power ostensibly demonstrated in the portraits turns each bishop's posture of authority into an iterative, performative act. The iconography speaks not only of the cultural hybridity of brown bodies wearing European costumes, but also of the orchestrated, globalized network linking Christian institutions around the world.

No wonder, then, that the two most compelling tropes through which photography has organized itself in high-art practices have been documentation and masquerade via performance. Perhaps these two even form an axis along which artistic photographic practice may be arranged. If the documentarian assumes the role of a cultural ethnographer, masquerade via performance offers the potential to explode the claims of documentary representation. Each undoes the function of the other.

There is another sense in which photography has captured the imagination of contemporary artists in India, and that is through its intimate links with "the contemporary." It is photography that best marks artists' being in the present. Even if it is impossible to grasp the contemporary because it is too close to us, photography becomes a metaphor for the contemporary because of its contiguity to the present through its capturing of an indexical image. No longer moved by the idea of utopia that led the modernists to imagine the future, contemporary artists are charged with the compulsion to occupy the present in all its imperfections.

Whether these artists inhabit the city or the village, none (at least, none in *The Matter Within*) subscribes to the idea of "India Shining," a piece of political propaganda generated by the Indian Right around 2000 to flaunt the country's entry into global capitalism. Far from ratifying excessively optimistic predictions about the future, these artists seem to take a hard look at the "real" political scene in India—and the underside of those claims—by focusing on the rural, the marginalized, and the underprivileged. In fact, globalization has opened up fractured spaces within the national modern, with its dreams of national unity and modernization as progress. If one looks beyond official rhetoric, the uprising in Kashmir in the north, counterinsurgency in the northeast, and Maoist-aided tribal rebellion in the heart of India make a mockery of the aspiration for superpower status.

For many artists, the underbelly of globalization is the crisis of democracy, the increasingly inequitable distribution of resources and technology. And crises in the arena of politics translate into the realm of the aesthetic. What is the most compelling mode of representation, if not photography, to attend to the ambivalent present moment? However bedeviled this moment may be, it also encapsulates much that can be celebrated through the poetics of the everyday, whether through an intimate glance shared by a gay couple, the spectacle of the masquerade, or the fragile fluttering of a butterfly.

The thread running through most of the works in this exhibition is the desire to be *in* "the contemporary" rather than to produce a belated or elevated response to the everyday. To be in the place of the here and now, to work with others in a simultaneous and concrete practice. To see the realization of work in the experience of connection with the contemporary. In a sense, this desire tends to raise the value of the performative aspect of practice and deflect the reflexive role of cultural production. Photography seems to be the answer to this cultural compulsion.

NIKHIL CHOPRA

Nikhil Chopra employs performance, drawing, photography, new media, and installation to create a parallel universe for his audience. Assuming different personae, he chronicles the world around him in murals on canvas while literally making himself at home for days at a time in crowded markets, abandoned buildings, galleries, theaters, and ordinary city streets. Viewers are free to come and go as they please as Chopra carries on with his daily routine of sleeping, eating, changing clothes, touring, and documenting his experiences and observations in large-scale, charcoal visuals. His characters invoke a different time and place, but are connected to the present through his personal history. His character Yog Raj Chitrakar is an amalgam of the artist himself and his real-life grandfather, a wealthy, landowning, British- and German-educated gentleman who spent his latter years painting the grandeur of India's Kashmiri Valley. The fluidly shifting character leaves the audience wondering, "Who is Chopra? Who is his grandfather? What is their relationship to the hybrid personality of Yog Raj?" as they attempt to decipher the multiple layers of identity in each performance.

Yog Raj Chitrakar: Memory Drawing (2010) documents a number of Chopra's live performances, each of which gives a fragment of the saga of Yog Raj Chitrakar's many faces and adventures. The artist meticulously assumes a series of avatars: Victorian draftsman, explorer, cartographer, prisoner of war, queen. He dedicates hours to shaving his head, face, and body in a near-ceremonial manner to embody each imagined identity. This elaborate transformation alludes to other kinds of changes that intrigue Chopra, in particular the evolution of urban spaces and societies. His drawings are not mere reconstructions of stagnant scenery, but documents of structures and spaces undergoing change—the collision of old and new, of past and present, of politics and nature. Through his drawings and performances, Chopra portrays a particular postcolonial subjectivity that is inherently ambivalent regarding change.

It is plagued by a wistful longing for the familiarity of the British Raj while simultaneously embracing the pride and promise of an independent India. In the words of Geeta Kapur in her 2001 essay "Dismantled Norms: Apropos Other Avantgardes," "Decolonization is an especially propitious moment to open the floodgates of the national/modern imagination, rupturing its too-conscientious project of identity with heterodox elements from the rest of the world." Free at last, Yog Raj looks outward into a new world, eager to discover, study, and examine external elements in the analysis and forging of a new individuality. Yet his depictions of a consistently transforming landscape suggest nostalgia for a time that will quickly become inaccessible, much like the Kashmiri Valley once painted by Chopra's grandfather.

Chopra presented the 96-hour performance *Yog Raj Chitrakar: Memory Drawing VI* (2009) in 2009 at kunstenfestivaldesarts 09, a theater festival in Brussels. The artist resided for the duration of the piece at Les Brigittines, a baroque chapel that has been converted into a theater. Each morning he set himself and his canvas up at the top of a hill overlooking the entirety of Brussels. He spent two days drawing the city on two separate canvases, referencing its political and cultural division: French on one side, Flemish on the other. He eventually sewed the two canvases together— an analogy for the forging of a unified and harmonious identity—and as a climax to his performance, hung the mural at Les Brigittines and posed in front of it dressed as a Greek goddess, in reference to the neoclassical architecture that so perfectly characterizes the identity of Brussels. This physical embodiment—the act of using his body to realize and communicate an idea—is a key feature of Chopra's work. Just as he uses his physical form to reference architecture, his transformation from gentleman to dandy to queen embodies the concepts of change and evolution, showing that one identity can have many faces, much like the city of Brussels.

···SR

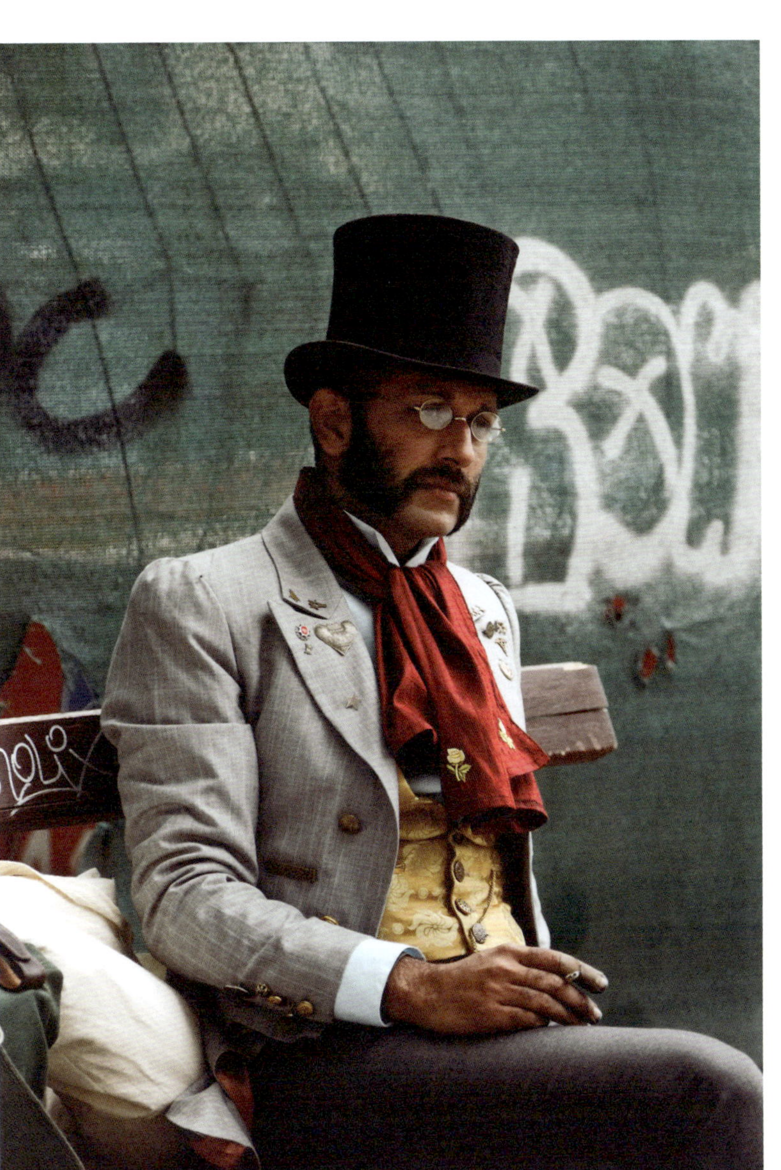

Yog Raj Chitrakar: Memory Drawing VI (16:00), 2010

60

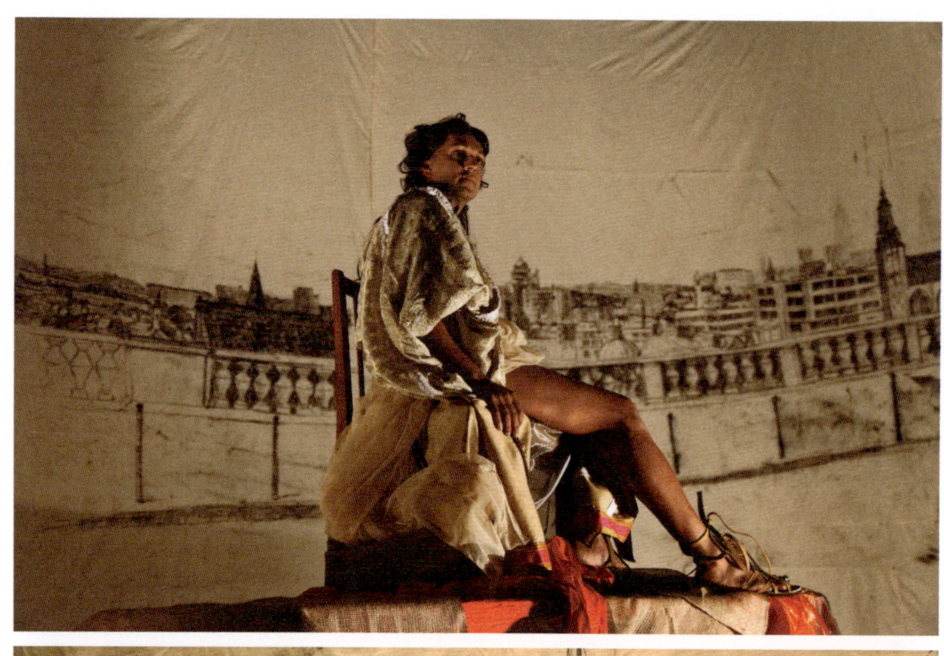

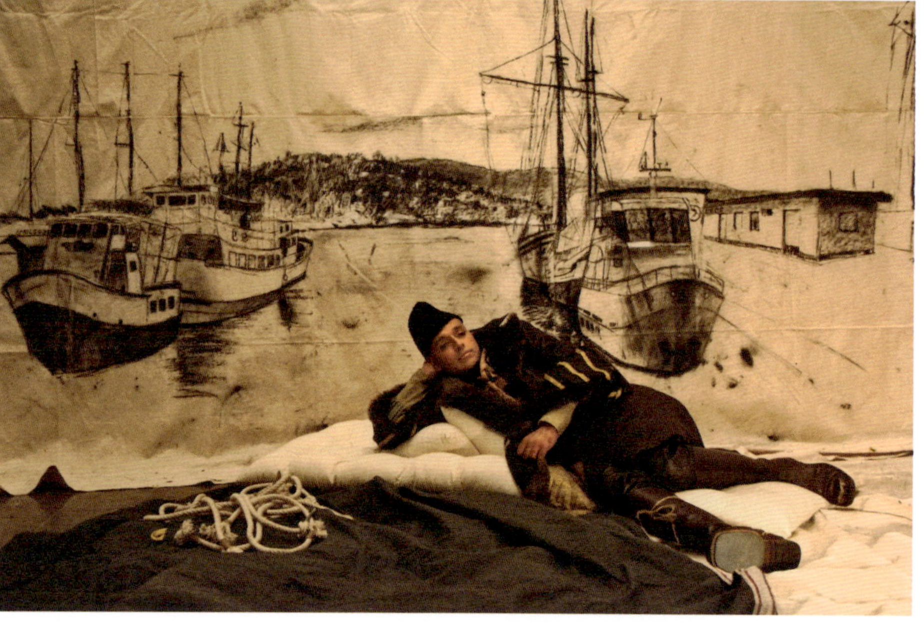

TOP | *Yog Raj Chitrakar: Memory Drawing VI (18:00)*, 2010
BOTTOM | *Yog Raj Chitrakar: Memory Drawing V (Part II)*, 2010

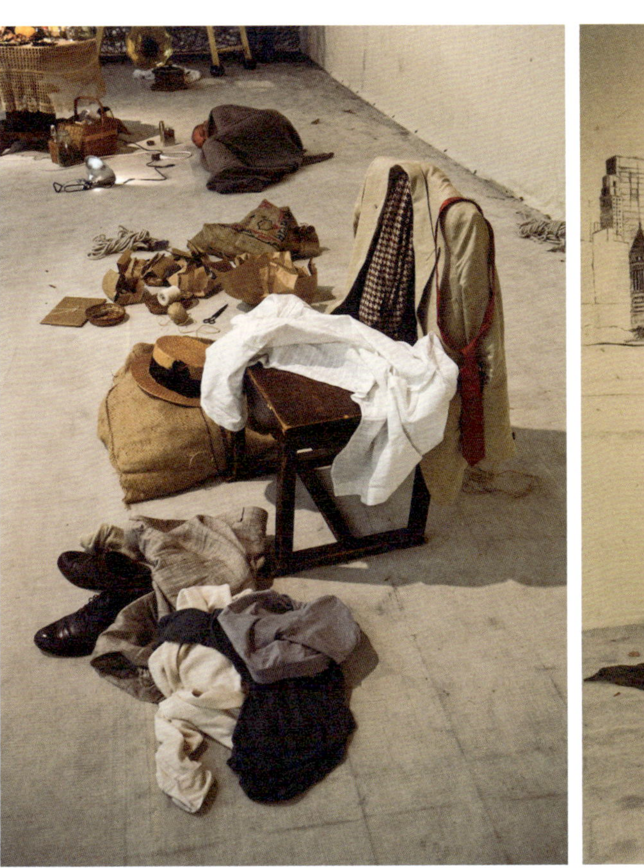

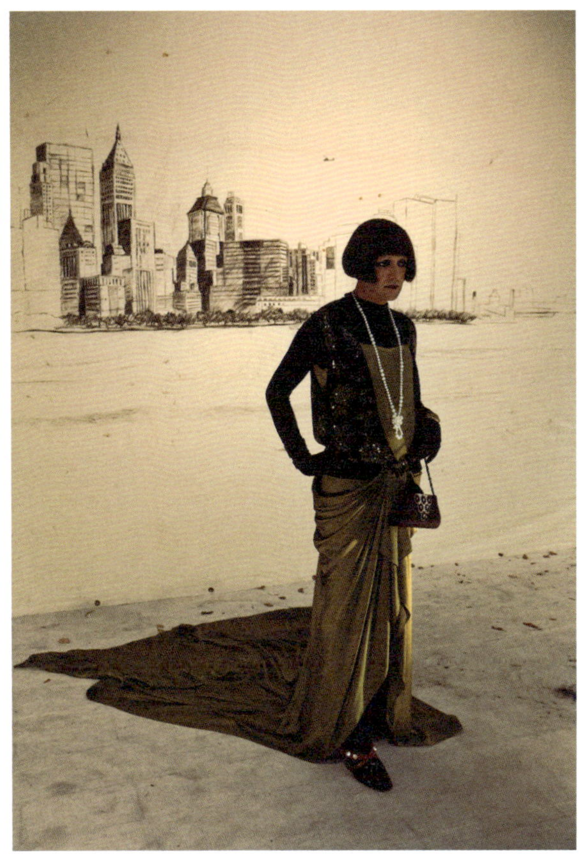

LEFT | *Yog Raj Chitrakar: Memory Drawing IX (14:00)*, 2010
RIGHT | *Yog Raj Chitrakar: Memory Drawing IX (17:00)*, 2010

GAURI GILL

Initially trained as a painter and an applied artist, Gauri Gill segued into photography because she felt that it allowed her to get out into the real world and record history. She worked for five years as a photojournalist for a news magazine (which informs her current documentary work), then eventually abandoned that in favor of a photographic practice that would allow room for "slow" thinking. She has made several series over long periods of time, from five to eleven years. These series manifest the social and political concerns of photojournalism while also being very personal.

Themes of migration, identity, and belonging run throughout Gill's work, as does an interest in portraying individuals living in communities that are underrepresented in the mainstream media. *The Americans* (2000–2007), a series depicting the South Asian diaspora in the United States, takes its name from Robert Frank's seminal photography book that captured American life in the 1950s, but it offers a more personal and expansive view of America in contemporary times. Gill shows the everyday lives of a diverse range of people—taxi drivers, IT professionals, housewives, farmers—and explores the adaptation of Indian individuals to a new country.

The series *What Remains* (2007) also examines migration and its attendant issues, this time by looking at generations of Afghani Sikh and Hindu immigrants in India. The photographs, taken in Kabul and Delhi, are presented together with pictures taken by the Indo-Afghani community on their visits back to Afghanistan, texts from interviews between Gill and the migrants, and other texts from a children's writing workshop conducted by the artist. The resulting installation is a reflection on locality, identity, and memory, from many different points of view.

Another side of Gill's practice avoids portraying people altogether, focusing instead on scenes that merely suggest human presence in the representation of modern buildings, structures, and cityscapes. The ongoing series *Rememory* (working title, begun in 2003) shows the metropolis in transition, where the rural intersects with the urban.

Notes from the Desert (1999–2010), the project included in *The Matter Within,* is entirely removed from India's cosmopolitan centers and focuses on people living in marginalized desert communities. An archive of more than forty thousand photographs taken over a span of eleven years, it contains several distinct narratives. It began with Gill's documentation of village schools in western Rajasthan and expanded in scope as she began personally visiting several individuals she met there, including a woman she befriended, who implored Gill to communicate the struggles of her small village to those outside. The artist eventually became well acquainted with many different communities in the desert, recording their daily activities and capturing the life cycle from birth to marriage, sickness, and death.

The length of time Gill devoted to the series allowed her to follow individual subjects from childhood to adulthood, as in *Jannat* (1999–2007), which focuses on one girl, Jannat, and her family. *Balika Mela* (2003/2010), another sequence within the larger series, shows portraits taken at a photo booth set up by the artist at a *balika mela,* or fair for girls. The teenage girls perform with props and stage their own shots for the camera, engaging with the artist in a creative dialogue.

The photographs in *Notes from the Desert* are printed in black and white with the grays at 50 percent; Gill's intent is to mute the vibrant, saturated hues for which the region is known and to imitate the effect of the harsh sun. This vast project reveals the widely diverse conditions of individuals in the Indian desert. While it is not meant to be didactic, it conveys a social message about the disappearance of rural India in the consciousness of the urban middle class, and its marginalization by the state. It is also a vivid account of a decade of encounters with people Gill came to call friends.

···TL

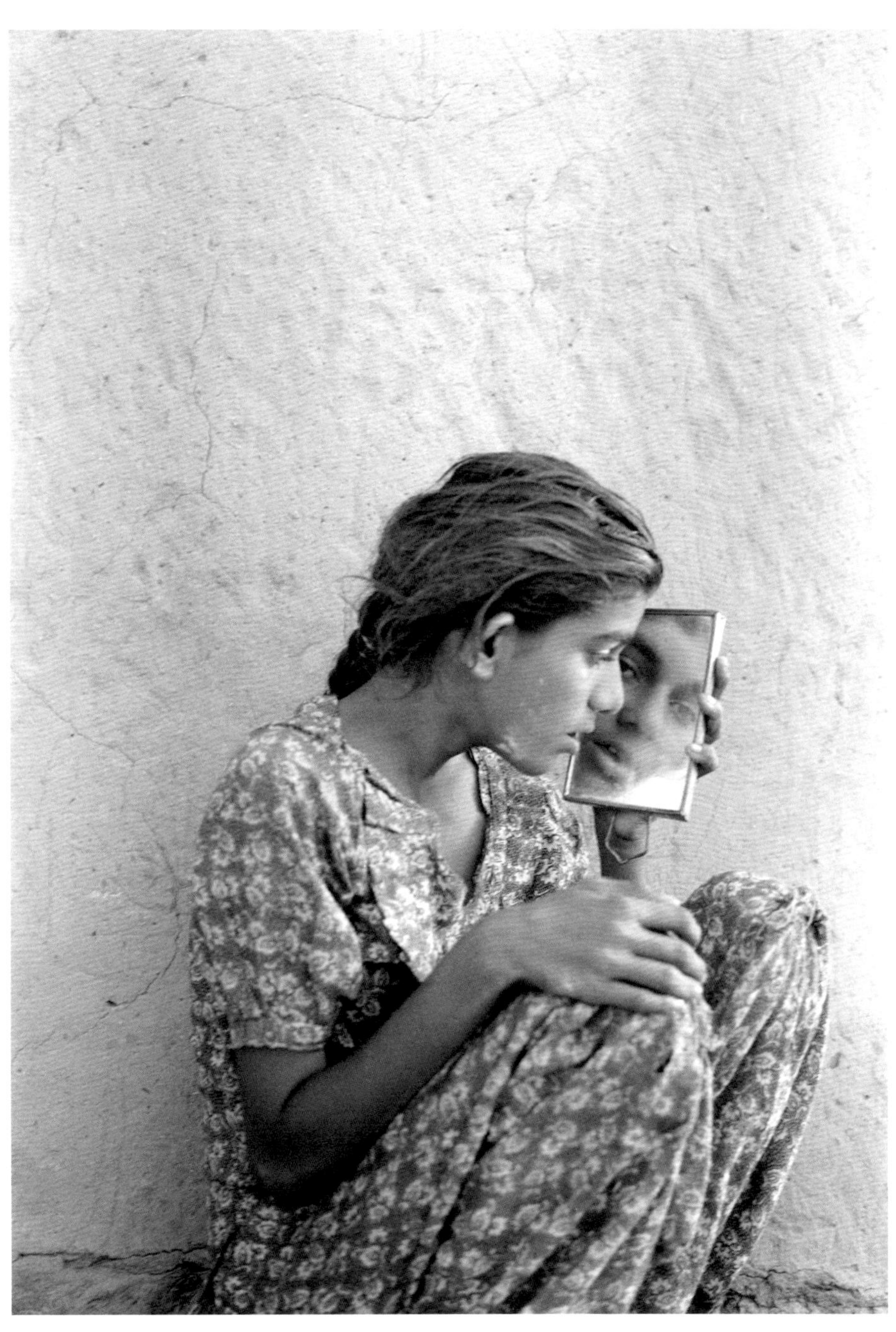

Ismat, Barmer, from the series Notes from the Desert, 1999

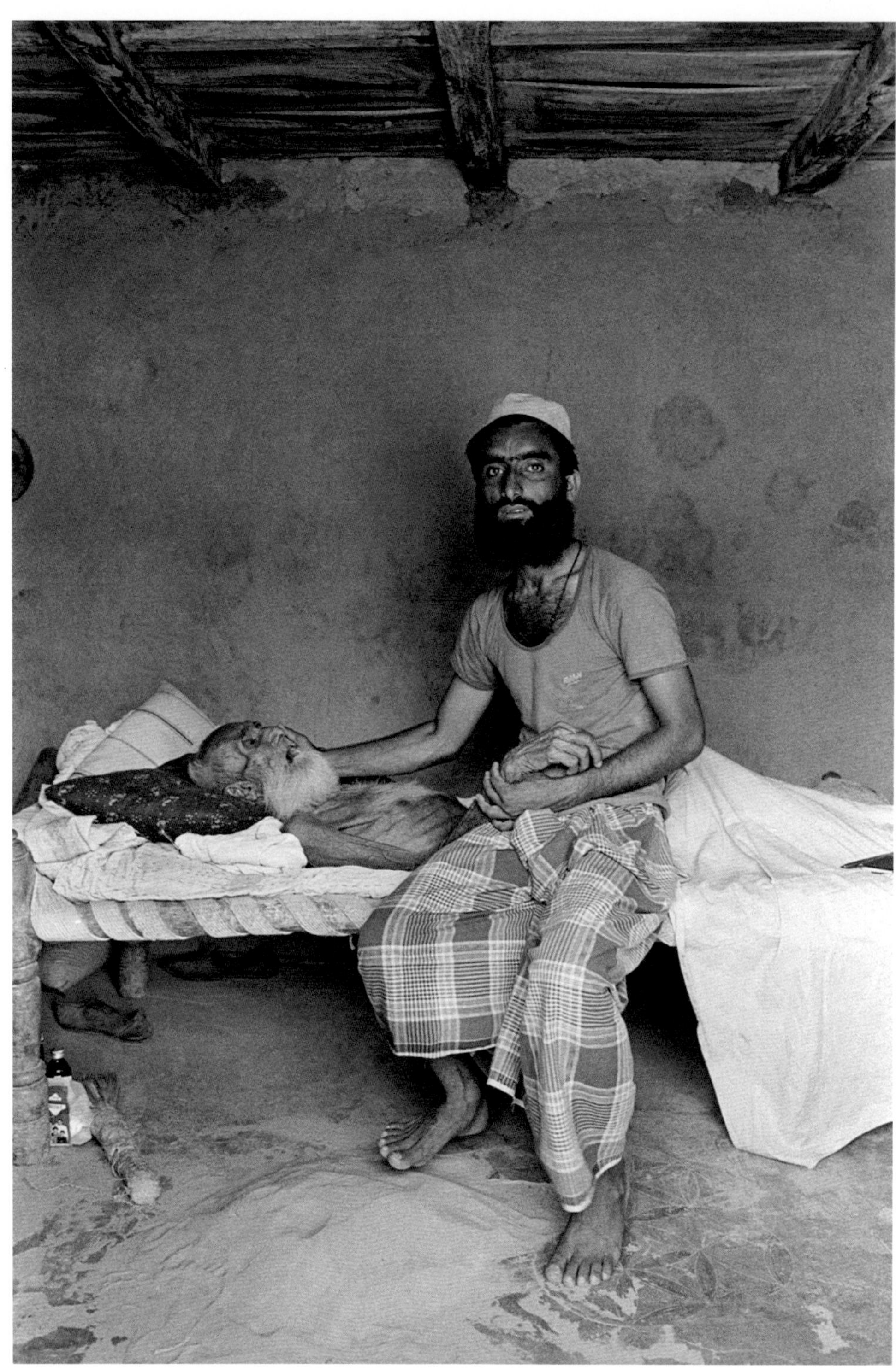

Mir Hasan with his grandfather Haji Saraj ud Din, oldest member of the community, in his last days, Barmer, from the series Notes from the Desert, 1999

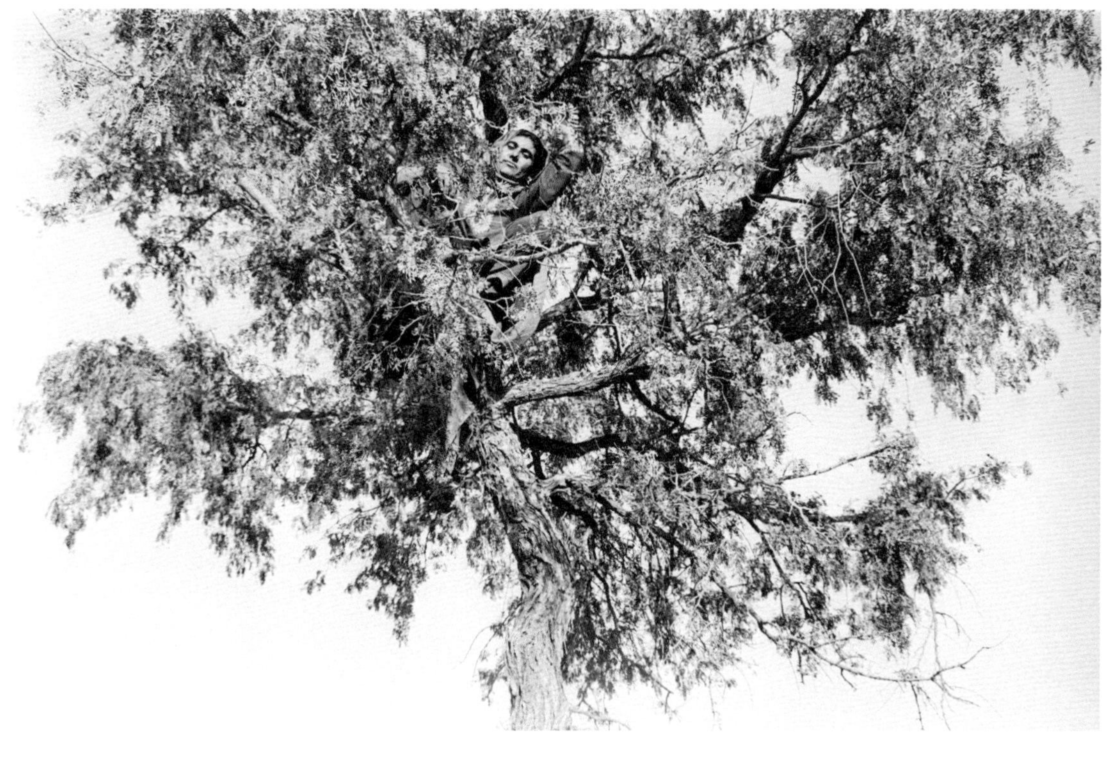

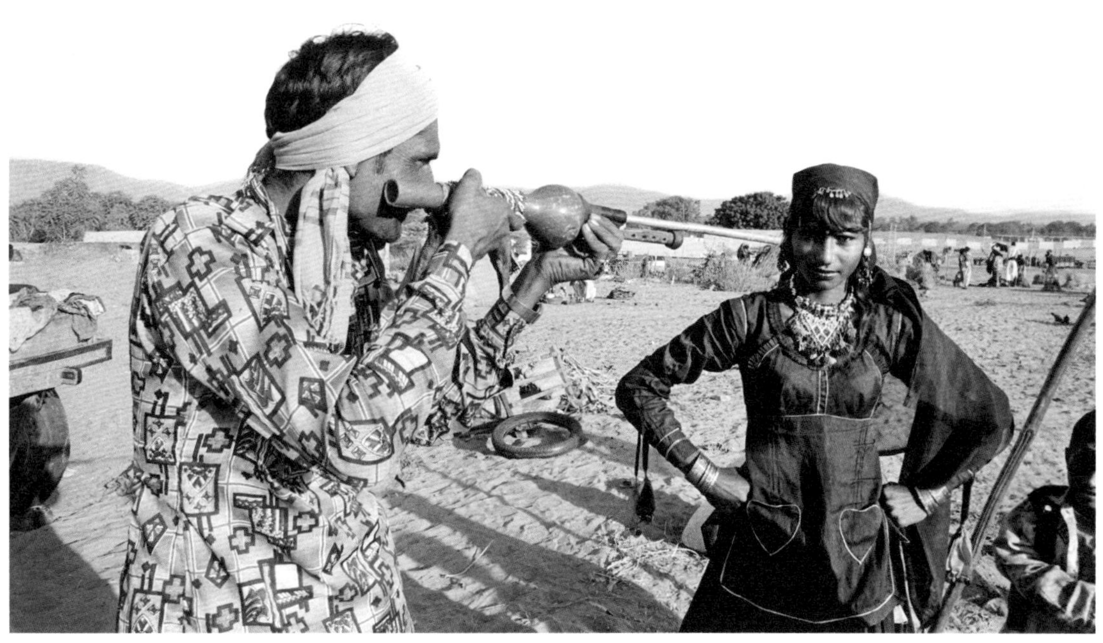

TOP | *Jannat, Barmer, from the series Notes from the Desert,* 1999
BOTTOM | *Marwar ke Nath, Bikaner, from the series Notes from the Desert,* 1999

Sunil Gupta

Born in New Delhi, Sunil Gupta moved with his family to Montreal as a teenager. In the mid-1970s he studied photography at the New School in New York, and then in 1983 completed his MA at the Royal College of Art in London. As both a photographer and an activist, his sensitivity to the politics of identity and representation was heightened after his HIV-positive diagnosis in 1995. In 2005 he moved back to India, where he continued to make work despite the pervasive public health crises there and the long-standing criminalization of homosexuality (which was not ruled down by the high court until 2009).

Politics and art, life and love—all rendered with a thoroughly transnational twist—are intertwined in Gupta's work. His photographs of marginalized subjects have been groundbreaking, but he cannot be reduced to a "queer artist" or any other single label. Indeed, one of the most consistent strands running throughout his work is the quiet but persistent struggle to unmask the myth of white male heterosexual subjectivity as the tacit default for the universal, while seeking to identify elements of universality in the lives of individual queer subjects. He is highly aware that our identities are always multiple, and that these different identities make themselves apparent in various contexts. Gupta's photography celebrates lives and creates zones of visibility for them in the public sphere.

For the series *Exiles* (1986), he photographed gay men in iconic historical and architectural sites in Delhi—such as Hauz Khas, Humayun's Tomb, and Nizamuddin— reclaiming India's history and public sphere as spaces for queer sexuality. The series *Mr. Malhotra's Party* (2007) takes its title from the local practice in Delhi of identifying gay nights at clubs as private parties held in the name of a fictitious individual— Mr. Malhotra—as a protection against laws at that time that criminalized homosexuality. Gupta's photographs show gay people occupying quotidian public space with a quiet defiance that valorizes the nascent emergence of a visible queer community in India.

Sun City (2010) is a staged work that borrows from the narrative of Chris Marker's 1962 film *La Jetée*. Gupta keeps Paris as the setting but reworks the story by making the protagonist a homosexual immigrant from India. The man always appears haloed by a yellow light that symbolizes, for Gupta, his sacred and innocent character. The narrative follows him through a series of encounters in his new and unfamiliar life—in public with his lover, and in the clandestine but egalitarian world of the Parisian bathhouse, "where communication does not involve speech, and everyone wears the same blue towel." There he is able to briefly transcend the cultural barriers and inequalities of his public life, and he grows increasingly intimate with the anonymous partners he meets. Gupta does not reveal the cause of the man's death, but leaves it open to interpretation.

In contrast, *Love, Undetectable* (2009) takes a more documentary form and reflects Gupta's preoccupation with the universality of love. The images capture real gay and lesbian couples in each other's thrall, entangled in intimate embraces or simply sharing the miracle of loving each other in their everyday lives. The title is a reference to his own crucible of living and loving as an HIV-positive gay man, measuring normalcy in his own body in terms of maintaining an "undetectable viral load," and thus holding his condition at a livable distance.

The artist has said that he remained single for nine years following his diagnosis, haunted by the specter of a loveless life, until he was able to come to terms with his condition and reopen himself to the possibility of love: "After more than a decade of just thinking of the body as a medical emergency to be endured, it once again became a tool of personal pleasure." Thus began his reengagement with love in his life and his art. The couples in *Love, Undetectable*, including Gupta and his partner, celebrate their physical and emotional bonds, and their love is immanently detectable in the poignant, intimate images. What is truly undetectable is any difference between their love and the love experienced by people everywhere, of all genders and sexual orientations.

···MK

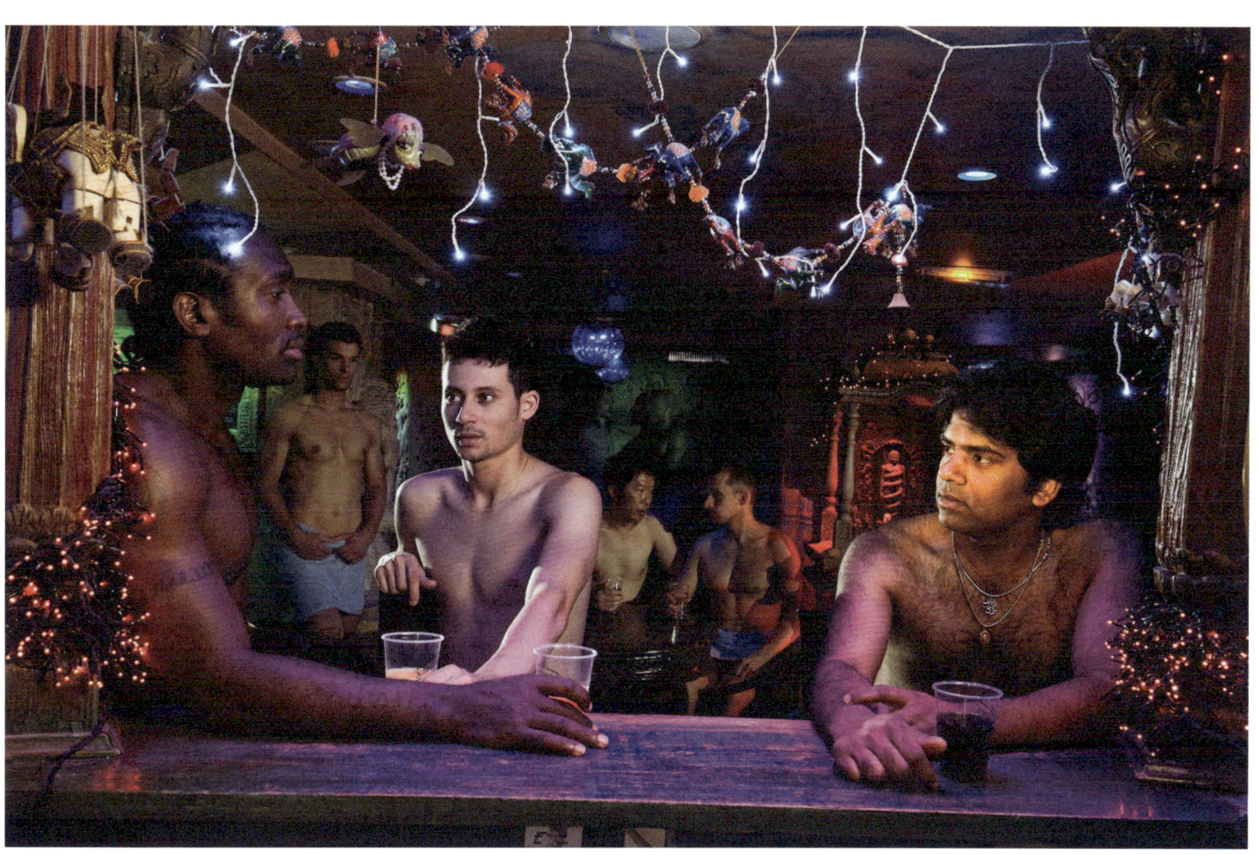

Untitled #7, from the series *Sun City*, 2010

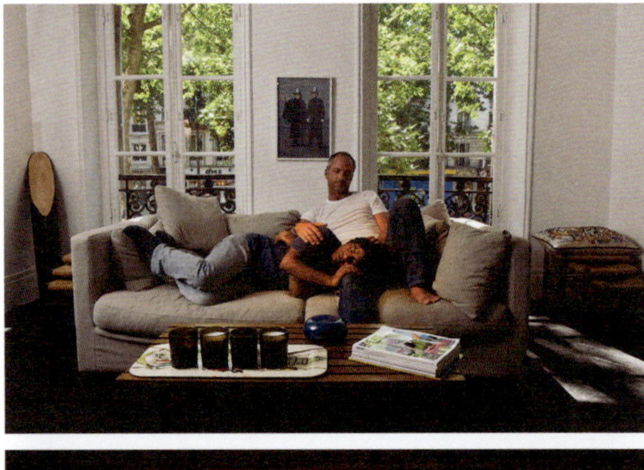 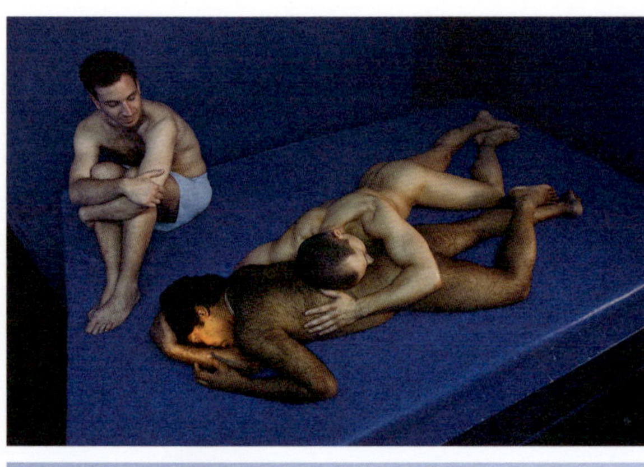

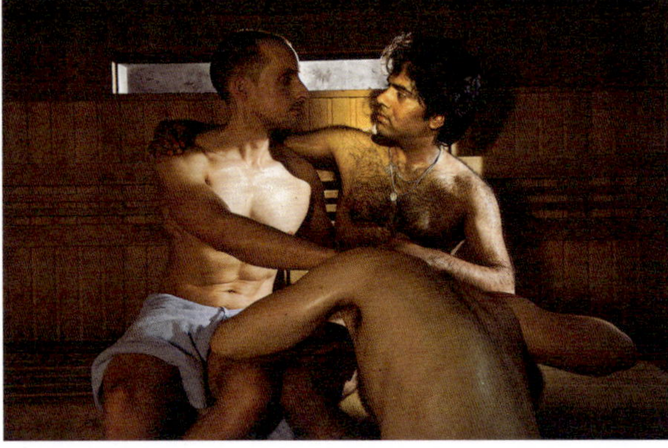 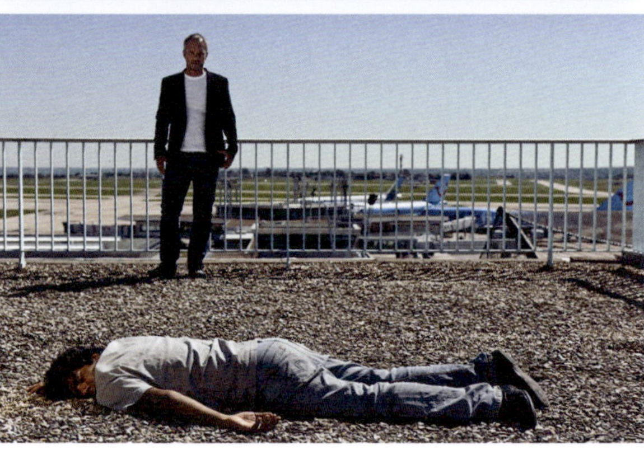

LEFT TO RIGHT, TOP TO BOTTOM | *Untitled #11, Untitled #13, Untitled #14, Untitled #16* from the series *Sun City*, 2010

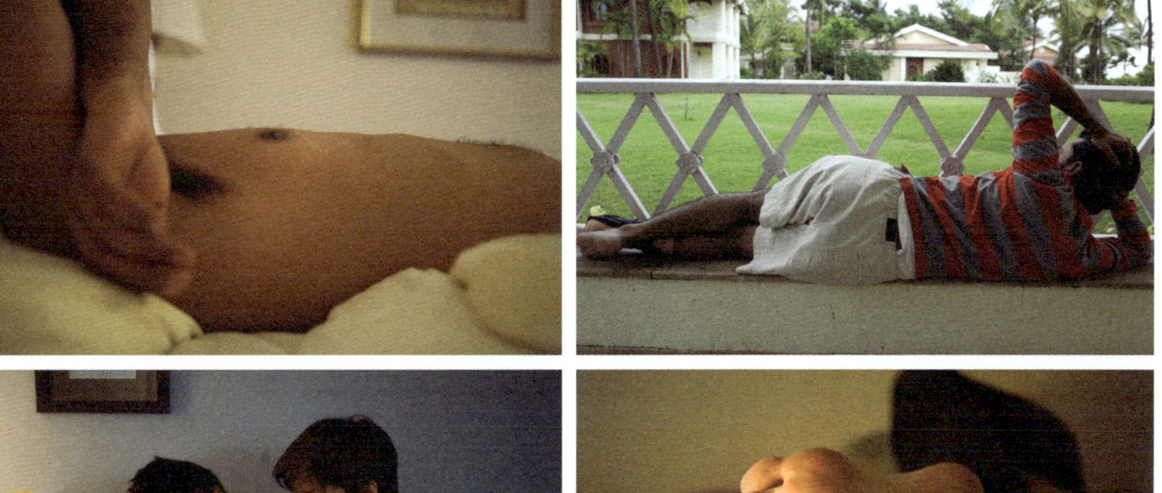
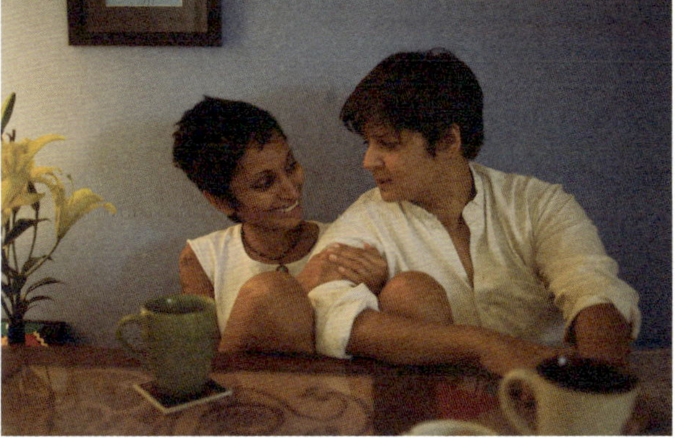
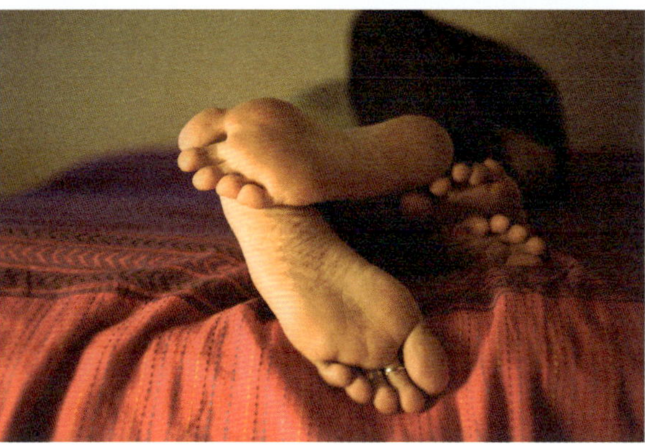

LEFT TO RIGHT, TOP TO BOTTOM | *Untitled #2, Untitled #5, Untitled #6, Untitled #8* from the series *Love, Undetectable*, 2009

Dhruv Malhotra

The photographer Dhruv Malhotra stalks India's capital city at night, not as a somnambulist but as an insomniac whose eyes never close; indeed, the eye of his long-exposure camera opens and shuts extremely slowly. He is capturing sleeping forms bathed in the sodium light of streetlamps. The bodies lie upon park benches or on rustic outdoor beds. Some are even under diaphanous mosquito nets, recalling the era of the British Raj. The pictures capture the changing seasons: The people may be wrapped in heavy quilts in winter, or clad in bare-minimum shorts and singlets in the hot Indian summer. In one, a worker sleeps in a glorious tent in which a huge marriage ceremony will take place the next day.

This collection of images reveals a seldom-seen aspect of the lives of India's millions of migrant or transient workers, for whom privacy, and real beds for sleeping, are rather remote realities. But there are many reasons why people might sleep outdoors, and in fact the artist is also interested in revealing to Westerners that sleeping under the open skies in India does not always indicate poverty or deprivation. In previous bodies of work, Malhotra also engaged with the idea of coaxing the poetic out of the mundane. He has wandered through concrete apartment blocks, mega malls, call centers, busy highways, and vast construction sites, capturing surreal scenes that feel dislocated from temporal and geographical specificity—that seem like anyplace in the world, at no particular time.

In his pictures of sleeping people, Malhotra is not simply delivering an essay on social customs or socioeconomic hierarchies. Rather, he also hopes that viewers will ponder the eventual awakening of these sleepers, and their inner dreams and aspirations. He believes that the power of a photograph lies in its ability to evoke something that isn't necessarily in the frame. He is inspired by Frank Herbert's *Dune* series of books, from which the phrase "the Sleeper must awaken" has long captivated his attention. While growing up, as he once mentioned in conversation, "like any young child I was reminded repeatedly of how much potential lies dormant, and

the work and effort it requires to be realized. It is this dormancy that the sleeping figure poignantly brings out for me." The sleeping state, even though it visually resembles death, is "never quite catatonic, never completely still. Death, dark and mysterious as it is, is also perhaps the ultimate awakening, one that transcends the borders of this familiar matter and lets the 'soul' take flight or return to the source."

How does Malhotra situate himself, his class, and his cultural background vis-à-vis his subjects? Are we supposed to understand these pictures as being partly about the photographer's own vulnerability? Malhotra is well aware of the slippages between voyeur and viewed, which is why he consciously underlines his own presence in these scenes. He says he "works himself up to be the voyeur, to approach his subject with stealth, and capture that candid frame." But other night creatures have their roles to play. Street dogs often bark at the crouching photographer, announcing his arrival, shattering that romantic barrier between the viewer and the viewed, and the sleeper sometimes wakes up. "Many times the people in my pictures awaken and look back at me. Sometimes I talk them into going back to sleep so I can complete my exposure."

For Malhotra, night photography has been a kind of therapy—a photographic yoga, one might say, with the silences, the stillness, the long exposures. The artist's muse is the sense of desolation he seeks even in highly illuminated, overbuilt urban environments. His ritual act of walking the streets of New Delhi was born of a time when he felt as if he was "sleepwalking through life." He shoots his nocturnal photographs with a long-exposure camera, the Mamiya 6x7. Working without a flash, he deliberately overexposes the color film for anywhere from twenty minutes to almost two hours, until a chemical reaction forces a distortion in the color. The process enables him to achieve the mysterious palette and light effects that are so crucial to the particular beauty of these works.

···GM

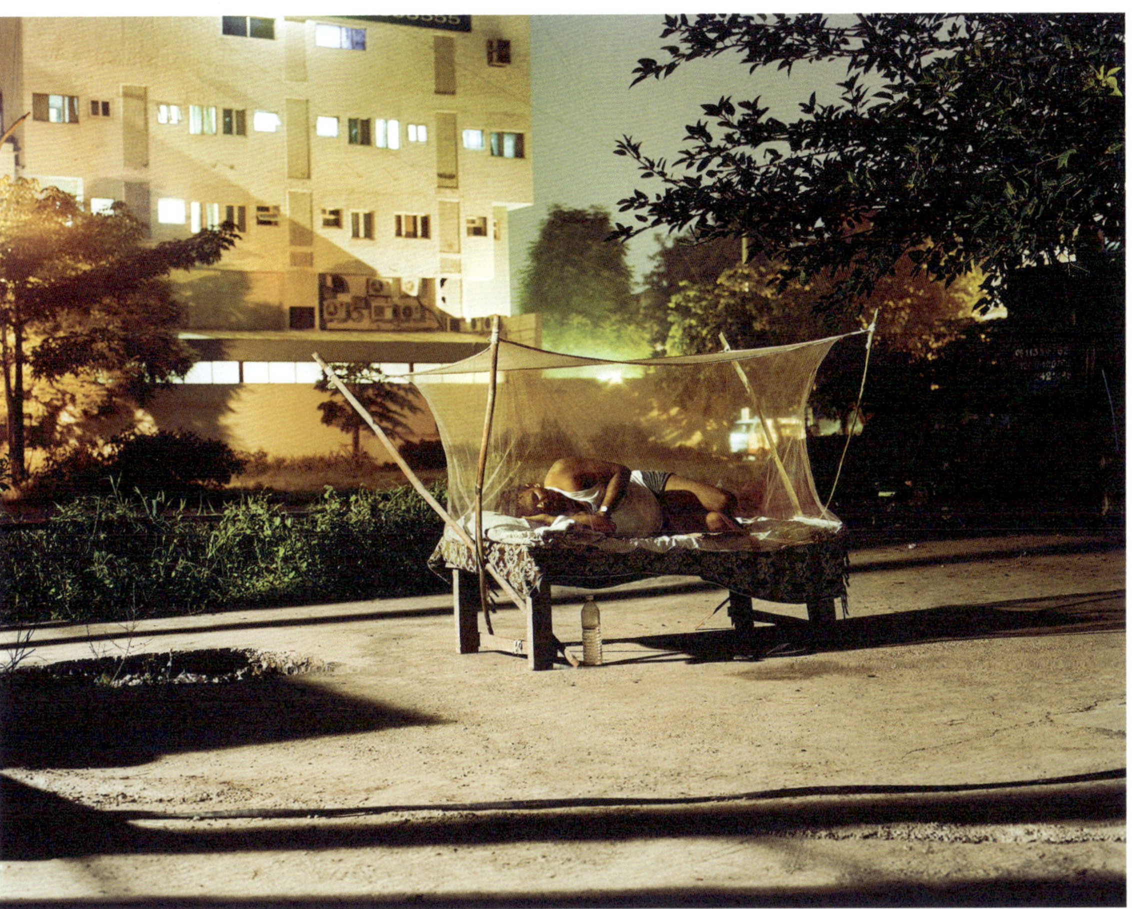

Untitled, from the series *Sleepers*, 2008–present

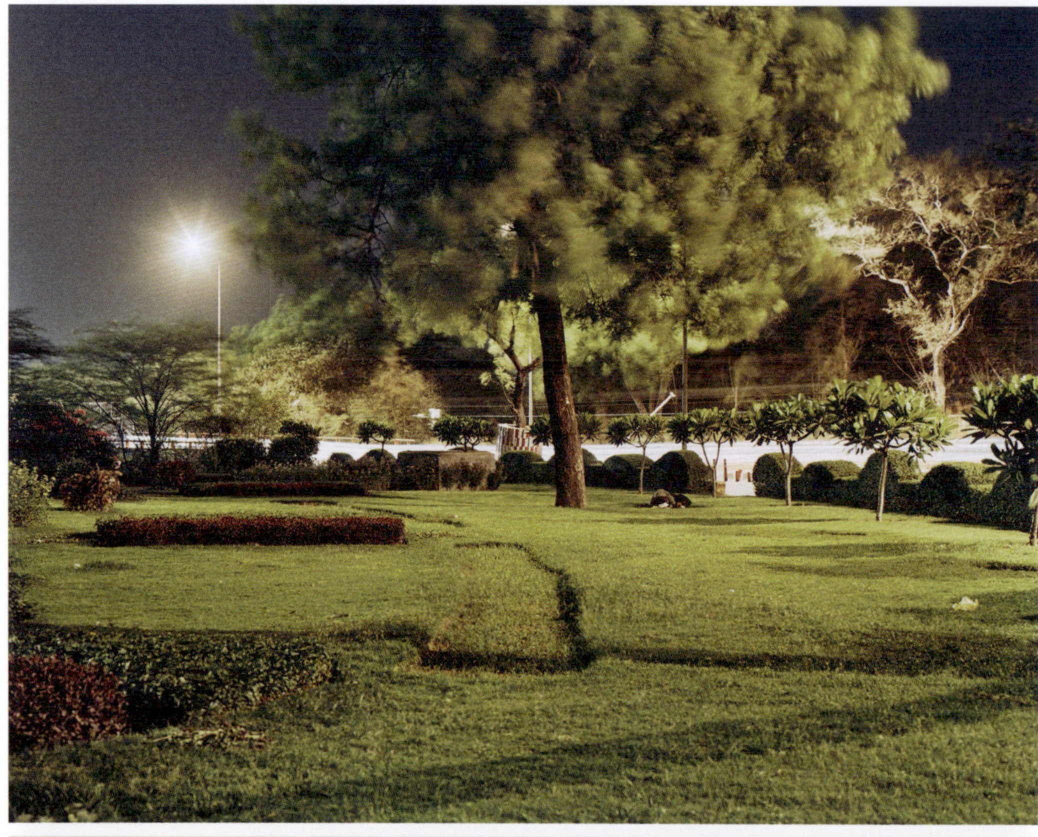

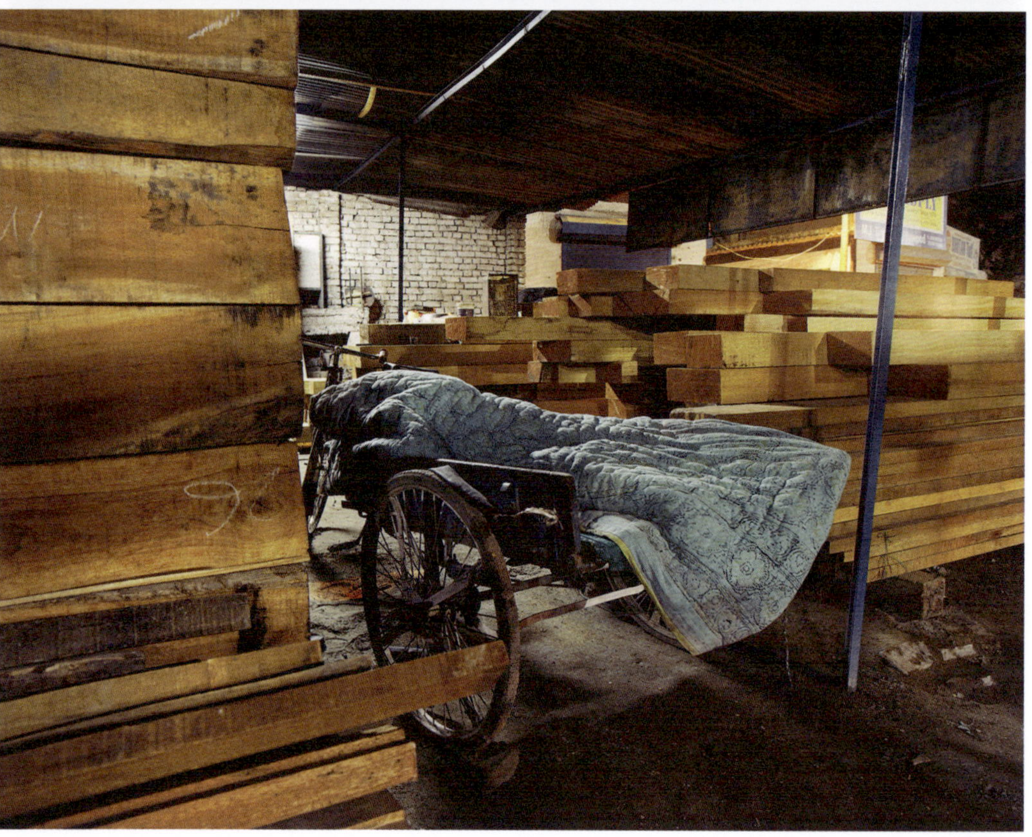

Untitled, from the series *Sleepers*, 2008–present

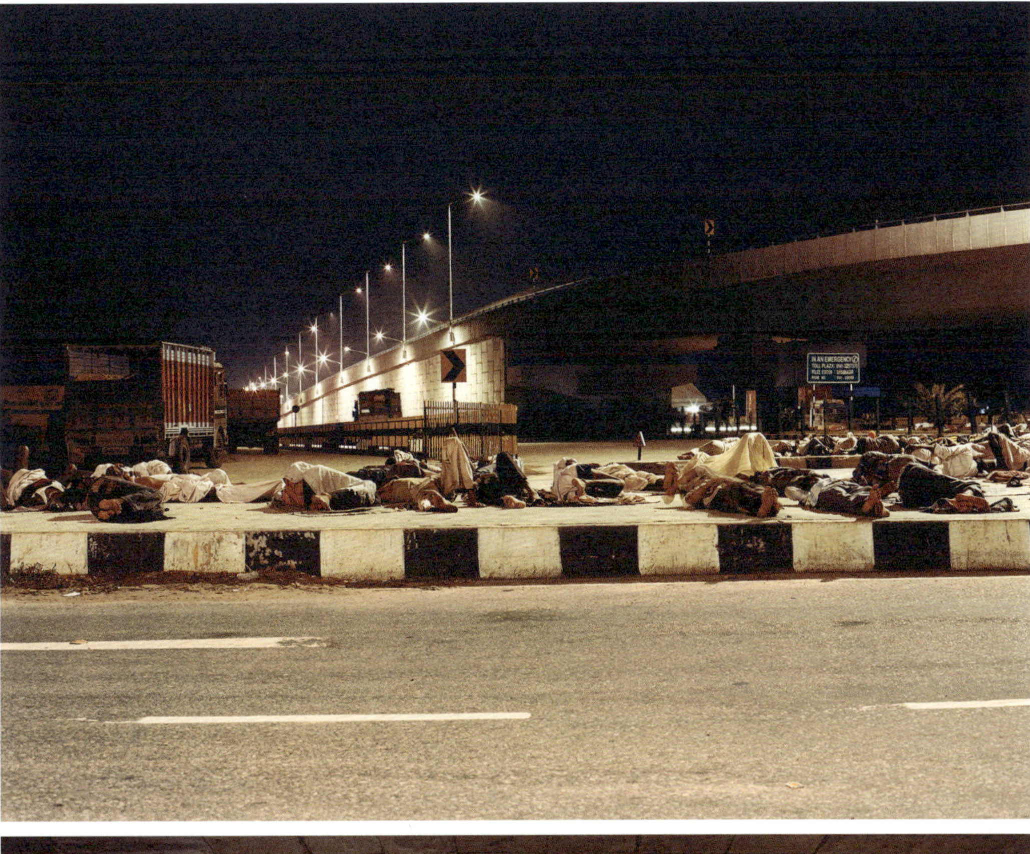

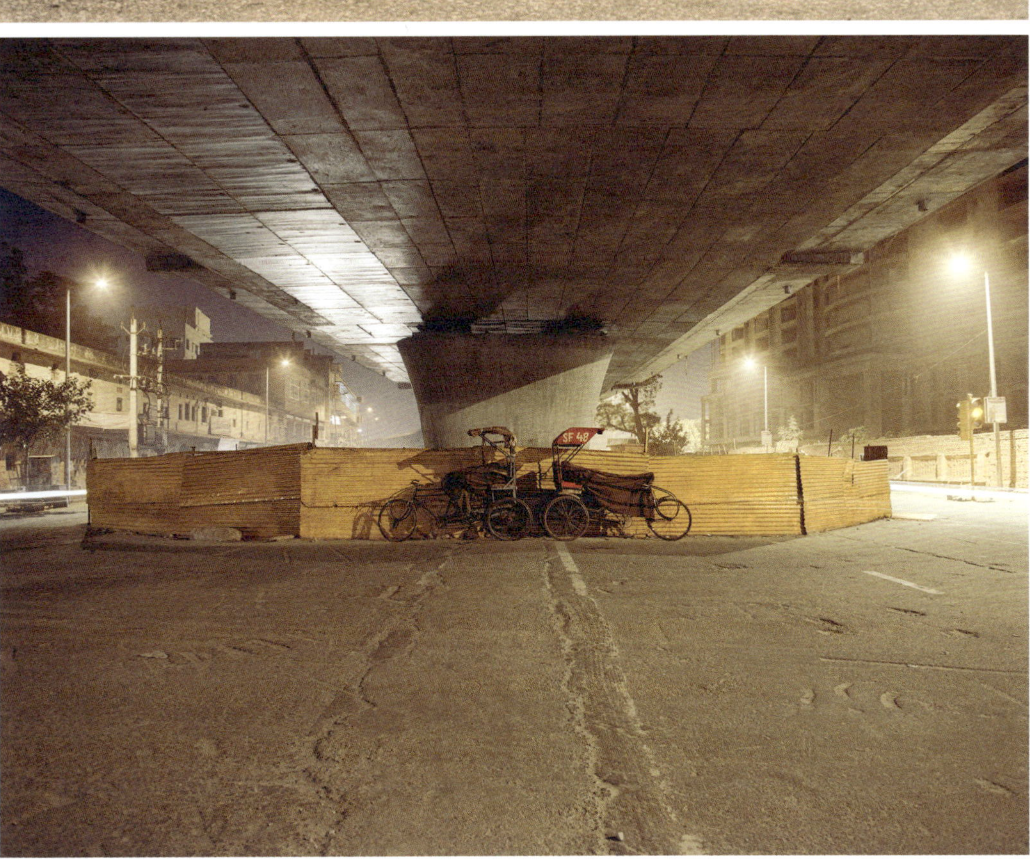

Untitled, from the series *Sleepers*, 2008–present

Pushpamala N.

Pushpamala N. is both director and actor in her prodigious body of work in photography and video. She uses performance-based mimicry to forge a fresh relationship to representations of women. Placing herself, as model and persona, into the center of established images in film, art, popular culture, and religion, she represents the female protagonist in varied sectors of Indian society and history, from perspectives of colonialism, Orientalism, ethnography, and the popular media. The artist approaches her work with a sense of irony while at the same time communicating a serious message about the assumptions behind characterizations of women over time. Her work highlights the power of print and other media to dictate how women are expected to look, act, and think, and investigates the role of photography and mass-produced print imagery in shaping female archetypes in the popular consciousness.

For the photographic series *The Native Types*, (2000-2004) the artist traced a journey from Orientalist ethnographic documents of Indian women as specimens of study to fantastical portrayals of women in contemporary media: the goddess, the flirt, the warrior, the circus performer. The series investigates, via appropriations of studio portraiture, popular cinema, and other media, the subconscious intentions of representation in the 19th and 20th centuries as they related to race and gender. By mimicking these images, Pushpamala N. deconstructs the relationship between the subject and the gaze, and by placing herself within the image, she humanizes and reclaims it, reversing the dynamic of observation. Her reenactment of each source image to its finest detail is a critical aspect of her successful triumph over that image. In some cases she spends months accumulating and re-creating the various props and costume elements in the scene, and of course in the process she develops a deep intimacy with the image, all the better to fully assume the character within it, much like an actress would, but with the end goal of undermining various aspects of the original.

This deliberate process of deconstructing and re-creating calls into question not only the genuineness of the original images, but also the authenticity of their subjects. In *The Native Types—Toda* (2001), Pushpamala N. refutes any belief in photography's ability to capture something as obscure as reality.

If encountered in an encyclopedia of anthropological study, her photograph would look like a convincing portrayal of a tribal woman in India in the 1800s. But this picture presents something far removed from the reality of that woman's life; it certainly conveys nothing about what would have been her frame of mind, her childhood memories, her ambitions, her fears. Pushpamala N.'s thoughtful impersonation of this source image stems from her desire to question its validity as a historical fact. Her deliberate assembly of costume, makeup, and props pushes the viewer to question the original Orientalist depiction of the woman as a "true" subject for anthropological study. The viewer is urged to ask, "Is the original photograph an accurate representation of a Toda woman?" thus confronting appearance for what it is and nothing more, while at the same time contemplating his or her own influences, biases, and motivations for interpreting the image.

Pushpamala N. is often compared to the American photographer Cindy Sherman, who also embodies classic female archetypes in her photographs, using herself as a medium for commenting on the role of women, of artists, and of media imagery in society. Both use themselves as models to represent and humanize iconic images of women, raising important questions about female stereotypes and the objectification of women at the hands of onlookers, whether these might be imperialists or fashion designers. But whereas Sherman's works are based on collective memories and icons, each one of Pushpamala N.'s photographs is a reenactment of a specific historical image.

Pushpamala N. draws inspiration from the early work of the famous Indian painter Bhupen Khakhar as well as from her mother, N. Vanamala. Khakhar, whose powerful figurative paintings grappled with issues of identity, gender, and sexuality, was the first contemporary Indian artist to create a series of exaggerated self-portraits. The series struck a chord with Pushpamala N., who was working primarily in sculpture at the time. Her first series of photographic self-portraits was a tribute to Khakar's early work. Her affinity for role playing and costumes stems from years of observing her mother who had a career as an actress.

···SR

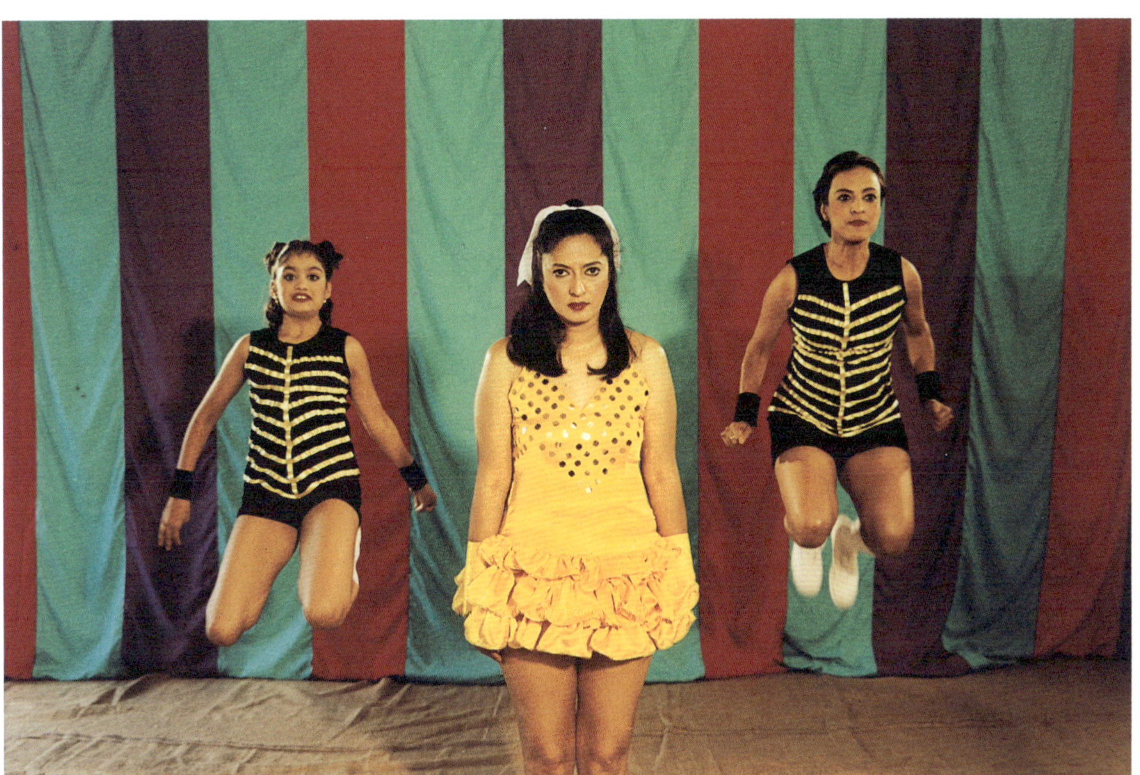

The Native Types—Circus (after a *Famous Circus* black-and-white photograph by Mary Ellen Mark), 2001

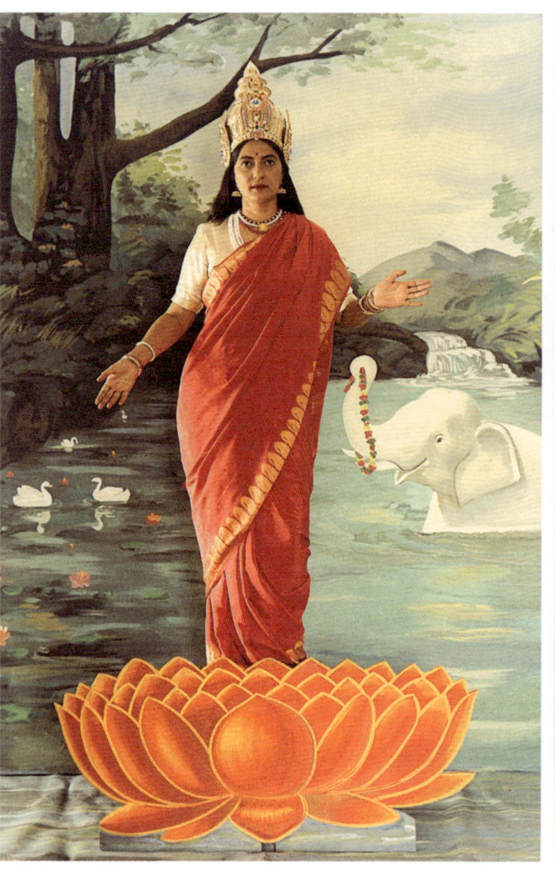

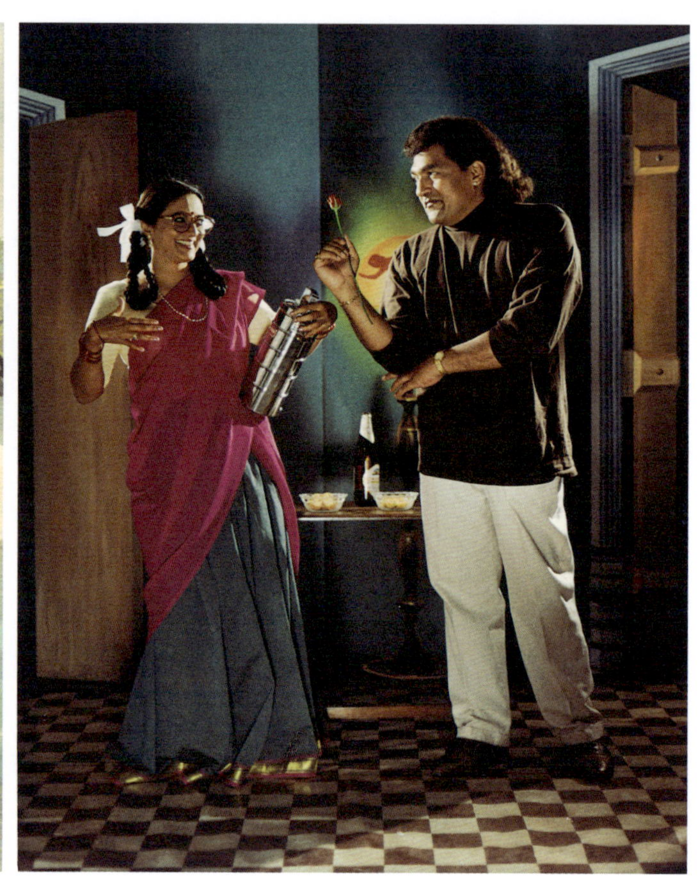

LEFT | *The Native Types—Lakshmi* (after an oleograph from Ravi Varma Press, early 20th century), 2001
RIGHT | *The Native Types—Flirting* (after a 1990s Kannada film still), 2001

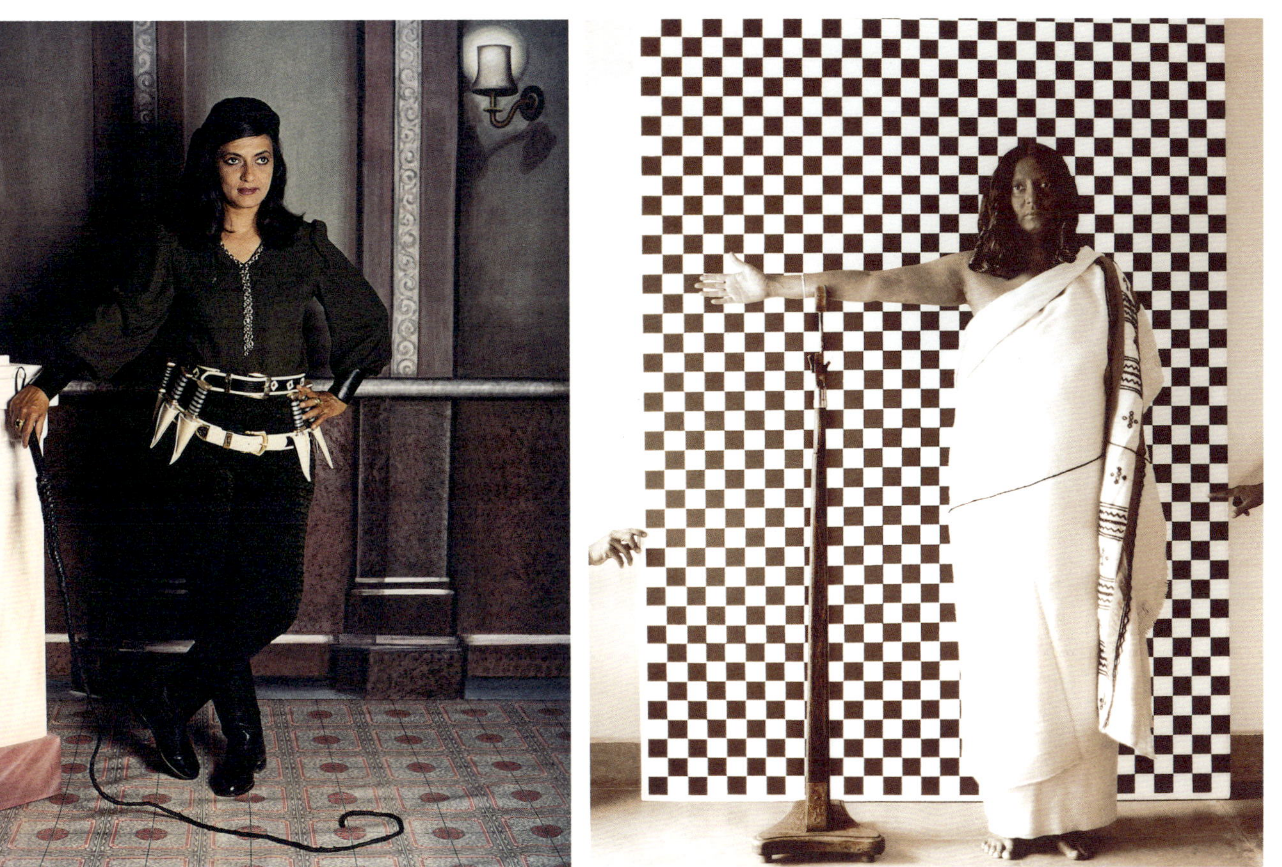

LEFT | *The Native Types—Cracking the Whip* (after a 1970s Tamil film still of Jayalalitha), 2001
RIGHT | *The Native Types—Toda* (after a late-19th-century British anthropometric photograph), 2001

TEJAL SHAH

Tejal Shah came to international prominence in 2000, at the age of twenty, with the groundbreaking video work *Chumma Chingari / Stinging Kiss*. It was a collaboration with the artist Anuj Vaidya that combined feminist porn, a camp aesthetic, and the transgressive power of consensual BDSM (bondage and discipline, dominance and submission, sadism and masochism) to create a clever subversion of the gendered tropes of mainstream Bollywood films. Since then her work has been shown in galleries, museums, and film festivals worldwide. Her multidisciplinary practice employs video, photography, performance, text-based art, kinetic sculpture, and installation. Shah is often branded as a "queer artist," yet this narrow label fails to capture the larger concerns that consistently inform and animate her work. Gender and sexuality are certainly important strands of her practice, as evidenced in the video installation *"What Are You?"* (2006) and the photography series *Hijra Fantasy* (2006), but she is actually most concerned with a variety of issues that hinge along the axes of what Michel Foucault called "biopower," relating to the disciplinary and regulatory techniques of "governmentality" for producing manageable populations. She explores interlinked aspects of the human condition connected to violence and power, identity and the body, the social construction of subjectivity and dominant norms, as well as the interpenetration of public and private. Her collaborative performance work *Encounter(s)* (2006), her recent series of photographs *Women Like Us* (2010), and the digital slideshow *I Am* (2009) all look at the gendered body in order to reflect upon questions of power and the social gaze.

Encounter(s) was a series of site-specific, interactive public interventions done in collaboration with the Bangkok-based artist Varsha Nair and enacted at the Turbine Hall of Tate Modern, at the National Review of Live Arts in Glasgow, and in various sites in the city of Turin. The artists, straitjacketed, jointly engaged the built environment in ways that stressed both the body and the costume. Their mutually constraining straitjacket was sewn from traditional Indian embroidered white cloth; it both connected the artists and also prevented them from touching. The work alluded to the violence of the mental institution as a regime of governmentality that punitively assigns normative value to particular states of being and subjectivities, and also to restrictive gender categories in Indian culture.

Women Like Us and *I Am* subtly explore gender, resistance, power, and the social gaze. Unlike in Shah's *Hijra Fantasy* series, which featured transgendered Indian women enacting their own fantasies of womanhood, the women in this series were born female but share characteristics with the dominant social construction of phenotypical masculinity in their external gendered characteristics. They come from all over India and occupy class positions across the social spectrum. Shah explores the external social gaze that is confounded by these seemingly masculine women. They are not necessarily self-conscious gender-benders, nor do they see themselves in terms of a politicized discourse about alternative gender identity or the social order. They simply *are* this way, and the way they are happens to be located outside the scope of what the dominant society in India perceives as feminine. Thus, regardless of their individual intentions or subjectivities, their appearances and modes of being offer an implicit challenge to the order of things that circumscribes Indian womanhood and femininity.

The title *Women Like Us* employs a double entendre. It can be read as a quiet manifesto or attestation of being that declares, 'There are many women like us out there. We are myriad, not marginal outliers.' But it can also be read in a more sexually provocative way, with "like" operating as a verb: "Whether or not the dominant society finds this mode of womanhood attractive, there are women out there who do like us this way.'

The digital slideshow of headshots in *I Am* also features so-called "masculine women." The power of the work lies largely in the heightened ambiguity of the headshot, where there is not even a hint of breasts or waist to clue the viewer into the gender of the person. The gazes, staring back at us, leave an arresting impression. On the one hand, the faces are as diverse as any population, yet on the other hand, the common factor of ascribed "female masculinity," amplified through the loop's iterative cyclicality, reinforces the strength behind their gazes, as if to say: 'Not only can the subaltern speak, but they can gaze back at power in a way that constitutes its own form of power.'

···MK

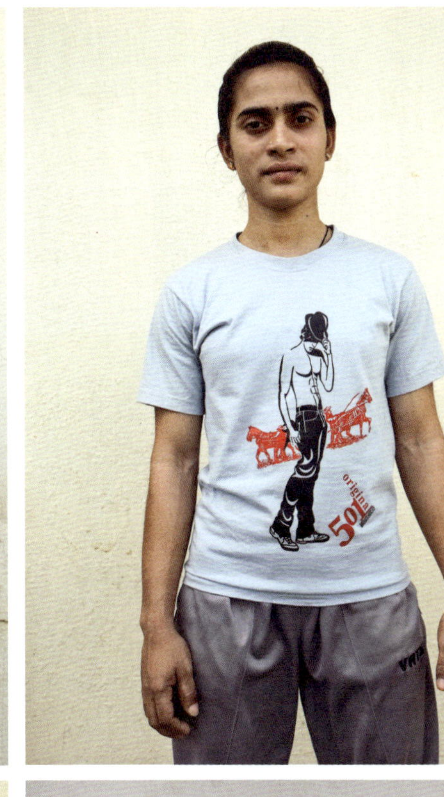
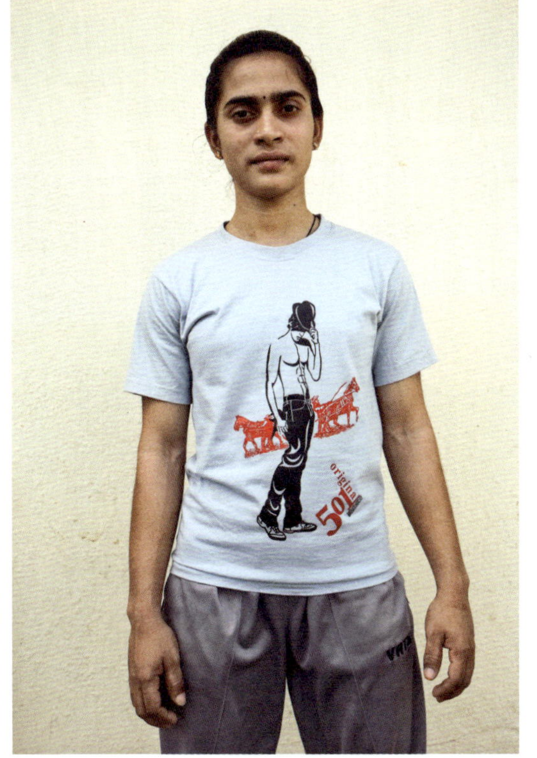
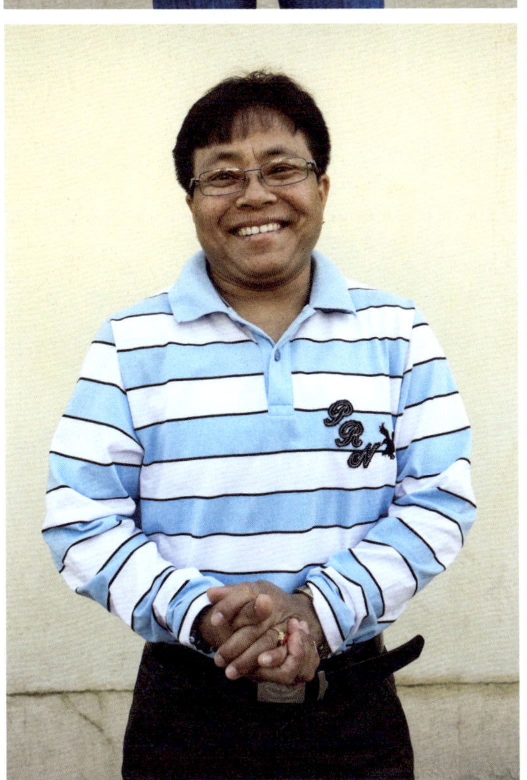
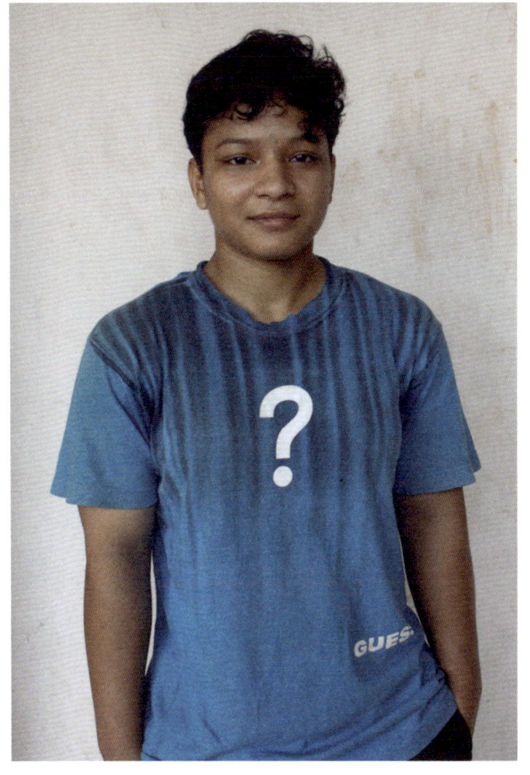

Women Like Us, 2010

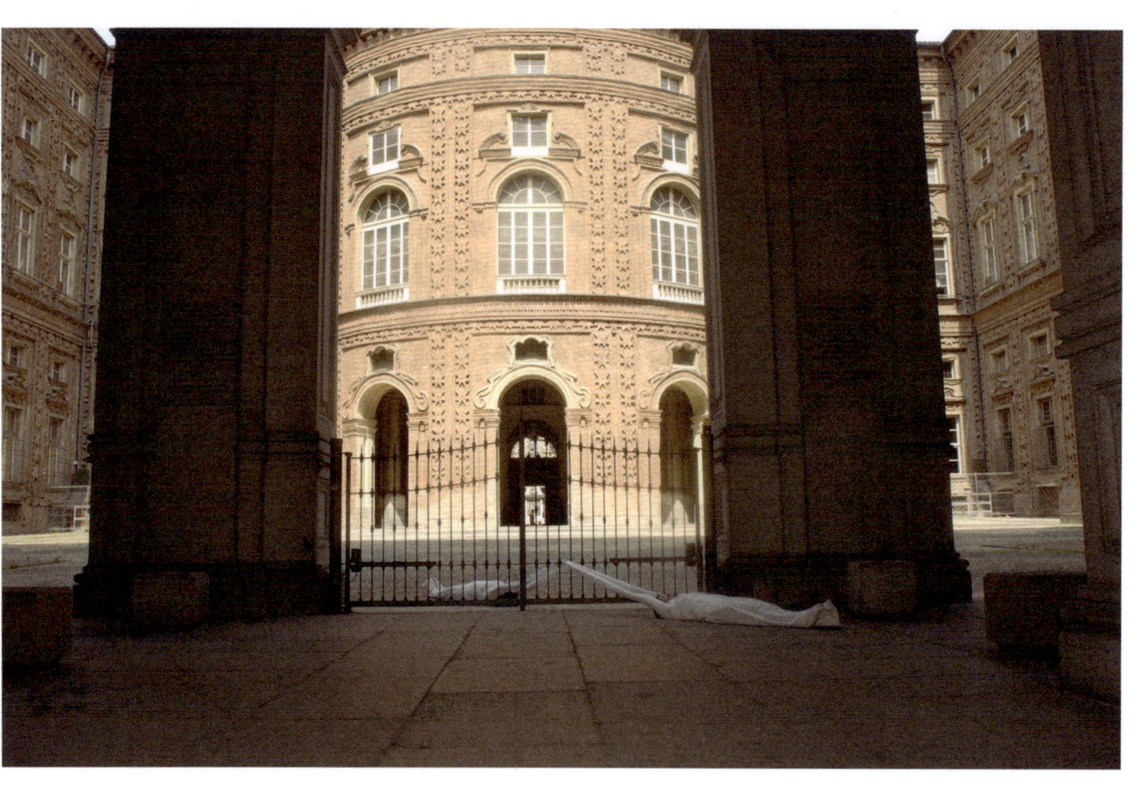

Tejal Shah and Varsha Nair, *Encounter(s) IV*, 2006

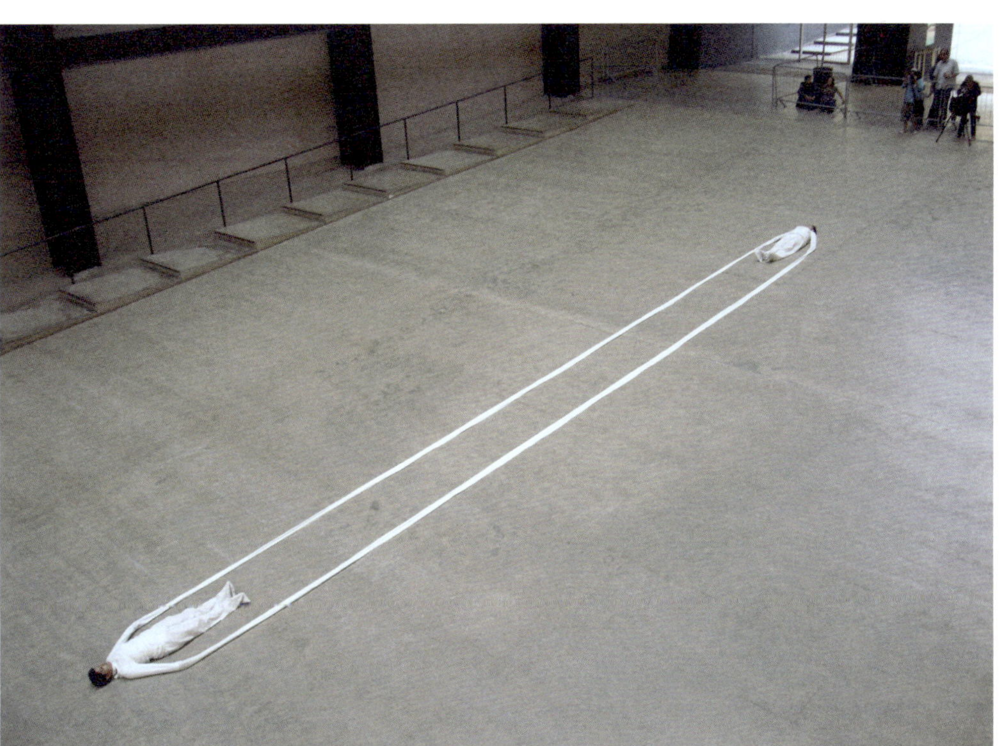

Tejal Shah and Varsha Nair, *Encounter(s) VI*, 2006

BHARAT SIKKA

Bharat Sikka's photographs evoke a haunting melancholy. Laced with mystery and a twist of magical realism reminiscent of a Gabriel García Márquez novel, the pictures often seem quotidian but subvert the mundane with an element of the unknown. While documentary in nature, they also have an air of the fictive. In an understated manner they evoke the surprise of serendipity or the shock of the surreal, eliciting a range of emotions that are gently thought provoking without being didactic.

Sikka's bodies of work in *The Matter Within* lack the usual mise-en-scène of his larger productions, which capture India's grand, globo-local settings or comment on its evolving urban landscape. Instead, these pictures offer up a series of intimate portraits. In one, a street musician self-consciously poses in a desolate New Delhi suburb with his trumpet under his arm. The band *wala*, as he is commonly called, is usually a working-class man who plays a brass instrument at large Indian weddings. He is a recurring motif among Indian painters and photographers, from the modernist painter Krishen Khanna to the Delhi-based Pakistani new media artist Bani Abidi. He is a metaphor for the strange coming-together of India's colonial military history and the vibrant kitsch that characterizes the Indian middle class, and his presence often adds a poignant note to a marriage celebration. In Sikka's photograph we get a sense of the past wrestling with the future. Perhaps this lone band *wala* has been left behind by a parade?

A dead pigeon, a septic tank, an unfinished clay statue of Lord Krishna, Delhi's deserted and foggy streets, a sprawling tree with a kite stuck in its branches: These images also clearly evoke melancholy, a similar sense of being left behind, lost, or forgotten, or of something having concluded. While endings are often inevitable, the sadness experienced after a period of giddy flight is also another inevitability—one that tinges even the moments of happiness immediately preceding it. This fraught sense of longing is a recurring concern for Sikka. He eschews the prosperous and the lively in favor of the desolate and the hopeless.

A series of informal photographs taken at the edge of the city, near the artist's home, captures the beauty of banal streets and byways. They represent the photographer's romance with the small things that make up the semi-urban scene, where nature encroaches on everyday life and vice versa. While of a specific place, they are almost common enough to stand in for every-place and every-person. They contrast with another thread in his work that captures anonymous landscapes, bare and barren like wastelands, that could belong to any part of India, though the presence of mountains and snow provides a hint that they were taken in the Himalayas. The lonely landscapes speak of spaces in between, neither urban sprawl nor rural idyll. These are zones of nowhere-land, abstract in the sense that they are overwrought with atmospheric indecision.

Another interesting set of images in *The Matter Within* is a suite of whimsical portraits involving hair. While in *Sonam* (2010) the subject's entire face is covered by his long, glossy hair and only his eyes and mouth peep out, the wild locks of *Chintan* (2010) are windswept by a theatrical breeze. It is tempting to interpret this series as a subversion of shampoo advertisements, which of course generally feature beautiful women and are aimed at a female target audience. Sikka's gender subversion here is odd and humorous, as he makes hirsute men the subject of his attentions. His poetic and sympathetic vision breathes life into any subject that attracts him. It is his focus on what is unusual or special in the visual world that feeds his far-ranging practice.

···GM

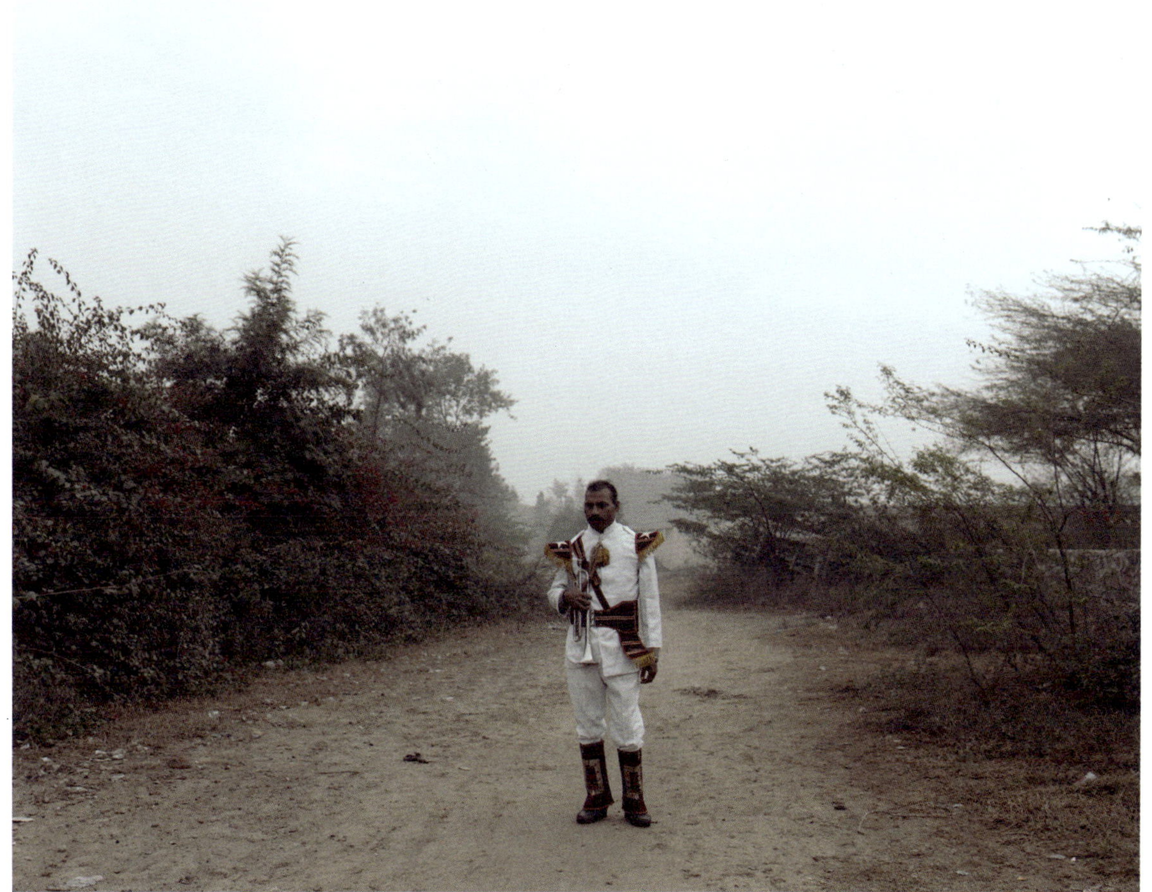

Opening Ceremony, 2010

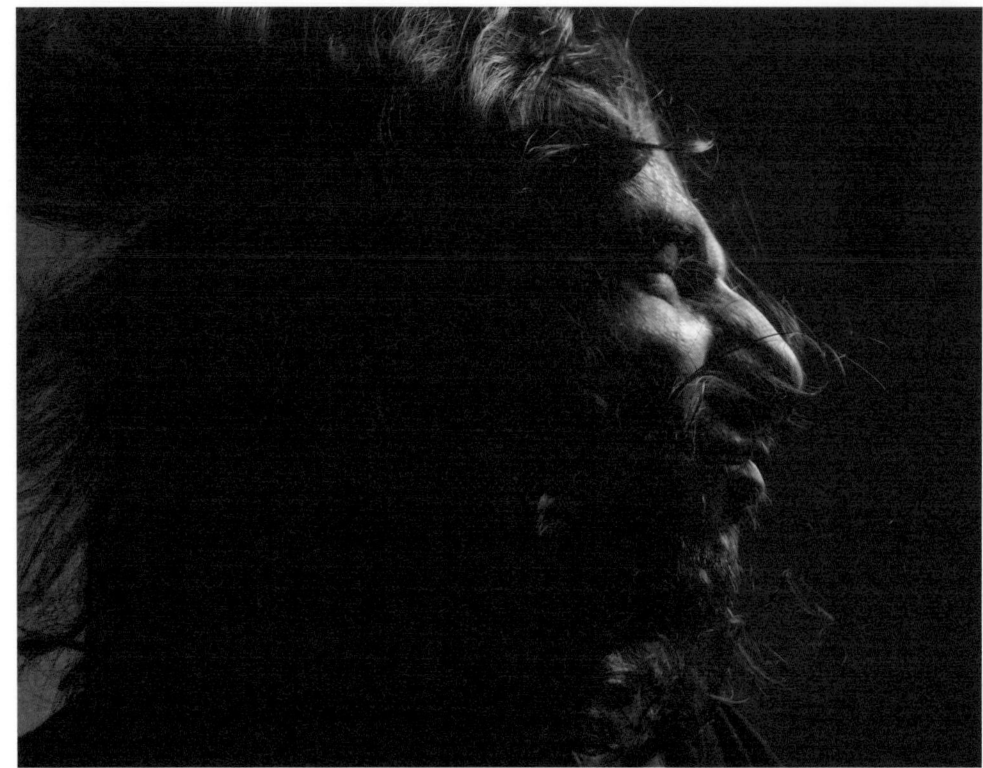

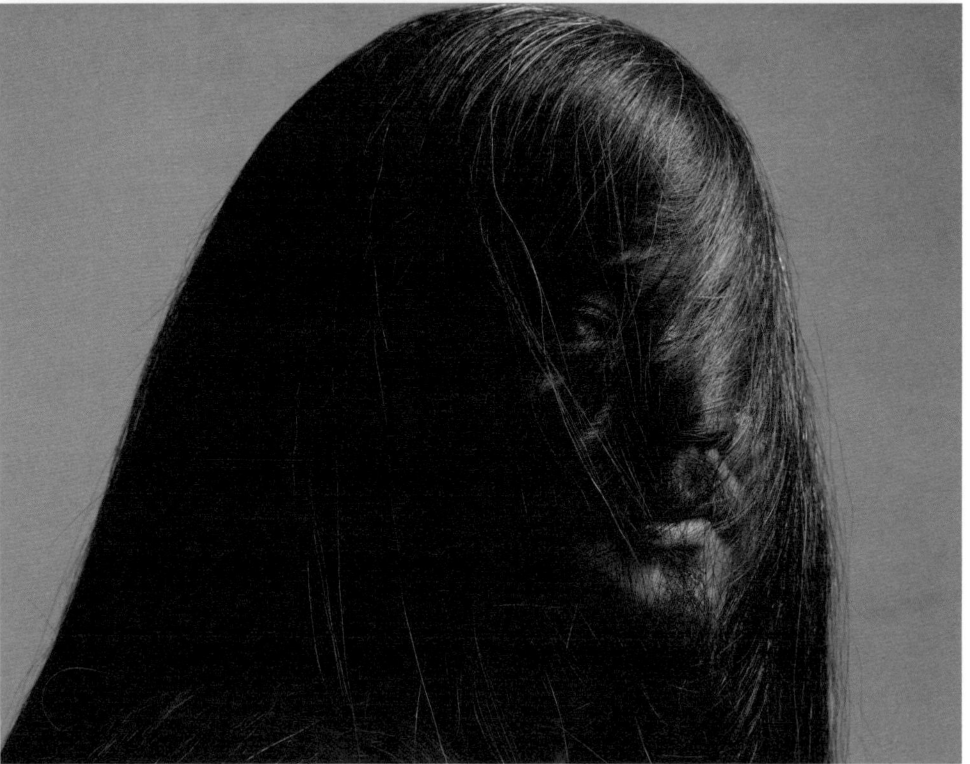

TOP | *Chintan*, 2010
BOTTOM | *Sonam*, 2010

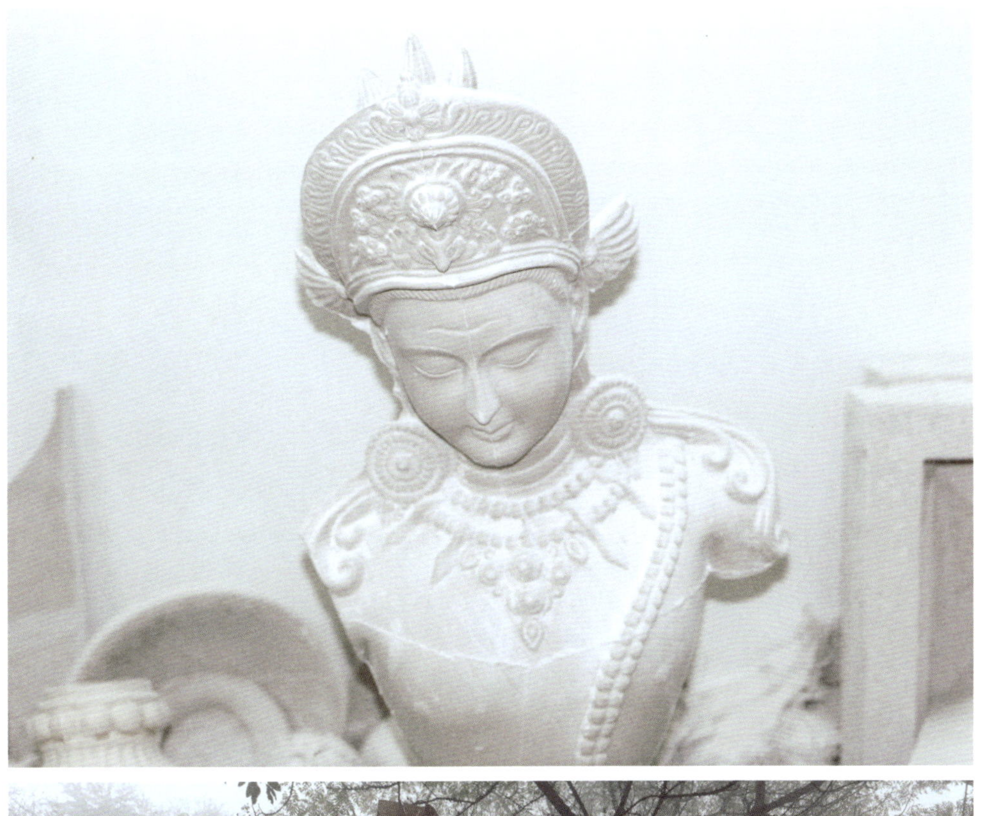

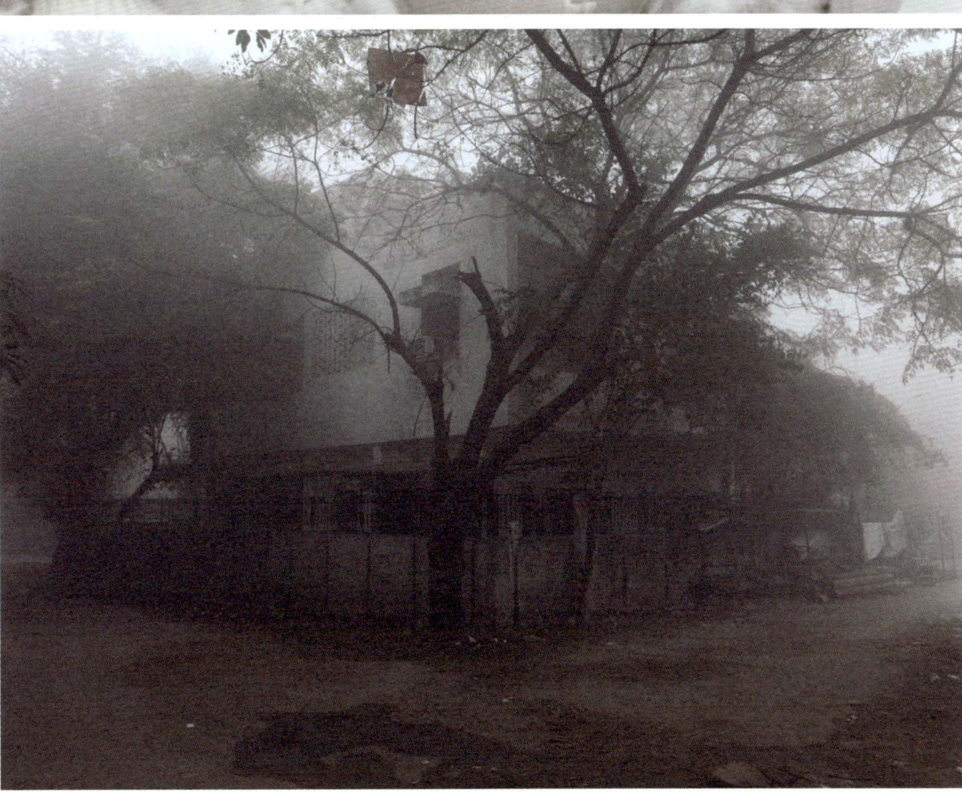

TOP | *Krishna*, 2010
BOTTOM | *The Kite*, 2010

ANUP MATHEW THOMAS

Anup Mathew Thomas's photographic practice focuses on social and power dynamics, specifically people in positions of authority and the impact of law on the general populace. In a variety of different formats, he questions the legitimacy of society's lawmakers and moral ambassadors who themselves are often driven by selfish politics and corrupt ethics. He is especially interested in these conditions as played out in the southern Indian state of Kerala, where he was born and raised. Documentary in nature, Thomas's pictures tell their stories through series rather than single images. The pictures are iterative, repetitive, and the method in which they are displayed is always important. His digital slideshows consist of anywhere from a dozen to five hundred images, and often they are incorporated into installations that set a mood and further an argument.

Thomas's early work was already exploring the concept of power, focusing on the authoritative figure with whom he was most familiar, his father. *Well, basically this is about Thomas Jacob* (2003) is the result of nine months of documenting the daily life of the head of household: at work, at play, and all points between. *NCA Library* (2006) continues the investigation of forms of authority, but with a more critical point of view. It documents the artist sneaking into the National College of Arts library in Lahore, Pakistan, and placing his own catalogues (of the *Well, basically this is about Thomas Jacob* project) onto the shelves, thereby offering a critique of institutional structures. It parallels the work of artists such as Banksy, who surreptitiously install their own works in major museums.

In *Cabinet* (2007), a slideshow of nineteen portraits, Thomas points his critical lens at a political subject. The pictures are of the cabinet members of Kerala's government at the time of the work's making. Flipping at regular intervals, each new slide introduces another member of the cabinet in a way that specifically highlights their similarities in appearance and posture. All are shown in three-quarter profile, and cropped in a way that mimics Roman sculptural busts of statesmen. The uniformity of the characters calls attention to the lone woman among the otherwise exclusively male group, a subtle commentary on the patriarchy of the Indian government.

Light Life (2005), a work featured in *The Matter Within,* is another series that employs the transitional moments of a slideshow as a visual enhancement. The series depicts empty dance bars: venues for adult entertainment involving women dancing for men in exchange for cash, but more akin to a cabaret than a strip club. The slides change slowly, almost imperceptibly, showing colored lights in different stages of brightness, producing a strobe-like effect. The photographs were taken the eve of the closure of these venues in response to a government ban; the fear was of possible corruption of young men and the breeding of crime and prostitution. The dance bars are animated with bright, pulsing lights but devoid of people, alluding to the disappearance of the workers, many of whom would ironically be forced to go underground into lives of prostitution and crime after the loss of their livelihood at the bars.

Not limiting the scope of his work to politics, Thomas also considers religion as an authoritative structure. *Metropolitan* (2006), also included in *The Matter Within,* consists of fourteen large-scale photographs of bishops of Episcopal churches in Kerala. A departure from the slideshow presentation, these large-scale photos are displayed in a grid and take up an entire wall. Their size and immediacy is meant to impress upon the viewer the power and grandeur of the bishops. Photographed in front of their official residences, they are dressed in an array of ecclesiastical robes, which highlight the diverse denominations of Christianity in the region; Kerala's Christian population is significant compared to the rest of the country (overall only 3 percent of India is Christian). While it does seem to be a celebration of religious pluralism in the state, *Metropolitan* may also be read as a critique of the spiritual leaders who—posed in front of their luxurious homes, dressed in their opulent gowns, and photographed at an imposing angle—seem not to adhere to the humble life they preach.

•••TL

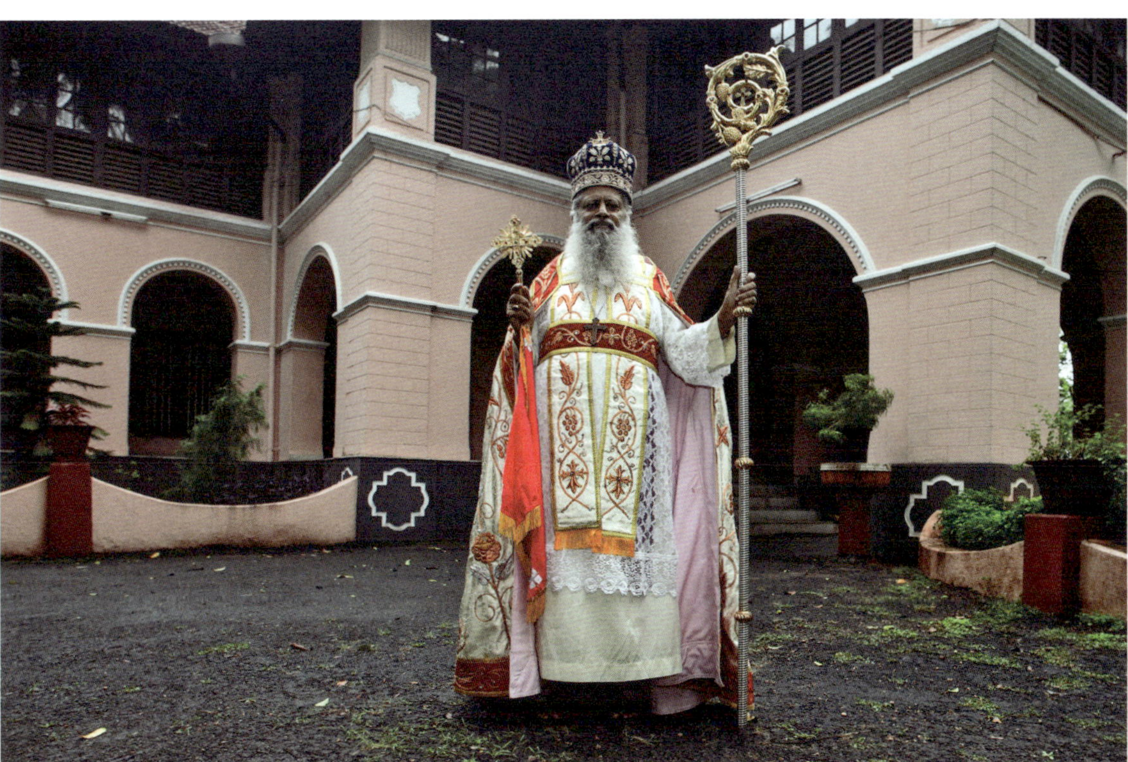

His Grace Dr. Mar Aprem Metropolitan, Chaldean Syrian Church of the East
from the series Metropolitan, 2006

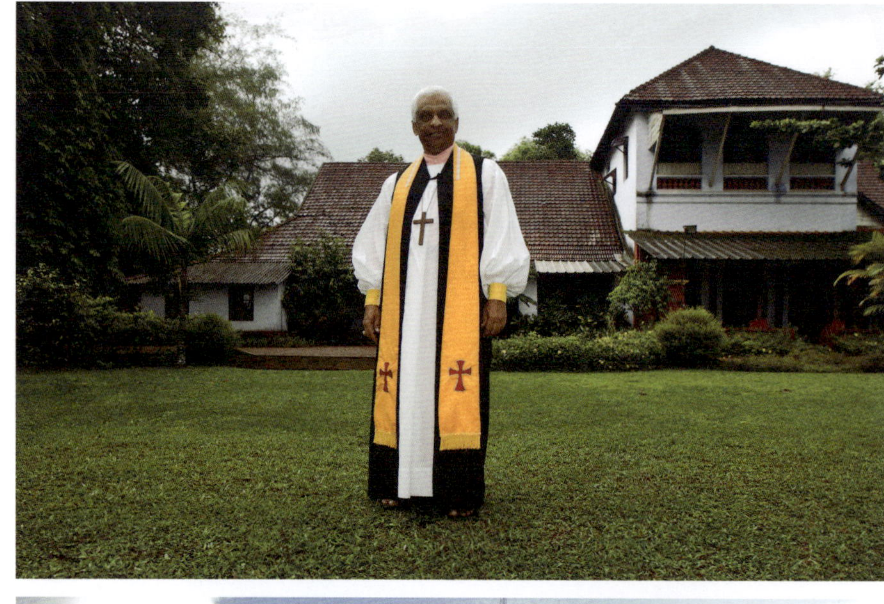

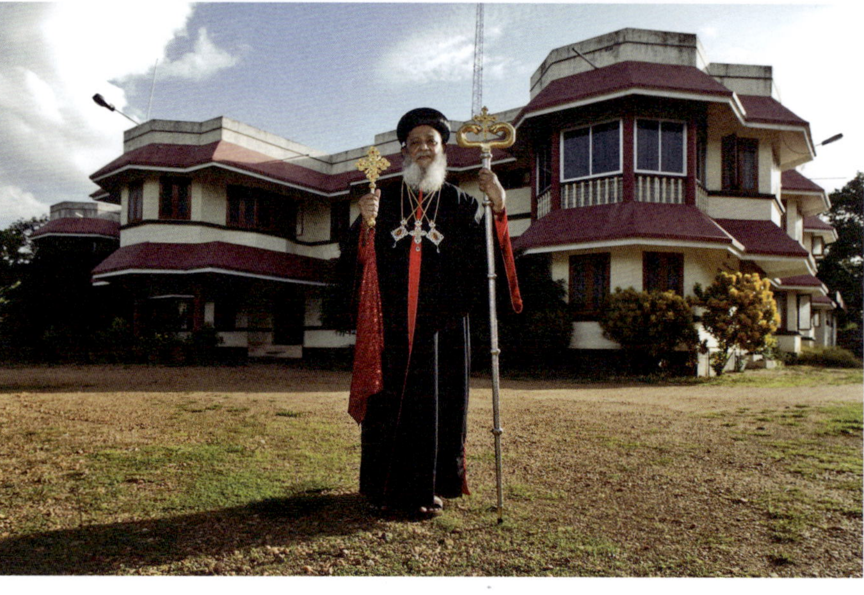

TOP | *Rt. Rev. Thomas Samuel, Bishop Madhya Kerala Diocese, Church of South India from the series Metropolitan, 2006*

BOTTOM | *His Beatitude Baselios Thomas I, Catholicose of the East and Metropolitan Trustee, Jacobite Syrian Christian Church, from the series Metropolitan, 2006*

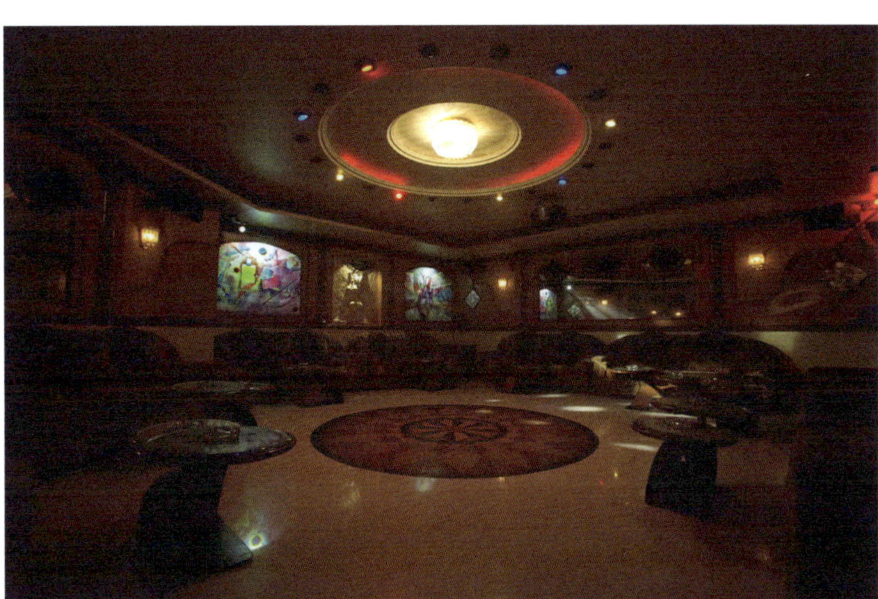

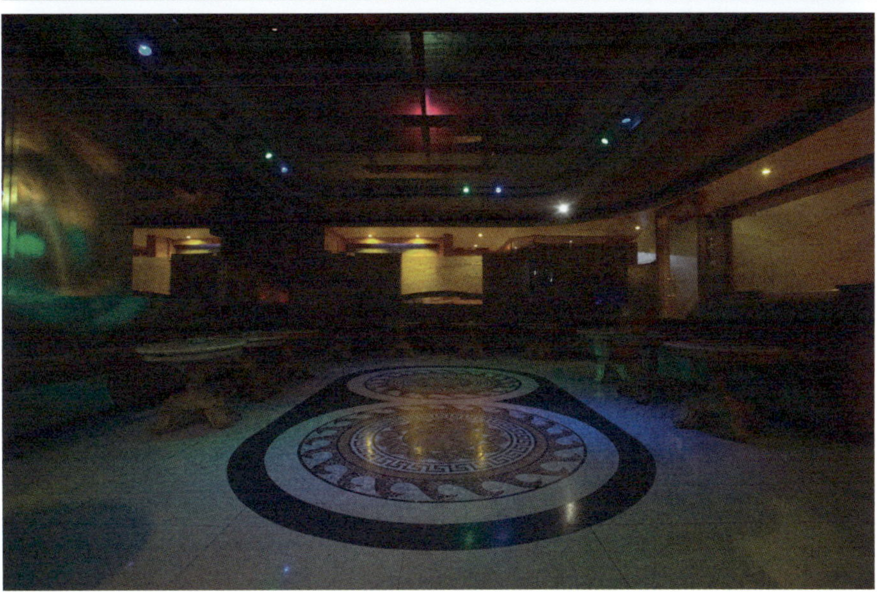

Light Life, 2005

Time for a Hundred Visions and Revisions, Which a Moment May Reverse

NANCY ADAJANIA

The first image he told me about was of three children on a road in Iceland, in 1965. He said that for him it was the image of happiness and also that he had tried several times to link it to other images, but it never worked. He wrote me: One day I'll have to put it all alone at the beginning of a film with a long piece of black leader; if they don't see happiness in the picture, at least they'll see the black.

This epiphany occurs at the beginning of Chris Marker's film *Sans Soleil* (1983). The film opens in darkness, with a voiceover recalling an absent cinematographer who has treasured the image of a group of Icelandic children held together by sunlight and a silken continuity of hands. This Arcadian image is briefly counterpointed by the image of a United States military aircraft, followed by the long piece of black leader: a darkness, a momentary extinction of image, voice, presence, narrative, and any memory of action; in the psychoanalytical sense, a fugue. We may like to believe that memory is a continent on whose resources we can draw as we establish the continuity of our selfhood. But that continuity is a fiction held together by intellectual effort and affective investment. Any breakdown in these mechanisms leaves us adrift and shows us that memory is not a continent but a long, uneven archipelago made up of islands of recall separated by the waters of amnesia.

In the space of a few minutes, Marker proposes a compelling meditation on memory, its representation, and indeed, most crucially, its *representability*. Why do we remember what we do, and how? Under what conditions do the contents of our memory become urgent? How does memory connect us to people, things, times, and places? And what measure of self-engagement and self-alienation are we guaranteed by the act of remembering?

The long piece of black leader in *Sans Soleil* reminds us with visceral force that the unitary self is a fiction, vulnerable to neurological schism and traumatic collapse, capable of exploding into multiplicities with the rise or fall in the level of a chemical. It dramatizes the fact that all experience is discontinuous and that art is an act of assemblage that tries constantly to bridge this discontinuity. Except that, in dealing with the deficit of memory, assemblage produces new alignments of the available material, thus generating new surpluses of meaning.

I have chosen to open this essay about four contemporary artistic positions exhibited in *The Matter Within*—CAMP, the Otolith Group, Ayisha Abraham, and Raqs Media Collective—with this Markerian prelude because it seems, to me, to signal the predicament of the contemporary subjectivity, a consciousness formed by multiple and competing histories, with which all four engage. I shall address and critically annotate these positions by reference to the following topoi: the retrieval and represent-ability of memory, the mediation of time and the articulation of entangled histories through the found and recycled image, the surpluses to be extracted from the historical remnant, and the archival residue.

He wrote: I'm just back from Hokkaido, the Northern Island. Rich and hurried Japanese take the plane, others take the ferry: waiting, immobility, snatches of sleep. Curiously all of that makes me think of a past or future war: night trains, air raids, fallout shelters, small fragments of war enshrined in everyday life. He liked the fragility of those moments suspended in time. Those memories whose only function had been to leave behind nothing but memories.[1]

Strangers' clothes hang from a clothesline and a lemon tree is dying in the courtyard of what was once home. This is a fragmentary detail from an account of a Palestinian family evicted by settler activity in East Jerusalem, presented in CAMP's film *Al Jaar Qabla Al Daar* (The Neighbor Before the House, 2009–11) (see pp. 107–109). But this film is by no means a documentary in the classical sense, where the subject is framed by the camera's omnipotent gaze and the image is precipitated through the complicity of performance and control. Instead, the representation of the situation develops from exchanges within a new coalition: one formed between the artist (as catalyst, facilitator, and co-conspirator) and the subjects/protagonists, who quite literally frame their own narratives rather than submit themselves to the preordained conclusion of an auteur interventionist.

Working in an intensely militarized zone where four hundred security cameras police one square kilometer of land, CAMP (founded by Shaina Anand, Ashok Sukumaran, and Sanjay Bhangar in 2007) turns the very act of surveillance on its head in this film. To make it they placed surveillance cameras on the rooftops of Palestinian homes and other neighborhood vantage points, and handed over the camera controller—a keyboard and a joystick with a PTZ (pan, tilt, and zoom) function—to the Palestinians themselves. Those who had been relentlessly spied upon were thus turned into agents who could actively reclaim and reassemble a new landscape of belonging for themselves, however transitory and ephemerally gathered together from dust and mirages.

In a zone of occupation, what is the ontological status of the neighbor? For instance here, in a neighborhood where Israelis and Palestinians live at such close quarters, and a *masjid* could abut on a Palestinian courtyard on one side and a *yeshiva* school on the other. Where the basis of coexistence is rivalry and contingency, can one rely on the relationships of trust and sharing that sustain the experience of neighborliness? Or do we find only shifting, unreliable, tactical adjacen-cies? When war is everywhere, the occupation viscerally invades not only the land but also the skin, air, and water of the occupied. As Anand says, "The project, if anything, is about what kinds of images are then possible."[2]

Intriguingly, when presented as an achieved work to its viewers, *Al Jaar Qabla Al Daar* may seem to possess the seamlessness of a classical documentary and thus may reflect a certain autho-rial presence. But this seamlessness is deceptive: The film does not try to conceal the footage-ness of the material produced by its protagonists. It retains the infinitesimal gap between what they see and what they say, a lag as well as in the anticipation between their voices and the images. Thus, it mirrors the differential temporalities by which recall becomes testimony and testimony reveals its lacunae.

It is important to note that *Al Jaar Qabla Al Daar* stems from Shaina Anand's rigorous and passionate critique of the potentials and limitations of the documentary mode of filmmaking. This critique has informed her probe into the politics of collaborative art making and her reinvest-ment of one of its pieties, namely "participation," with a fresh surplus of meaning: one that takes account, in various contexts, of the reconfiguration of class, gender, ethnic, and caste align-ments within emergent communities. CAMP's use of technology is neither instrumentalist nor dogmatic; it is a means toward the production of transformative action.

And I deploy the latter formulation cautiously. Its seed lies in early 2000, when Anand

1.
From the *Sans Soleil* voiceover. For the complete text see http://www.markertext.com/sans_soleil.htm.

2.
From a conversation with the artist on August 30, 2011.

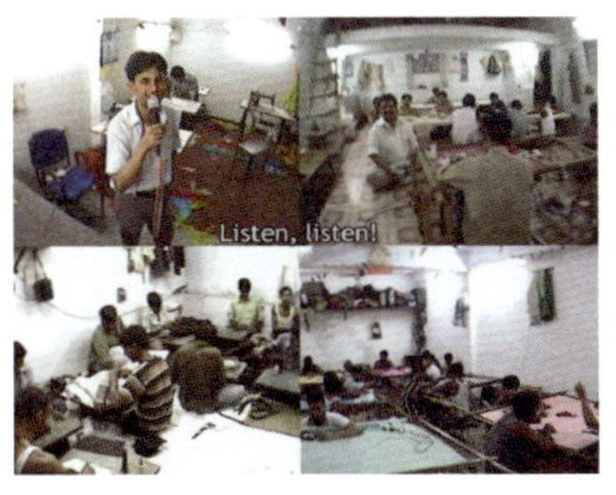

SHAINA ANAND
Khirkeeyaan Epsiode 4, Factories
(video still), 2006
Courtesy the artist

3.
Shaina Anand in conversation
with Ashok Sukumaran in *The Khoj Book
1997–2007: Contemporary Art Practice in
India*, ed. Pooja Sood (New Delhi: Harper
Collins, 2010): 621.

4.
From a conversation with the
artist on August 30, 2011.

5.
From the *Sans Soleil* voiceover.

6.
See George Clark, "The
Otolith Group Talks to George Clark,"
February 18, 2010, http://www.apengine.
org/2010/02/the-otolith-group-talks-
to-george-clark/. All statements by
Anjalika Sagar and Kodwo Eshun in
this section are
from this interview.

preferred to leave a documentary film project (*Tellavision Mumbai*) incomplete because of her disappointment with the Indian Left's inability to intervene creatively and critically in the public sphere. The immediate provocation was 9/11 and its viral televisual manifestations. The Left in India was in no position to counter the shock-and-awe propaganda of the United States and the anti-Islamic rhetoric that underwrote the soon-to-unfold invasions of Afghanistan and Iraq. Its response to the manifestation of a new geopolitics after 9/11 was to hold a few ineffectual public meetings. Anand says, "The film project 'failed' because I could never edit it into a coherent or *hopeful image*. [italics mine] The map was there, but what emerged was not a useful vision. It was turning into a lament on the death of the Left, which was not at all what I wanted to do. . . . All the creative . . . editing skills that I could bring to it could not present a 'critical public culture' where there really wasn't one."[3]

Anand's will to produce a "hopeful image" should be read not as a commitment to falsify ground reality (hers is not, after all, a sunshine documentary vision) but rather as a commitment to affirm the promise of the Left, and by extension the documentary film as a medium of justice and the transformation of consciousness. In the seminal experiment *Khirkeeyaan* (2006) she accomplishes this not by entangling herself in the grand ideological narrative of a moribund Left, but by retooling the micropolitics of a neighborhood so that the subaltern can speak in his or her own voice.

Al Jaar Qabla Al Daar similarly "pokes at the promise of documentary."[4] The protagonists are neither resigned to their circumstances nor nostalgic for what cannot be recovered. Rather, I would contend that they are complicit with CAMP in the mobilization and performance of history as a memory recharged by political desire: The intifada remains a subliminal presence in the field of this work. The work is an assemblage constructed from a re-membering, a gathering together of the broken limbs of what the Palestinian poet Mahmoud Darwish visualized in his great poem "We Travel Like Other People" (1984) as a people who have only a "country of words," who travel but "return to nowhere." In this film, set in the intermediate zone where the narratives of Shoah and Nakba intertwine, what cannot be spoken comes to light.

While the self-operated PTZ movements of the protagonists overwrite official records with memory, and rewrite memory with prognostications for the future, we know that even an infinite zoom cannot calculate the incalculable violence that will be unleashed. It cannot, for instance, penetrate below street level to reveal the tunnel built by the IDF (Israeli Defense Forces) to advance the state's program of military control.

CAMP has made a journey from the aspiration to produce a "hopeful image" to a place where grief, reason, despair, and hope all find themselves weighed in the balance.

> *He wrote me: I will have spent my life trying to understand the function of remembering, which is not the opposite of forgetting, but rather its lining. We do not remember, we rewrite memory much as history is rewritten. How can one remember thirst?* [5]

The London-based Otolith Group, comprising Anjalika Sagar and Kodwo Eshun, produces atmospheres rather than images as evidentiary material in their eponymous trilogy. They create an environment, a mood, where there is no true north but where personal memory conspires with collective history to produce a state of disorientation. The Otolith Group infuses creative instability into the very act of image making by naming themselves after a delicate part of the anatomy (the inner ear) which is meant to retain our balance against the pull of gravity, but which, if damaged, can bring about a loss of equilibrium.

The Otolith Group creates idiosyncratic narratives that yield critical insights into that large-scale programming of nations and societies which was a major feature of post–World War II modernity, and specifically of the forms of modernity released by the decolonization process. As Eshun reflects, "A lot of what we're interested in isn't necessarily visible, speculation, master plans, pre-emption, these are abstract modes of power, they're not things you can easily illustrate, or if you can they wouldn't be very successful."[6] But instead of being overwhelmed by these epic narratives, Otolith finds entry points through fugitive details (such as the laboring body), forgotten microhistories (such as the Soviet space program) and unrealized projects (such as Satyajit Ray's film *The Alien*).

What is truly captivating is the group's ability to generate a sense of deep cosmic time—not without irony—within which the history of the 20th century can be contextualized and the 21st and 22nd centuries can be speculated upon. The trilogy *Otolith I, II,* and *III* functions like a memoir for an entity larger than itself, fashioning at once a sci-fi inscrutability and a global historical consciousness—both important features of the 20th century that were strengthened in the 21st. It is then not surprising that Otolith cites Marker's *La Jetée* (1962) and *Sans Soleil* as major influences on their filmmaking. Given their affinities with the "left wing essay form," they draw for themselves a lineage that goes back to Dziga Vertov, passes through Chris Marker, and continues through the Black Audio Film Collective and the work of Harun Farocki. Like Farocki, they exhibit a fundamental mistrust of words and images, and have steered clear of the clichés of the "essay" film. Farocki laments its uncritical usage: "In television when you hear a lot of music and see landscapes—nowadays that's called an essay film, too. Lots of atmosphere and fuzzy journalism is essay. . . . It's so vague."[7] To counter the depoliticization of the essay film, Eshun argues that, for the Otolith Group, "The essayistic is dissatisfaction, it's discontent with the duties of an image and the obligations of a sound. It's dissatisfaction with what we expect a documentary to do especially."

Otolith I (2003), a work cast in the mode of science fiction, envisions a future utopia of "agravic" human habitation: a no-place where the rules of gravity do not apply. But this freedom from anchorage is, paradoxically, anchored in very specific histories. In a narrative structured in concentric circles, each a memorial to a female ancestor, each a site of contending histories, we encounter Sagar making an epistolary connection with her grandmother, Anasuya Gyanchand, a feminist and Communist who was enthusiastic *about* the Soviet space program. Gyanchand's narrative in turn revolves around and abuts on the life and work of Valentina Tereshkova, the first woman in space, whom she admired and had met.

The mode of science fiction, with its model of an "agravic," gravity-free existence, holds in reserve the real and deep disquiet that afflicts the artists. They do not seek freedom from the political; they confront what they perceive as a general lack of commitment to a specific position on collective life, which Sagar terms a "suspension of political will." The voiceover says, "It is my great misfortune to belong to a generation with no political vision to betray or to fulfill."

An attempt is made to mark a dissenting note by filming American protestors opposing their government's invasion of Iraq in 2003. But the slow, hypnotic treatment of the protest is quickly undercut by an escapist, even levitationist gesture as Sagar, the protagonist, leaves for Star City to conduct experiments in microgravity. The contradiction deepens when we encounter the artist in an Ilyushin 76, a troop transport plane from the Soviet era that is now being used as a laboratory for the space program. To see the artist levitate tranquilly in an airplane of the kind once involved in military interventions in Central Africa (exporting Communism via the Che Guevara route) is somewhat disconcerting. But these are productive contradictions. The valorization of the Soviet past, the simultaneous Gandhian and Communist agendas of the grandmother, and the performance of the peaceful cosmonaut at the end all reveal various models of revolution, the entangled mythologies of emancipation, the rival soteriologies of Gandhi, Marx, and Lenin that have contended for space in the postcolonial imagination. Anasuya Gyanchand, Anjalika Sagar, and Kodwo Eshun appear as multifrequency consciousnesses, conveying both signal and static, which we sometimes mistake for one another. As viewers we find ourselves at a finely tuned pitch of alertness here.

Otolith II (2007) cannot afford the luxury of "agravic" levitation. Its exploration of labor performed under extreme conditions, in a society transiting between postcoloniality and globalization, ranges from the register of melodrama to that of melancholia. Its Mike Davis–like apocalyptic forecasts of Bombay's ready-to-explode slums and brazen real estate greed (all of which are true) fail to account for interventions made by the city's denizens against the official master plans at the micropolitical level. In this labor-intensive film ("We were interested in the labor of watching labor"), the act of observing the body at work becomes a cathexis. As a result, instead

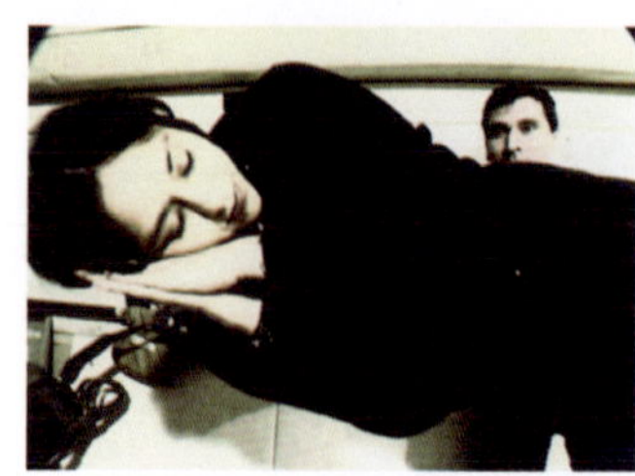

THE OTOLITH GROUP
Otolith I (video still), 2003
Courtesy the artists

7.
See "Neun Minuten in Corcoran. Uberwachung, Krieg, Montage. Der Filmemacher Harun Farocki in Gespräch mit Rembert Huserm," *Jungle World* 45, November 1, 2000.

of achieving its avowed intention of blocking "visual pleasure," it ends up attaining the opposite goal: fetishizing laborers by dwelling relentlessly on their bodies. The only moment of compassion in the film appears as a vision in an abandoned mill, when the child protagonist from Ray's *The Alien* plays hide and seek with the red-eyed extraterrestrial creature. The alien could be parsed variously here: the artists as critical outsiders investigating a city in a transitional society and finding their one zone of liminality in the afterlife of labor, or the denizens of the city themselves portrayed as aliens, migrants, or foreigners who will never feel at home and yet may never be able to return to where they belong.

Ray's unrealized film *The Alien* is the subject of *Otolith III* (2009) (see p. 111), which was included in *The Matter Within*. The artists were not attempting to make Ray's film, but to redeem what mainstream cinema would call a failure because of its unfinished status. Even though the film performs an elaborate charade—looking for people who might be cast as the characters of the Boy, Industrialist, Engineer, and Journalist—the casting is never meant to come to fruition. The characters are meant to be placeholders for the artists' politics and ideas and theories about filmmaking. The figure of the alien, although sketched into various abstractions, never achieves final, material form. It remains a black surface, an atmosphere. The unrepresentability of the alien attunes us to the realization that an unfinished project and the afterlife of a failed project form the archetypal dual paradigm of modernity. The utopic vision is a surplus that can never be achieved; in its very spectrality, it always exceeds representation and possession, and is available only through yearning or eschatology.

He wrote me that in the suburbs of Tokyo there is a temple consecrated to cats. I wish I could convey to you the simplicity—the lack of affectation—of this couple who had come to place an inscribed wooden slat in the cat cemetery so their cat Tora would be protected. No, she wasn't dead, only run away. But on the day of her death no one would know how to pray for her, how to intercede with death so that he would call her by her right name. So they had to come there, both of them, under the rain, to perform the rite that would repair the web of time where it had been broken.[8]

Ayisha Abraham has interceded with death on numerous occasions to save an orphaned film from crumbling to dust or being reduced to a sticky mass. Her archiving of amateur films—8-millimeter, Super-8, and 16-millimeter—and research into their social and cultural history forms the basis of her experimental documentaries. Instead of looking at amateur film as the "other" of commercial cinema, essentially lacking in technical expertise, Abraham points to a unique feature of its morphology. She writes, "Although home movies expose a temporality filled with beginnings, such footage seldom provides any closure. The shot might end because the three-minute reel of raw stock ran out or the subject walked off the frame. An embarrassing moment transpires and recording stops. The viewer, then, is propelled to imagine beyond the visible frame."[9]

If intimacy and interiority are the primary characteristics of amateur films, it is impossible to achieve narratival closure. This impossibility condition is not only a result of a lack of resources or professionalism, but inherent in the very nature of the experience itself. The amateur film is marked by the contingent, the aleatory, and the fugitive, where that which is "beyond the visible frame" takes on a greater importance than what is recorded. In salvaging this material Abraham attempts to repair the broken web of time, but the assemblages born of this rescue operation (*Straight 8* [2005] and *I Saw a God Dance* [2011]) (see pp. 103–105) do not aspire to closure; in fact, they actively resist it. The memory joints are missing here, and the image ghosts and doubles itself. And when the convulsive frame stabilizes itself for a moment, we see it pockmarked with dust and fungus, appearing like a perforated lung dying on its breath.

Abraham's investment in the afterlife of amateur films, or what she calls the "private archives of memory," creates an overpowering phenomenological impact on the viewer. But this evocation of the sensorium conceals a quiet politics: that of acknowledging the unofficial stories and memories of anonymous figures such as colonial subjects, grandmothers, and amateur filmmakers. Trinh T. Minh-ha, whose experimental films Abraham admires, for instance, questions the reasons behind privileging a written history over a storyteller's account, the polarization of

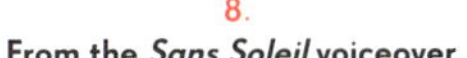

8.
From the *Sans Soleil* voiceover.

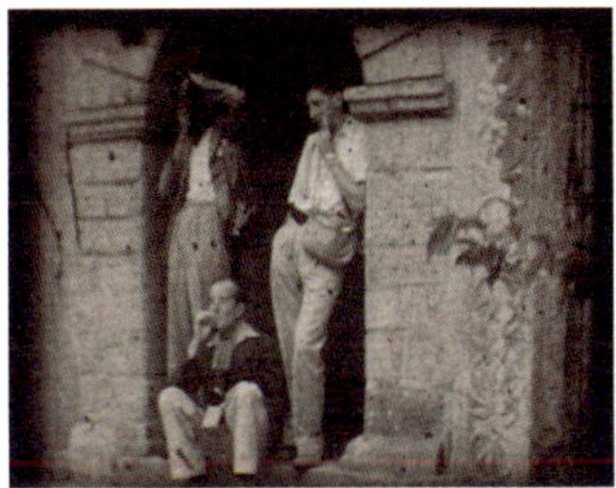

AYISHA ABRAHAM
Straight 8 (film still), 2005
Courtesy the artist

9.
Ayisha Abraham, "Deteriorating Memories: Blurring Fact and Fiction in Home Movies in India" in *Mining the Home Movie*, eds. Karen L. Ishizuka and Patricia Zimmermann (Berkeley: University of California Press, 2007): 171.

fact and fiction, and the competing claims made over a mediated truth. She argues: "If we rely on history to tell us what happened at a specific time and place, we can rely on the story to tell us not only what might have happened, but also what is happening at an unspecified time and place. No wonder that in old tales storytellers are very often women, witches, and prophets. The African *griot* and *griotte* are well known for being poet, storyteller, historian, musician, and magician—all at once. But why truth at all? Why this battle for truth and on behalf of truth? I do not remember having asked grandmother once whether the story she was telling was true or not."[10]

But before Abraham was able to explore through her work the spaces of liminality where the magical and the uncanny happened in an "unspecified time and place," she had to wrestle with an educational system that privileged dogma over the experientiality of practice. Between 1983 and 1987 she studied painting at Maharaja Sayajirao University, Baroda, where the narrative-allegorical style had become entrenched as a hegemonic trend. It was at the Whitney Independent Study Program in New York in the early 1990s where she received a life-changing caveat from her teacher Silvia Kolbowski: "Thought is material itself; trying to reconstruct your feelings is not enough."[11] She was intellectually stimulated by the concerns of artists such as Mary Kelly (the deconstruction of motherhood) and Kolbowski herself (deployment of the gallery as artistic material) as well as the art historian Hal Foster, who was theorizing the concept of site specificity.

Abraham's distance from home brought her in touch with questions related to memory and migration. While research into photography theory familiarized her with notions of gaze, pose, and subjectivity, she found herself deeply exercised by the performance of memory among older people and in migrant communities. She recalls, "I had two grandmothers who lived across the 20th century and both died close to one hundred years and it seemed like they were *griottes* (as Trinh T. Minh-ha would describe them) who carried experience of the world through their subjective lives."[12] In 1998, while her exhibition . . . *Looks the Other Way*, consisting of digitally manipulated images of her family photographs from the colonial era in New York, was on view at Franklin Furnace, New York,[13] she also attended the Flaherty Seminar, which brought her into contact with people who drove around the United States collecting home movies in pickup trucks and storing them in warehouses. Thus began Abraham's obsession with rummaging and scavenging for home movies. Tom D'Aguiar's home movies from the 1940s, on which her film *Straight 8* is based, were found by the artist in plastic bags at his home in Bangalore as it was about to be demolished.

D'Aguiar's home movies are full of joie de vivre, a passion for representing the everyday, and a capacious imagination to dream up adventures when reality falls short of expectations. An Anglo Indian, D'Aguiar lived in the British cantonment of Bangalore, actively participating in its cultural scene, which followed the principle of racial segregation in bars and clubs. He captured on film his neighborhood, family picnics, parties, and his travels through Karnataka along with directing and editing the home movie *Well Done Walter*, a spoof on a spy thriller enacted by European fighter pilots waiting to be called up for combat in Southeast Asia. So much of the context of an amateur film remains undecipherable, and Abraham's annotation in the form of documentary interviews makes it somewhat less opaque, but there are clues embedded within the material that we need to be alerted to: Why, for instance, do we not see the Kannada-speaking native town? How does the affinity between D'Aguiar and the Burmese-Rajput dancer Ram Gopal go beyond a mutual passion for the arts and strike at the very heart of their condition of in-betweenness, as figures inhabiting the threshold spaces of colonial society?

Abraham encodes this disquietude at the very beginning of the film by choosing to begin with an image of a man walking along the boundary of a wall with a sheer drop. It could be read as an intriguing metaphor for the poetics of the edge. The edge is the liminal threshold where transformation can occur, but also where death lurks. The edge is the point where slippage occurs as well. *Straight 8* self-reflexively deploys the instability of the medium to ask difficult questions about the very idea of retrieval: the retrieval of memory, of the self, and of the archive, which are in the final analysis unknowable, never fully recoverable.

Abraham's most recent film, *I Saw a God Dance* (see pp. 103–105), which is about the dancer Ram Gopal (1912–2003) and was included in *The Matter Within*, may have begun life as one of the nested narratives within *Straight 8*. Abraham expanded the work to include archival footage by the

10.
Trinh T. Minh-ha, "Grandma's Story" in *Woman, Native, Other: Writing Postcoloniality and Feminism* (Bloomington and Indianapolis: Indiana University Press, 1989): 120.

11.
From a conversation with the artist on September 1, 2011.

12.
Ibid.

13.
Read Saloni Mathur's essay on the larger context underpinning the exhibition, "Re-Visualising the Missionary Subject: History, Modernity and Indian Women" in *Third Text* 37 (winter 1996–97): 54–61.

filmmaker Claude La Morisse and recent interviews with the dance critic Sunil Kothari and the dancer Kumudini Lakhia. But these articulations and supporting materials come to us in fits and starts, with audio and video freezes and a series of caesurae that are so regular and mesmerizingly rhythmic that we might be confused into believing that the art of the pause is not an exception but the rule here. The speech is broken up. The face, disfigured, caves into itself. The image is gradually stripped away. These devices stop the flow of time but also provide the shock of mortality in a film addressing the manifestation of the divine. These provocations may create anxiety, anticipation, and unease in the viewer, but they might equally create pause for reflection.

It is the gaps in the narrative flow that alert us to Ram Gopal's adroit art of the masquerade. He is believed to have said that it is not enough to act and dance like the gods, but to *be* a god. Playing god had its uses, especially during the colonial era, when many Indian subjects became adept at what Ranjit Hoskote has elsewhere called "auto-Orientalism," the internalization of Western imperial stereotypes about Eastern society, religion, and culture. Auto-Orientalism was thus a self-essentializing strategy meant both to ward off Western reformist interference as well as to elicit Western praise for the exotic and beautiful Other.

Ram Gopal skillfully used his threshold position to exoticize himself as the transracial, gay aesthete exhibiting a confident androgyny. In his dance performances in East Asia and Europe he refined the notion of the "Hindu dance," which combined elements of the devotional, the erotic, and the spectacular. In the film, we see Ram Gopal—the Hindu divinity come to life— being comically pursued by middle-aged women fans at a London matinee show, or Ram Gopal the pseudo-spiritual dance teacher leading a class of enthusiastic Western students.

The moment of revelation comes in the form of the resplendent Garuda dance (Garuda the mythic bird is Lord Vishnu's mount) where Ram Gopal achieves liminality as opposed to performing the liminal. The archival footage shows him transiting the proscenium with the sweep of his dazzling golden wings as he dances across a mountainside and a river. He finds his ultimate release when a bird cuts through his trapped reflection in the water and flies across and beyond the frame. As Trinh T. Minh-ha would have said, "Truth is when it is itself no longer."[14]

Then I went down into the basement where my friend—the maniac—busies himself with his electronic graffiti. Finally his language touches me, because he talks to that part of us which insists on drawing profiles on prison walls. A piece of chalk to follow the contours of what is not, or is no longer, or is not yet; the handwriting each one of us will use to compose his own list of "things that quicken the heart," to offer, or to erase. In that moment poetry will be made by everyone, and there will be emus in the "zone."[15]

The Surface of Each Day Is a Different Planet (2009) (see pp. 113–115), made by Raqs Media Collective (Jeebesh Bagchi, Monica Narula, and Shuddhabrata Sengupta), is a conversation with the investigative essay film form, as refined to a fine pitch by Marker and Farocki. At the very beginning, we might think that it conforms to a reasonably classical model of symphonics, in which various separate lines of narrative development will eventually come together. But as we go deeper into the narrative we realize that its structure is, in fact, diaphonic: We are being led in different directions through a series of related but not identical pursuits, which take us as far away as possible from the idea that there is a singular truth. The film, as Raqs puts it, is open-ended, with no inclination toward a determinate closure.

The film takes as its basic premise Elias Canetti's account in the 1966 book *Crowds and Power* of how crowds play a key role in the evolving social dynamics of representation and authority. Canetti, having enumerated a slightly idiosyncratic typology of crowds (flight crowds, baiting crowds, feast crowds, and so on), goes on to meditate on the role played by different kinds of crowds in establishing collective identities, producing political change, and articulating the most turbulent impulses of a society. At the core of this meditation is Canetti's sense of wonderment at how the crowd can produce a strange doubling within the same person, who is both individual and person-in-the-crowd, the latter identity overwhelming the former.

The Surface of Each Day Is a Different Planet is a concatenation of textual quotations and archival material, and an index of Raqs's theoretical explorations. Raqs might agree with Farocki, who

14.
Trinh T. Minh-ha, "Grandma's Story," 121.

15.
From the *Sans Soleil* voiceover.

proudly proclaimed, "I film my library."[16] One of their abiding concerns is an inquiry into the construction of identity and the forms of interpellation that are imposed on it through diverse apparatuses of control, surveillance, and taxonomy (whether these apparatuses belong to the state, science, or historical master narratives). For more than a decade now, Raqs has been engaged with the forms and strategies by which these insidious forms of interpellation may be resisted.

The film reveals, for instance, the flaws in the 19th-century statistician Francis Galton's project of predicting behavioral tendencies from such evidence as fingerprints and facial types. In retrospect, we may see the work of Galton, Cesare Lombroso, and Paul Broca in such fields as cranial anthropometry and physiognomic reading as efforts made by science to reclaim the prerogatives of divination. Raqs sifts through historical evidence with a surgeon's adroitness: Their scalpel takes apart the claims made in the name of science or of photographic representation. They astutely deconstruct the itinerant Italian-British photographer Felice Beato's account of the Indian war of independence, which took place in 1857 (Beato would have referred to it as the Indian Mutiny), by analyzing the manner in which he "staged" the aftermath of the upheaval in his iconic 1858 photograph, thus contributing to the amplification of this event into a major component of imperialist mythology.

The film's diaphonic structure articulates, within itself, the nature of the crowd it depicts; lines and knots of distinctiveness emerge briefly before dissolving once again into a turbulence of patterns. The nature of its construction is poetic. It works through a system of floating allusions, assonance, and rhyming events and structures. In the same register, its garland of quotations is illuminated by interludes of sensorial encounter: the sea brimming over with emotion, or traffic lights in a nocturnal landscape reducing human beings to hyphens and ciphers.

Raqs asserts that the work is "anti-documentary." The group began life as a collective of documentary filmmakers and writers in the 1990s; even at that time their films were questioning the claim to a monocultural truth made by most conventional documentaries. Indeed, Raqs's earliest anthology of essays, *Double Take: Looking at the Documentary* (2000) invited documentary filmmakers to write about their practices in a heuristic manner (this lacuna still remains largely unaddressed in current discourse on Indian documentary films).[17] The book was the product of inquiring minds who privileged the pioneering spirit over institutional dogma and who did not treat any knowledge—technical, political, or aesthetic—as too small or marginal for the purpose of scrutiny. Above all, Raqs's practice has always laid an emphasis on the ethics of creativity.

In 2002 Raqs was invited to participate in Documenta 11. Thus began its engagement with the contemporary art world. A year before that, Raqs had co-initiated Sarai, a program of the Centre for the Study of Developing Societies in Delhi. Living up to its name, it became an oasis for those who wanted to break through the boundaries of disciplinal knowledge. It has functioned in various avatars: as a research and conference center, an artist residency, a cinema, and a software lab. In a decade that reveled in "privatism" (the philosopher Jürgen Habermas's term for the retreat of citizens from politics due to their disillusionment with the state and a turn toward the enhancement of private life), Sarai fought hard to activate and sustain a critical public sphere by debating issues related to urban culture, history, technology, and law through its various symposia and colloquiums.

Sarai is one of those rare places where greater knowledge has *not* brought greater suffering (to adapt a dialogue from Andrei Tarkovsky's *Andrei Rublev*). Instead, it has encouraged its large network of colleagues and friends to desire new lists of "things that quicken the heart" so that "in that moment poetry will be made by everyone, and there will be emus in the 'zone'."

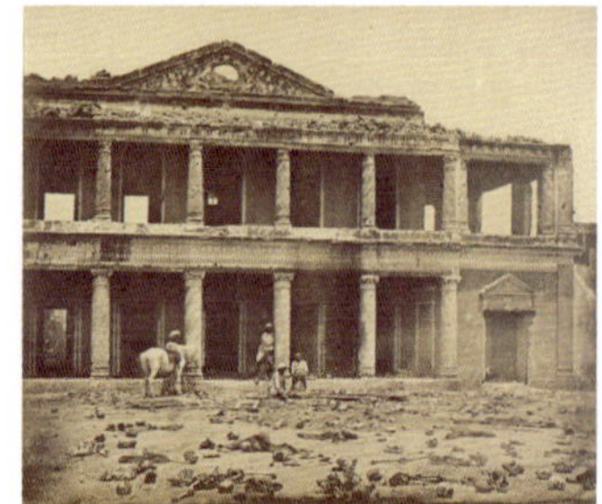

16.
The quote is from Harun Farocki's 1978 film *Zwischen Zwei Kriegen*.

FELICE BEATO
Interior of the Secundra Bagh After the Slaughter of 2,000 Rebels, Lucknow, 1858
Albumen silver print
10 ³⁄₁₆ x 11 ¼ in.
Courtesy The J. Paul Getty Museum, Los Angles, Partial gift from the Wilson Centre for Photography

17.
Raqs Media Collective, *Double Take: Looking at the Documentary* (New Delhi: Foundation for Universal Responsibility in association with Public Service Broadcasting Trust, 2000).

Ayisha Abraham

Ayisha Abraham moves comfortably between conventional and experimental documentary. Her films combine new and archival footage, telling personal stories that also engage larger issues relevant to India's history and cultural identity. Her accounts of the marginal histories of Bangalore have little to do with the official narratives found in books and newspapers.

Similar to how today's information age has democratized news, journalism, and communication, the availability of affordable home movie cameras democratized movie making starting in the 1930s, opening the door for ordinary individuals to document their lives and for amateur filmmakers to stretch the boundaries of artistic creation in an entirely new medium: first 16-millimeter, then 8-millimeter and Super-8. Abraham's films resurrect the artistic forays of ordinary people living in India in the mid-20th century, providing a glimpse into everyday life at that time as well as into the creative ambitions and preoccupations that prevailed during this crucial transitional period in India's modern history.

Much of Abraham's work interlaces narrative fragments from various sources—found footage, interviews, archival photographs—with footage she shot herself, in her own style, to present a layered experience that is both individual and collective. In *I Saw a God Dance* (2011), commissioned for *The Matter Within*, Abraham seamlessly blends her own recent video footage of interviews with people who knew the dancer Ram Gopal with 8-millimeter footage of Gopal dancing on an outdoor verandah shot by the Anglo-Indian amateur filmmaker Tom D'Aguiar in the 1930s.

Abraham salvaged D'Aguiar's films from his old home, where they had been stored in obscurity for decades, only hours before the home was demolished. Since then D'Aguiar's work has come to play a prominent role in many of Abraham's films, including *Straight 8* (2005), an experimental documentary combining footage of a spoof spy film, shot by D'Aguiar and his friends in the 1940s, and an interview with the elderly D'Aguiar in which he reminisces about his younger days. By bringing these experiences and memories to life on the screen, Abraham unveils a side of British colonial life in India that is seldom seen, thereby filling a gap in the sociological study of that era. Moreover, in both *I Saw a God Dance* and *Straight 8,* by cutting and layering archival footage with recent narratives, Abraham refashions a piece of history as her own creation while at the same time carefully preserving the voice of the subject.

I Saw a God Dance explores the life and adventures of Ram Gopal, the world-famous pioneer of classical Indian dance whose career spanned from the 1930s through the 1950s. The concept of embodying a character is commonplace in the performing arts, but Gopal was remarkable for his attempts to truly transcend mortal being and embody divinity. To Western audiences, many of whom were unfamiliar with classical Indian dance (or with India at all), Gopal was not just performing as a god but actually incarnating a god. While he was loved and celebrated in the West, however, he was regarded as somewhat of an outsider in India because of his mixed Indian-Burmese heritage, his homosexuality, his unconventional style of dance, and his eventual departure from India. It was perhaps due to these prejudices that for most of his life Gopal aspired to assume a different identity—one that was bigger and more powerful than his own—for example by dressing as Indian royalty offstage, and assuming the avatar of a god onstage.

A desire to decipher the varied faces of the outsider is central to many of Abraham's films. In *Straight 8*, she slowly reveals the nuances of D'Aguiar's identity as a third-generation British officer living in India, neither completely British nor entirely Indian, and thus an outsider in both cultures. In *One Way* (2007) she discusses the changing demographics of Bangalore, and specifically its growing Nepalese migrant population, by bringing forth the untold story of a Nepalese immigrant, Shyam Bahadur. As yet unassimilated in mainstream society, Bahadur and his community represent yet another face of the outsider. *One Way,* and also the works *Straight 8* and *I Saw a God Dance,* are examples of biographic portraiture through film. They are in different ways all about outsiders, inviting the viewer to identify with a person who is classified as different within the established social order.

···SR

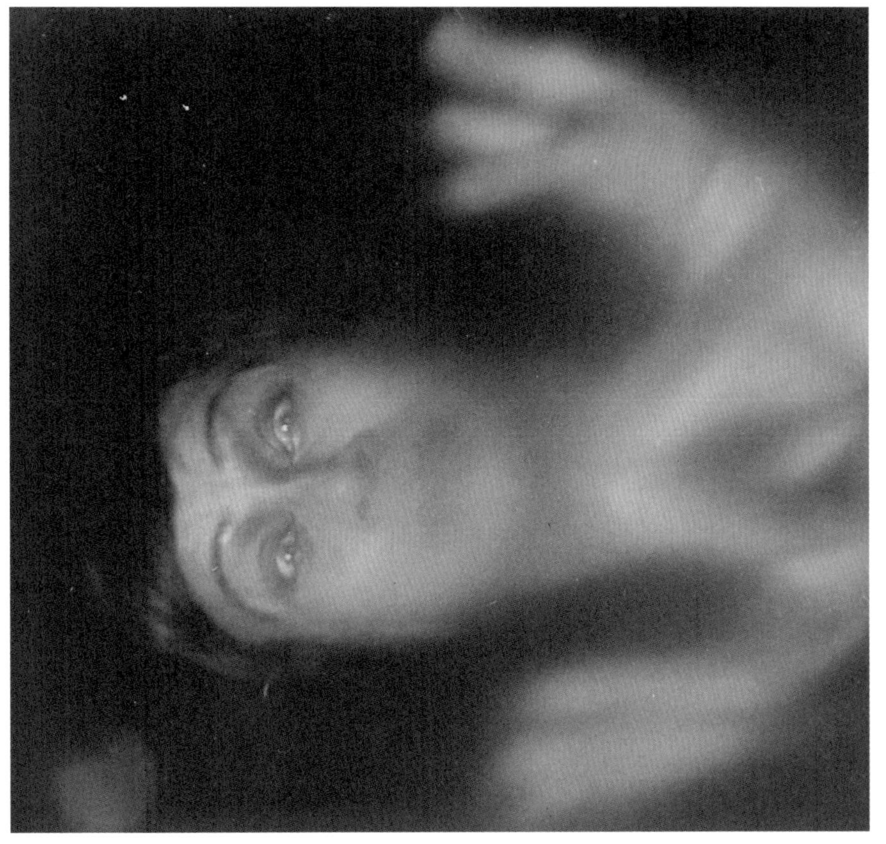

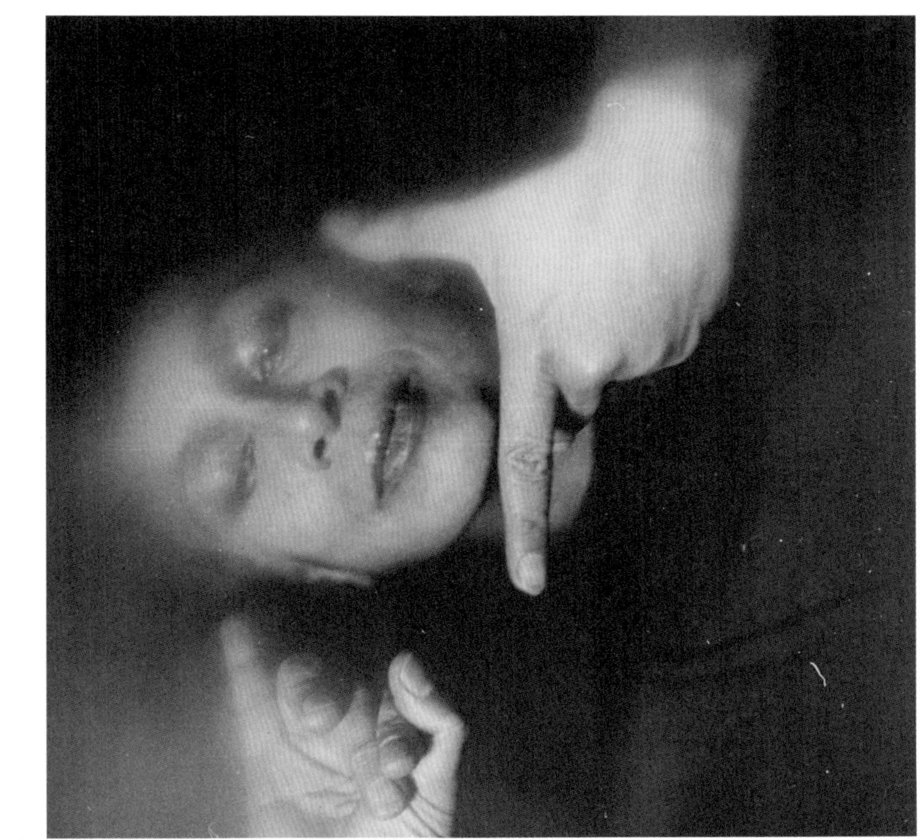

I Saw a God Dance (video still), 2011

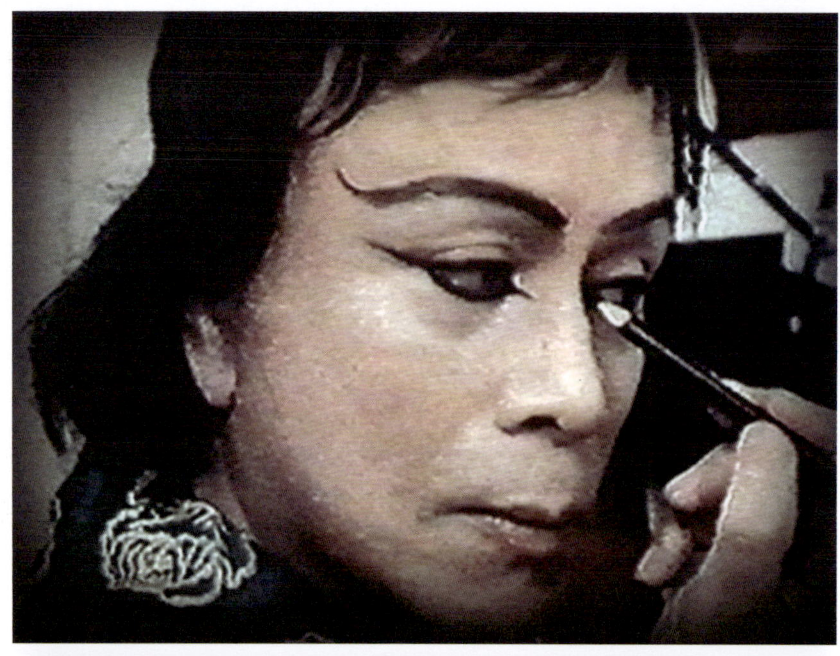

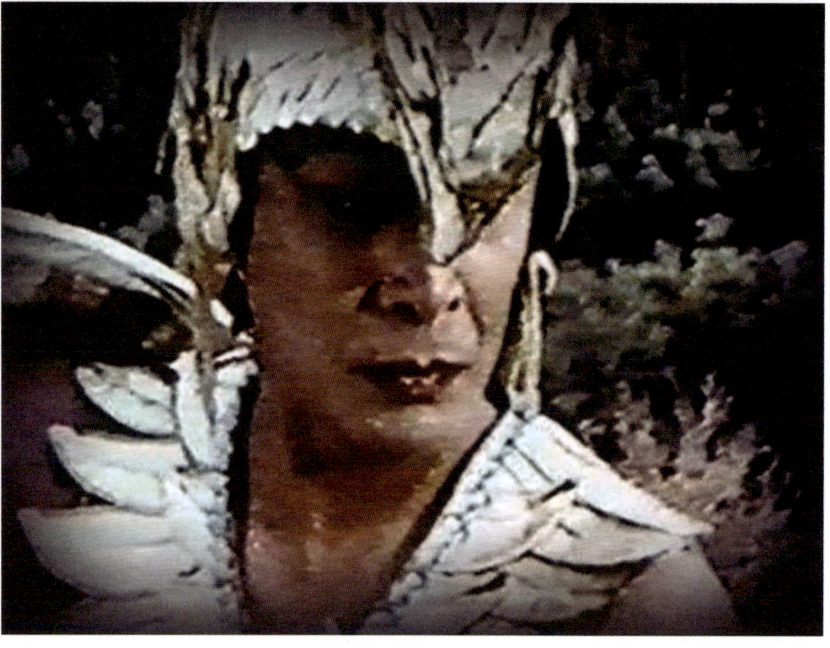

I Saw a God Dance (video still), 2011

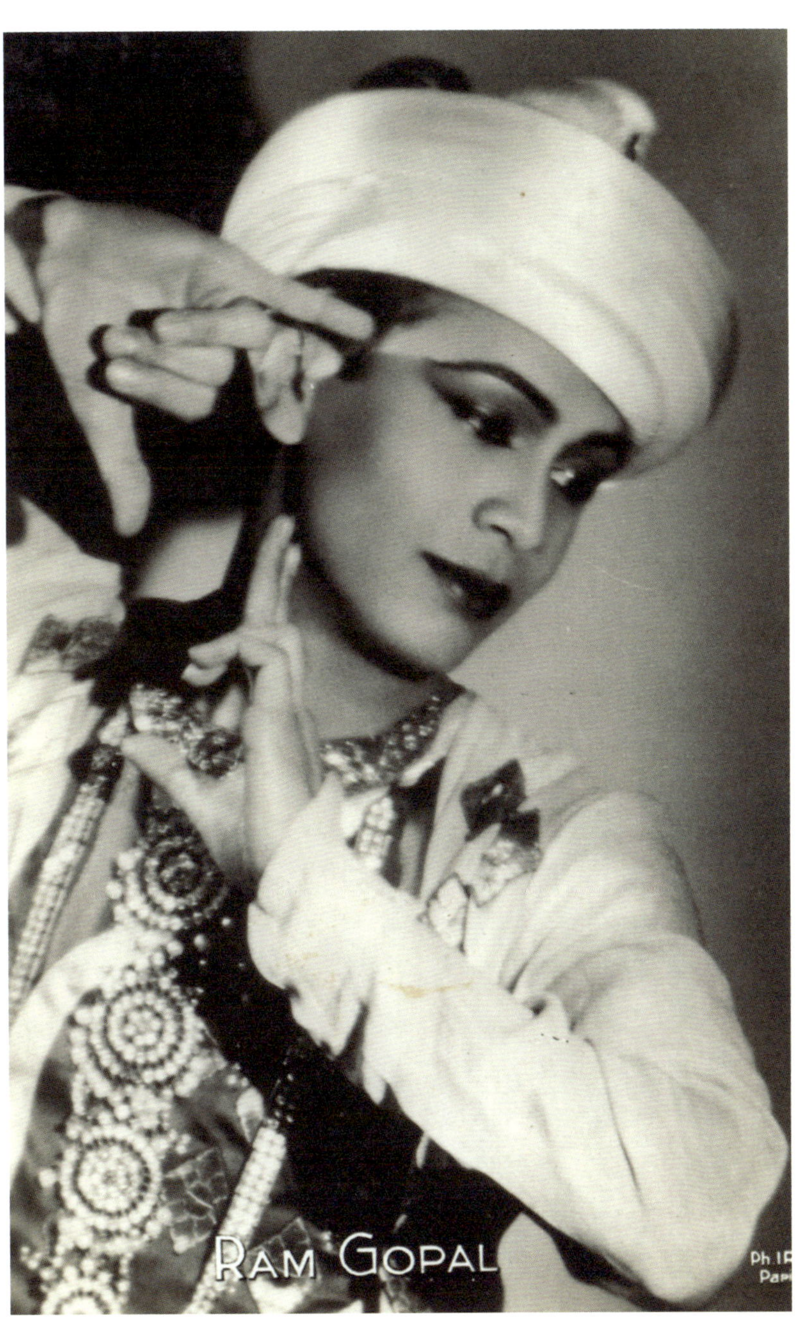

I Saw a God Dance (video still), 2011

CAMP

According to its founders, Shaina Anand, Sanjay Bhangar, and Ashok Sukumaran, CAMP is not an artists' collective, but a space in which ideas and energy gather, and become interests and forms. CAMP's central preoccupations revolve around challenging conventional notions of authority and ownership, as well as triangulating the multiple relationships among public, private, and political. They are intimately concerned with the workings of power in relation to technology, authorship, and the decentering of the gaze. Their ideational concerns are empirically anchored in the material, infrastructural, and systemic, and are often instantiated in systems of communication, surveillance, distribution, and social practices surrounding means of communication, tools, public utilities, and facilities as well as the dissemination of information and the politics of knowledge making.

Their ongoing online project Pad.ma, for example, is a publicly accessible digital media archive of documentary video and film footage, images, and related annotated texts, archived with searchable time codes. The logic of the project resembles that of the Open Source movement, but in the context of digitized visual material. The public can use these materials for research, look for writings, offer annotations, and so on, making Pad.ma a visual Creative Commons: a source for creative works and a site for public discourse.

In a number of recent works, CAMP appropriates and inverts the usual uses of CCTV, CATV, and other omnipresent scopic systems typically used for closed-circuit, covert recordings of individual and collective behavior. For *Khirkeeyaan* (2006) they set up a system of security surveillance cameras, linked to family television sets, in the working-class, municipally "unauthorized" colony of Khirkee Extension in New Delhi. Four sets of monitors, microphones, and cameras were dispersed and their recordings fed back through a central mixer, turning the footage from the four locations into a live and shared "community media" source. The project collapsed the usual binaries between subject and performer, viewer and audience. The recorded video material was transformed into seven separate "episodes," which were re-consumed by the local community through the same broadcast system.

Al Jaar Qabla Al Daar (The Neighbor Before the House, 2009–11) draws its title from the Quranic maxim that exhorts people to consider their neighbor before considering themselves, but it has a corresponding vernacular usage that means something more like 'Check out the neighbors before moving into the neighborhood.' Set in East Jerusalem, this major work extends and expands CAMP's characteristic practice of appropriating the gaze. The individuals who were once being watched become the watchers. To make the piece, CAMP worked with eight local families in Palestinian neighborhoods in East Jerusalem, where Palestinians are being systematically evicted from the homes they were given by the United Nations in the 1950s. To map the residential topography that is being transformed by patterns of Israeli settlement, the artists placed the same kind of high-powered security cameras usually used by Israelis to police the area on rooftops, terraces, and balconies, and gave the controllers to the families. The cameras recorded a landscape of disenfranchisement, community dismemberment, and ethnic interpolation. In cases where the houses of the families shooting the footage had been seized by Israeli settlers, they used their neighbors' homes as sites from which to record the interlopers occupying their stolen homes, which fostered a sense of solidarity by underscoring the pervasiveness of this experience in the community.

CAMP wired connections from the rooftop cameras directly to the families' television sets, allowing them to control the pan, tilt, and zoom functions from their own living rooms, which became makeshift CCTV control rooms. They recorded their own live observations about the scenes taking place outside. Unlike typical voiceover commentary, the speakers' voices have the texture of raw footage, which creates a sense of direct, intimate proximity between the viewer and the subjects. The various commentaries wed historical context with personal accounts of recent evictions. The grainy, crude audio and video defy aestheticization.

The ability of the families to spy on the people who routinely spy on them reverses the power equation, if only momentarily, and tethers larger political tensions to a horizon of quotidian, personal stories. *Al Jaar Qabla Al Daar* stitches together a patchwork of everyday history, locating individual loss in a shared and shifting geography of dispossession and displacement. These accounts form a matrix of counterhegemonic micro-narratives about life under siege and surveillance. Appropriating technologies that traditionally serve that systemic disempowerment in order to reclaim and reconstitute public and private space, the work shifts the focus from the representation of spatial politics to the spatial politics of representation.

···MK

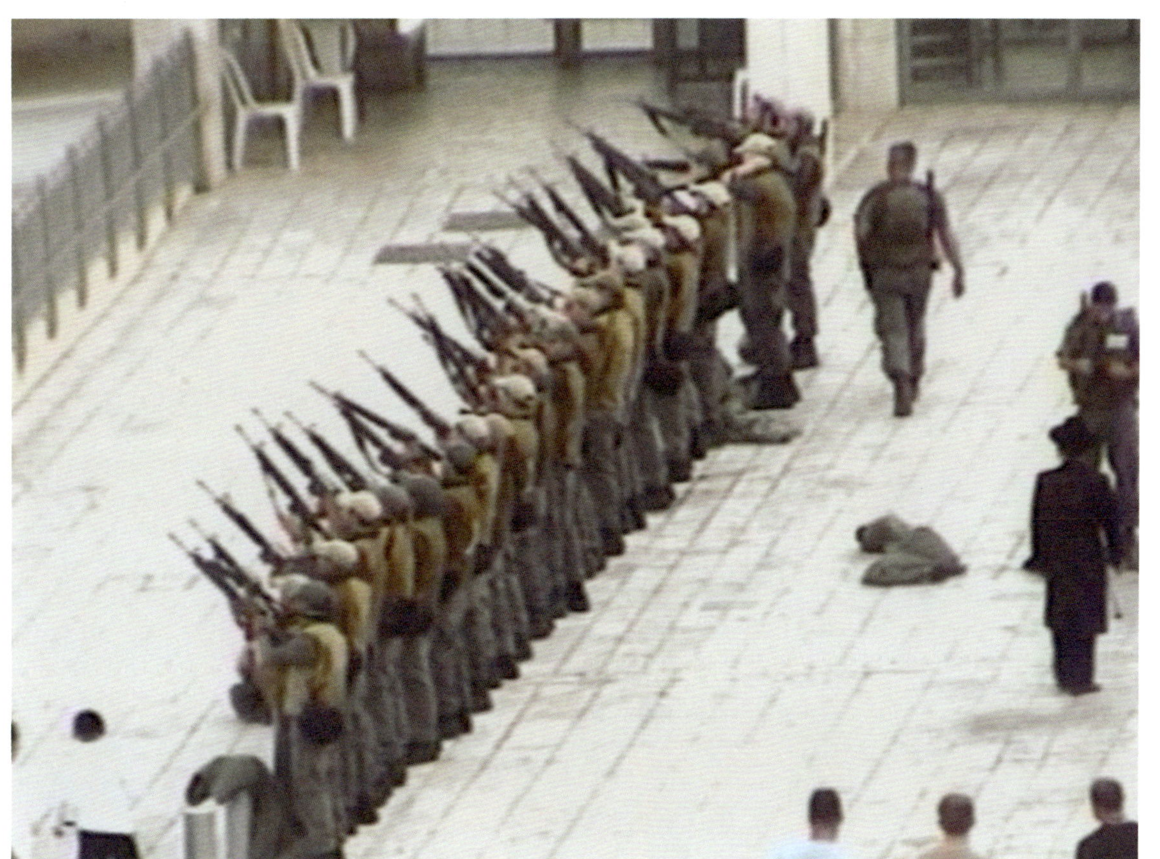

Al Jaar Qabla Al Daar (The Neighbor Before the House), 2009–2011

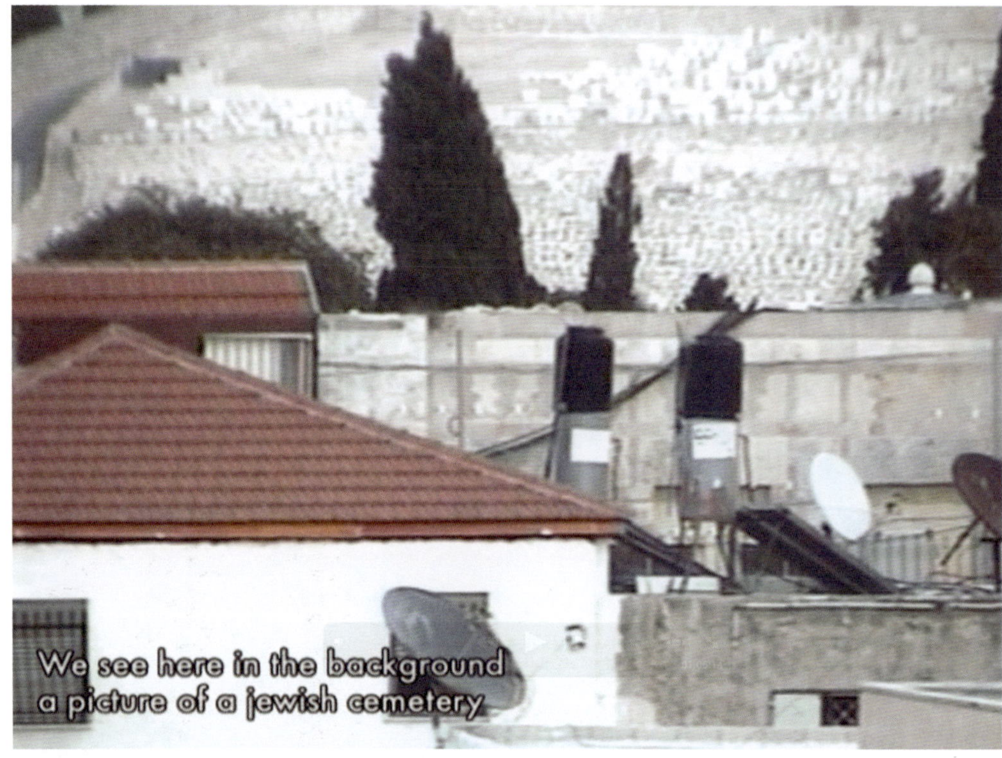

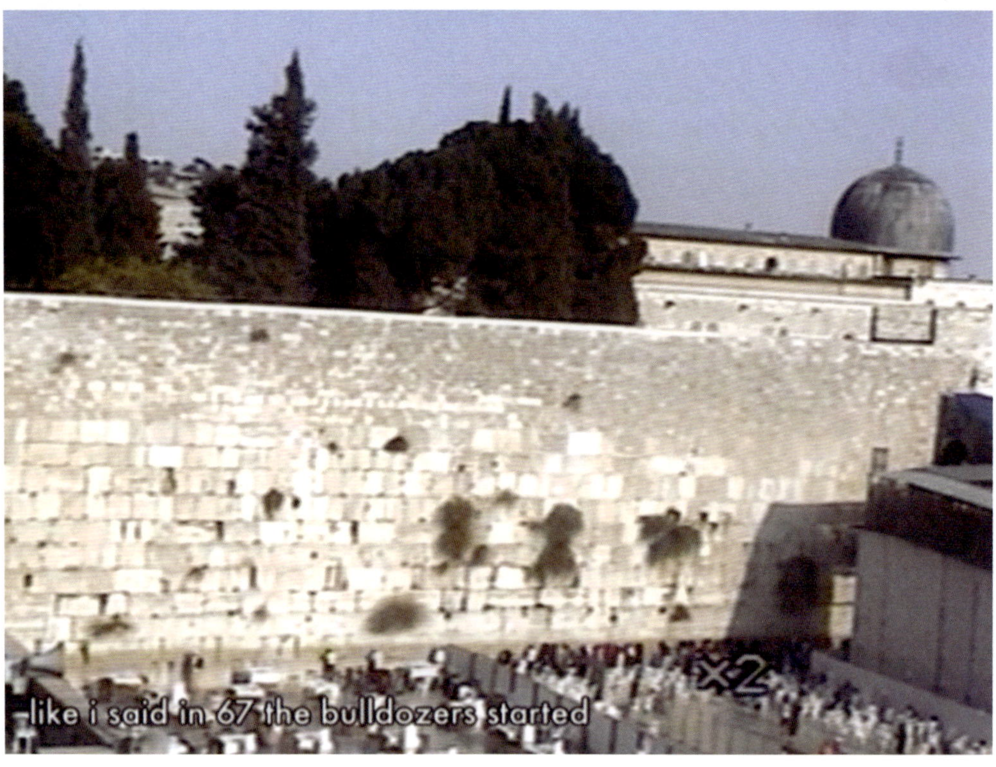

Al Jaar Qabla Al Daar (The Neighbor Before the House), 2009–2011

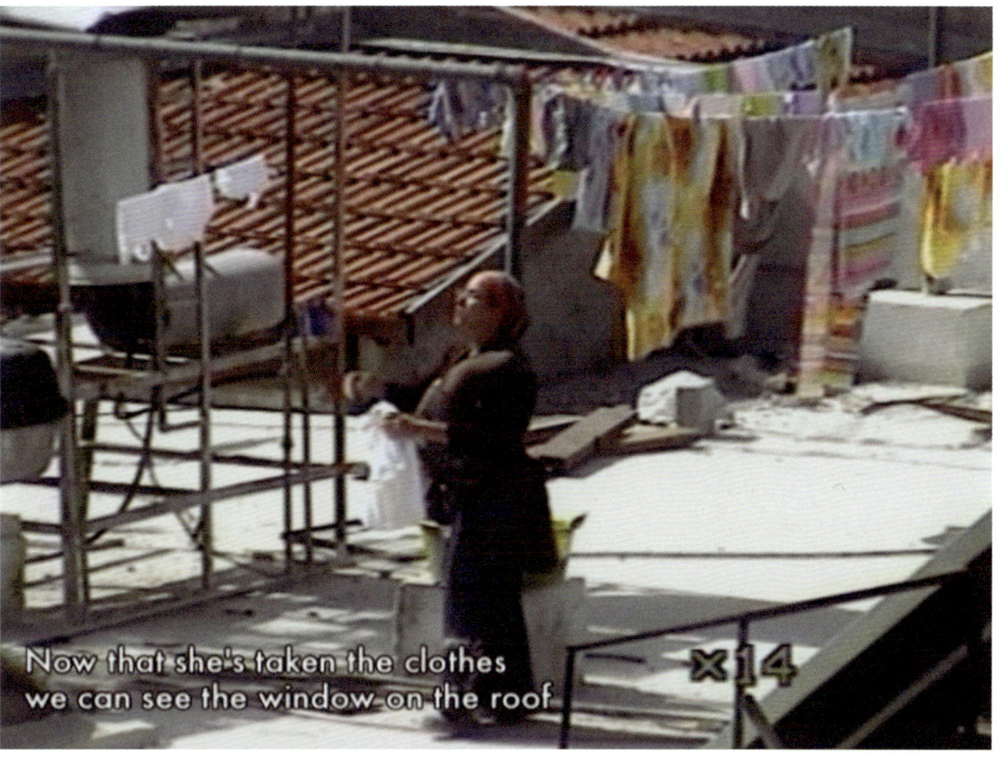

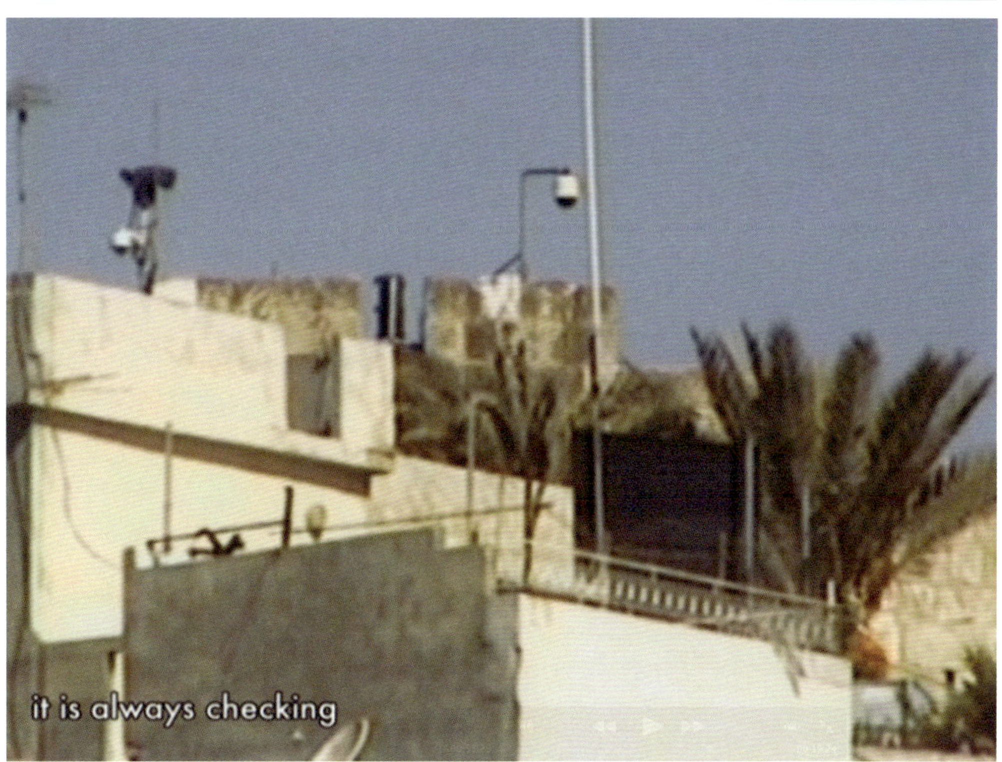

Al Jaar Qabla Al Daar (The Neighbor Before the House), 2009–2011

THE OTOLITH GROUP

The Otolith Group, based in London, was founded by Kodwo Eshun and Anjalika Sagar in 2002. The group's practice spans filmmaking, events, publications, and exhibitions, all of which are informed by research-based activities. Much of its work takes a speculative approach to the archive, focusing on topics that illuminate the future through investigations into the past. Its logo—a zero with three parallel lines underneath—was appropriated from Jean-Luc Godard's film *Le gai savoir* (The Joy of Learning, 1969), in which it symbolizes both a future world and a return to zero. That film's analysis of images and sounds exemplifies the genre of the essay film, which also prioritizes thoughts and ideas, often making abstract concepts visible through an unfolding of images representative of different viewpoints, some of them fictional. Other influences on the duo include Chris Marker, Harun Farocki, and Black Audio Film Collective, all of whom are masters of the essay film form.

The Otolith Group's films also draw upon the experimental documentary, a genre that developed from early experiments with found footage and nonlinear narratives during the Russian avant-garde period. References to other films, literature, and art are detectable from one film to the next. The artists enjoy working in series, especially trilogies, as in *Hydra Decapita* (a planned series; the first of which was completed in 2010), which touches on slavery, finance, and water to comment on globalization, capitalism, and climate change.

The title of the group's first film, *Otolith I* (2003), which would later evolve into the first part of a trilogy, gave rise to its name. The word refers to a structure in the inner ear that establishes one's sense of gravity and orientation. A collaboration with the artist Richard Couzins, *Otolith I* is set in the year 2103. In it, the artists imagine a future in zero gravity, and portray three generations of the Sagar family. Two (Anjalika Sagar and her grandmother, Anasuya Gyan-Chand) are factual, and one (Dr. Usha Adebaran-Sagar) is fictional. The work also includes some archival footage, for instance sequences showing the Russian astronaut Valentina Tereshkova and the 2003 London protests against the Iraq war. This combination of personal and public histories is common to the essay film genre;

in this case it provides a platform for an exploration of utopian ideals.

Otolith II (2007), again narrated by the fictional Dr. Adebaran-Sagar, is set in Mumbai's Dharavi slum and the modernist city of Chandigarh; the latter was designed by Le Corbusier in 1963. The film looks at the effects of architecture on the psychological makeup of a city, avoiding stereotypical shots of poverty in order to thwart any quick path to empathy. Dr. Adebaran-Sagar observes in *Otolith II* that Satyajit Ray, the great Bengali filmmaker, might have changed the path of science fiction if his film *The Alien* had been completed.

This observation becomes the basis of the last installment in the trilogy, *Otolith III* (2009), the work included in *The Matter Within*. *Otolith III* is an homage to Ray's unrealized film *The Alien;* the artists describe it as a "premake," or a remake that precedes the original. Footage from fourteen of Ray's other films is intercut with dialogue in which the characters from the unmade movie question the director as to why he never made the film and push him to finish it. This recalls the personages in the 1921 Luigi Pirandello play *Sei personaggi in cerca d'autore* (Six Characters in Search of an Author). Just as Pirandello's play puts the theater and its processes themselves on stage, the Otolith Group reveals the inner workings of a film via their method of street casting for the roles of the Boy, the Engineer, the Journalist, and the Industrialist. This technique was inspired by Pier Paolo Pasolini's short documentary *Appunti per un film sull'India* (Notes for a Film on India, 1968), in which the director travels around India interviewing people from all castes as research for a planned movie that never came to fruition. The inclusion of illustrations by Jack Kirby from an unrealized screenplay of Roger Zelazny's 1967 novel *Lord of Light* continues the theme of incompletion.

Whereas history usually regards unmade films as failures, the Otolith Group sees them as important—perhaps even more important than finished works. Their attempt to recover this particular unmade film also highlights the contradictions of Ray's career: He was the most important filmmaker in India, but was never able to break into Hollywood.

•••TL

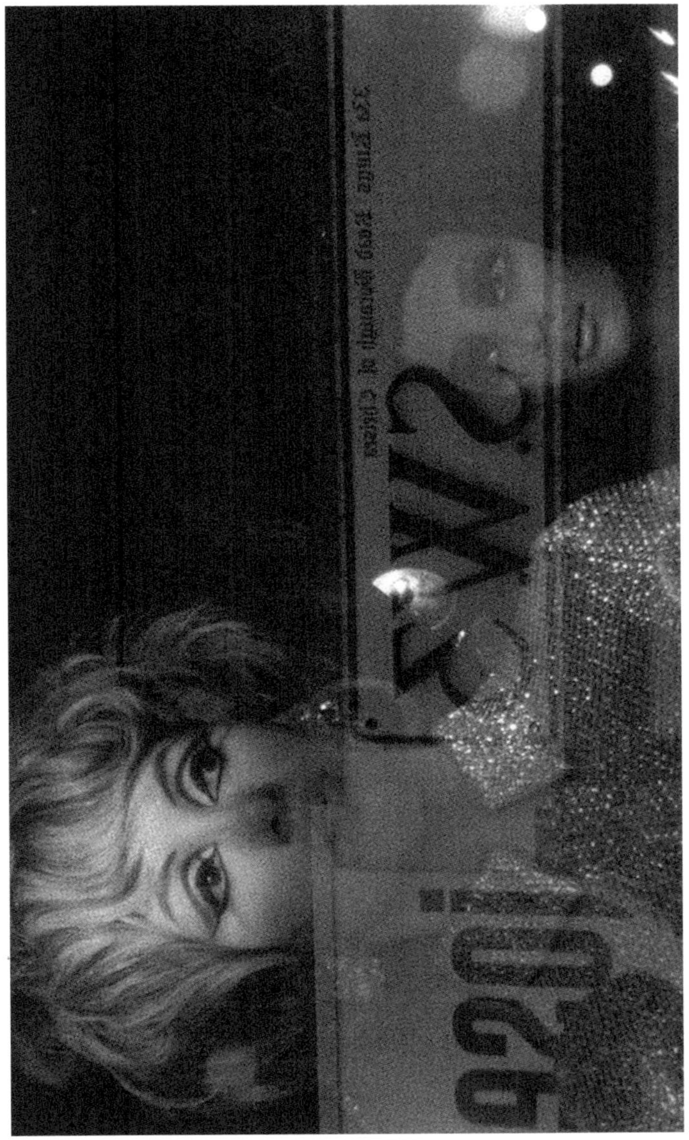

Otolith III (video still), 2009

Raqs Media Collective

Jeebesh Bagchi, Monica Narula, and Shuddhabrata Sengupta founded Raqs Media Collective in 1992. A commitment to the analytical and the poetic shapes their practice. They ask epistemological and political questions related to measurement, knowledge systems, and the human condition under global capitalism, without polemics.

Raqs's major works that grapple with this cluster of concerns include *On the Question of Standards While Considering the Freedom of Speech, After Duchamp* (2006), which plays on the arbitrary power of standard units of measurement. *Escapement* (2010) is an array of twenty-seven clocks with human emotions in place of hours, with a heartbeat soundscape and an ageless, genderless, ambiguous, pan-human subject in the accompanying video. *The Untold Intimacy of Digits (UID)* (2011) uses the 1858 handprint of the 19th-century peasant Raj Konai, which was the forerunner of the modern fingerprint in Indian criminology, and references India's invasive new Unique Identification Database (UID). The installation *When the Scales Fall from Your Eyes* (2009) features glass busts whose heads have been replaced by weighing scales, playing on the absurdity of measurement by replacing the "fish scales" of the original idiom (which was a metaphor for obstructed sight) with scales used to weigh quantities. While some things are quantifiably measureable, like a kilo of fish, how can we measure abstractions such as justice, or happiness?

The question of how "to bury the casualties of the accumulation of capital" permeates the video diptych *The Capital of Accumulation* (2010). How do we calculate and account for the immeasurable losses inflicted by the dominant order of things? Raqs takes Rosa Luxembourg's classic critical book *The Accumulation of Capital* (1913), and the mystery of the author's murder and missing body, as the primary plot and protagonist in this non-narrative narration of the intertwined strands of history, ideas, industries, labor, lives, and lore. Fighting capitalism through images is futile, Raqs's narration suggests, for capitalism is not an image but a set of social relations. Why is it common practice to "recognize" the "limits to what can be altered," but accept the limitlessness of "that which cannot be altered"? Raqs pushes viewers to reassess who the protagonists of history in fact are.

These interwoven themes come together in *The Surface of Each Day Is a Different Planet* (2009), commissioned by Tate Britain for their *Art Now Lightbox* series. This video installation is comprised of illumination, furniture, animation, soundscapes, archival photographs, and a characteristically cryptic, poetic, non-narrative spoken narration that moves between juxtaposed historical references and philosophico-poetic insights. The work is about the failure of measurement and the limits of knowability. In the discussion of massacres, the narration asks the rhetorical question: "Forensically distinct, but existentially uniform . . . can the remains of any charnel house not speak for the tragedy or banality of every massacre? Must we always weigh massacred crowds and mounting statistics into heaps of greater and lesser significance?"

Meditating upon places and "people cast off as the residue of history"—the individual and the crowd, the present and the absent, the knowable and the unknowable—*The Surface of Each Day Is a Different Planet* explores how people, and their ways of life, disappear. Sometimes populations, even cities, vanish, gobbled up by "hungry gods," exploitative impersonal industries, or rival states, simultaneously obliterating memories, histories, people, and places. Engulfed in the crowd, the powers potentially constituted through numbers are rendered impotent by anomie: "In the crowd we lose names, because the crowd erases distinctions, and gain numbers because the crowd is nothing if it is not an accumulation." And in that "crowded compound of absence and presence, a trespasser can only feel like a visitor from another planet." The title of the work invokes themes of irreducible difference and questions the very knowability of life itself.

Throughout their oeuvre, Raqs questions the politics of epistemology. How are we to know unknowable Others, or enable our myopic gazes to take in the vast diversity of meaningful modes of being, with the limited, fallible optics at our disposal? Overcoming our own poverty of vision, they suggest, is a journey that will lead we know not where. Returning to the question of power and the protagonists of history, Raqs leaves us with a haunting provocation: What does it take to transform the crowd and all the individuals in it into agents of history? To borrow the penultimate line from the work, "Further investigations will continue to be necessary."

···MK

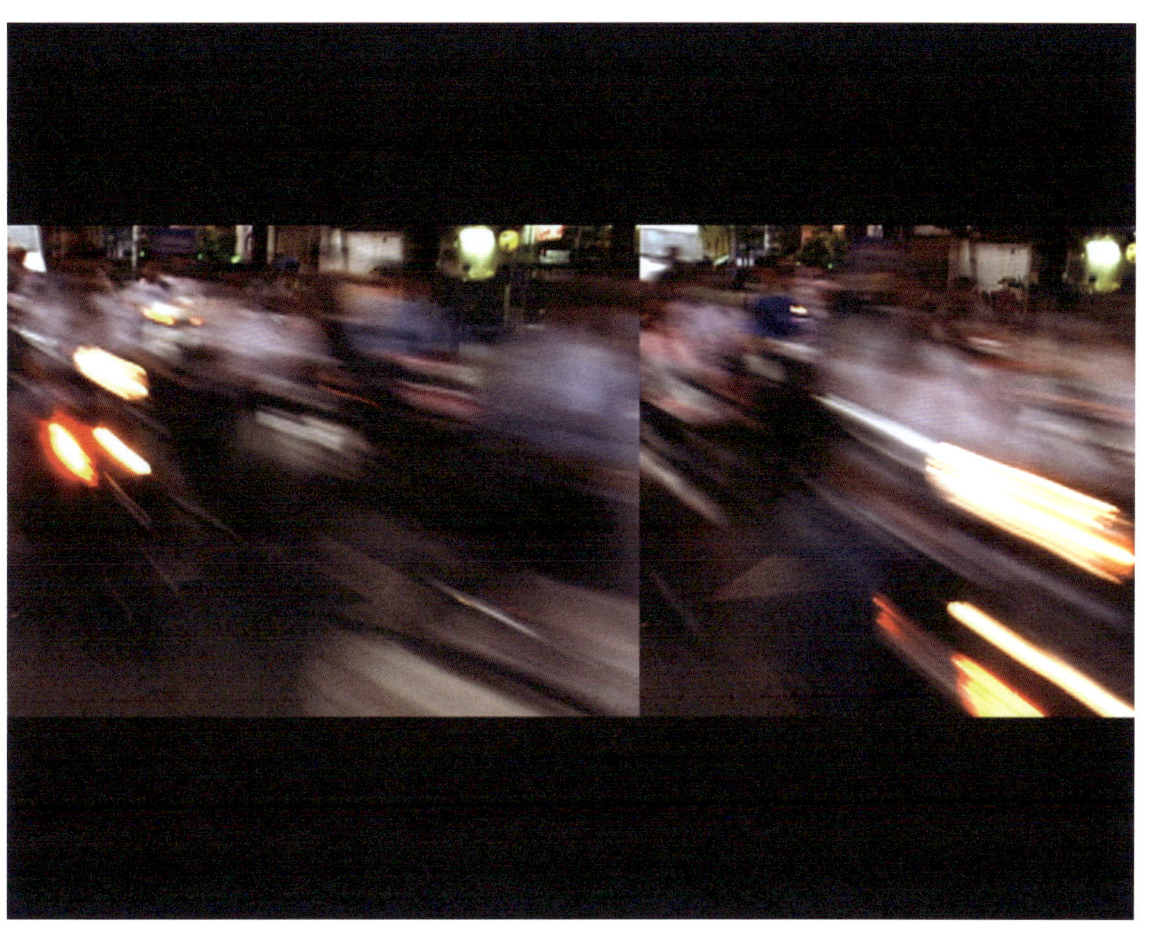

The Surface of Each Day Is a Different Planet (video still), 2009

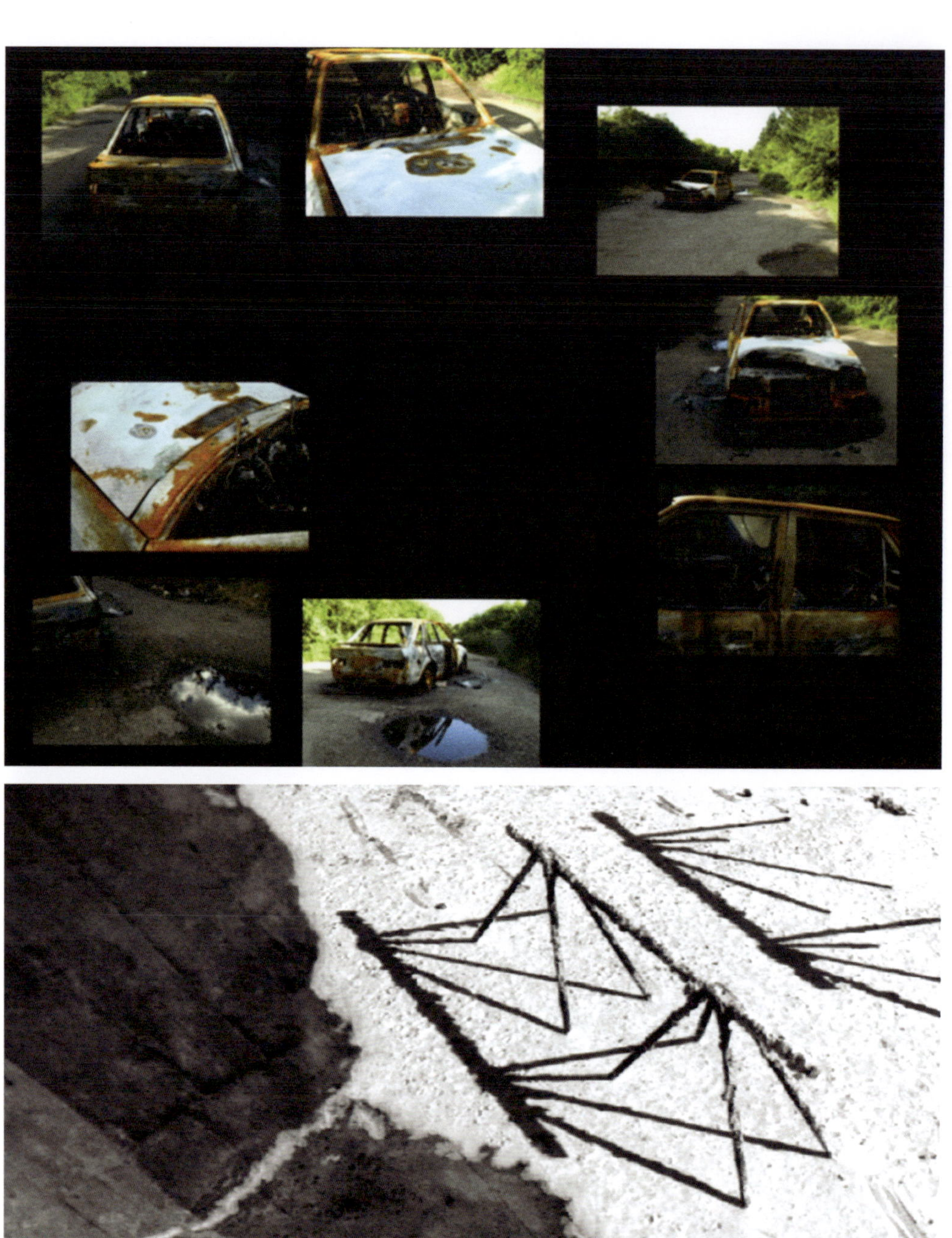

The Surface of Each Day Is a Different Planet (video still), 2009

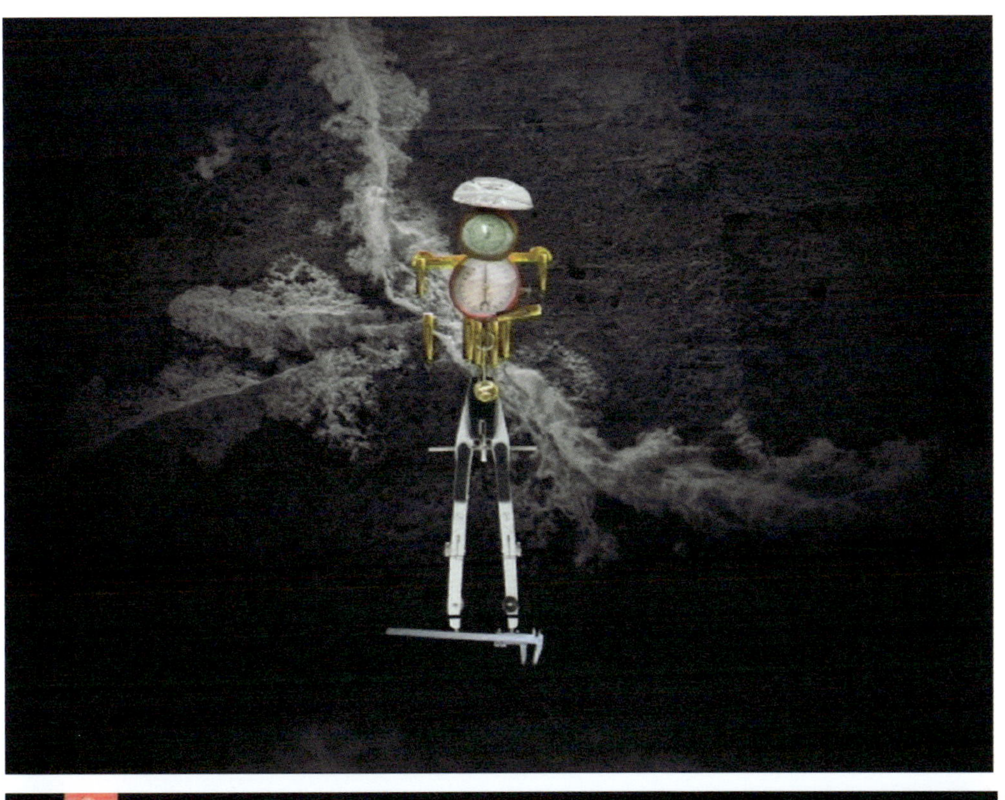

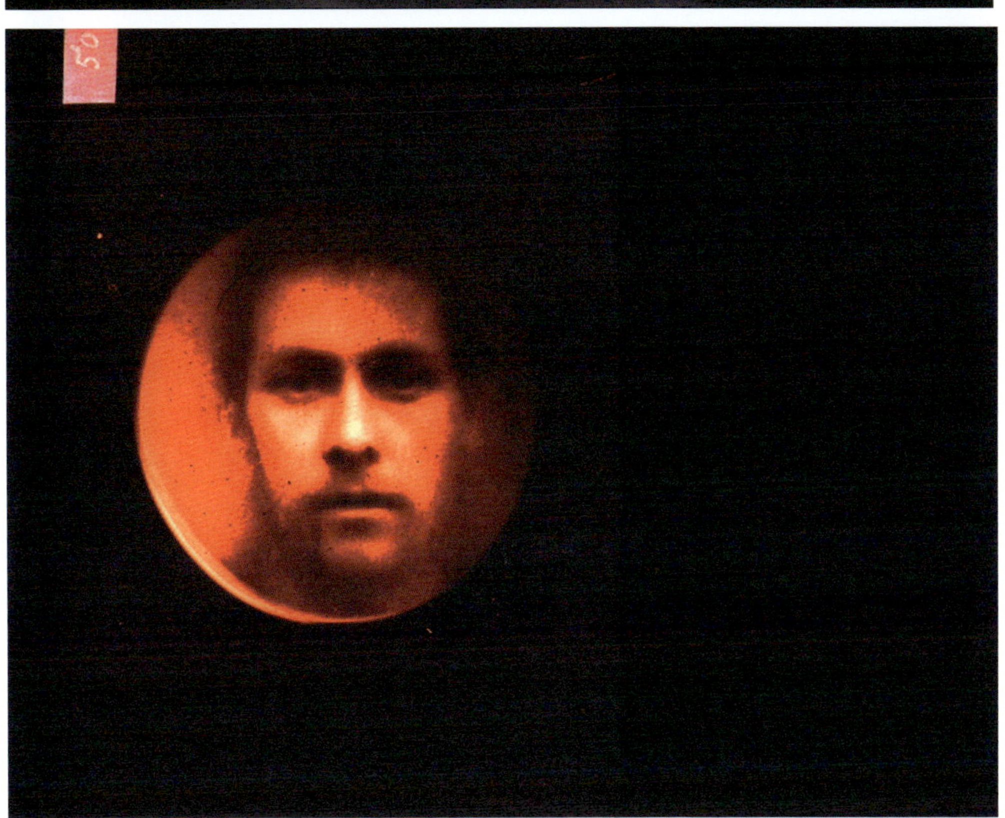

The Surface of Each Day Is a Different Planet (video still), 2009

The Exhibition

The
Matter
Within

NEW CONTEMPORARY ART OF INDIA
OCTOBER 15, 2011–JANUARY 9, 2012

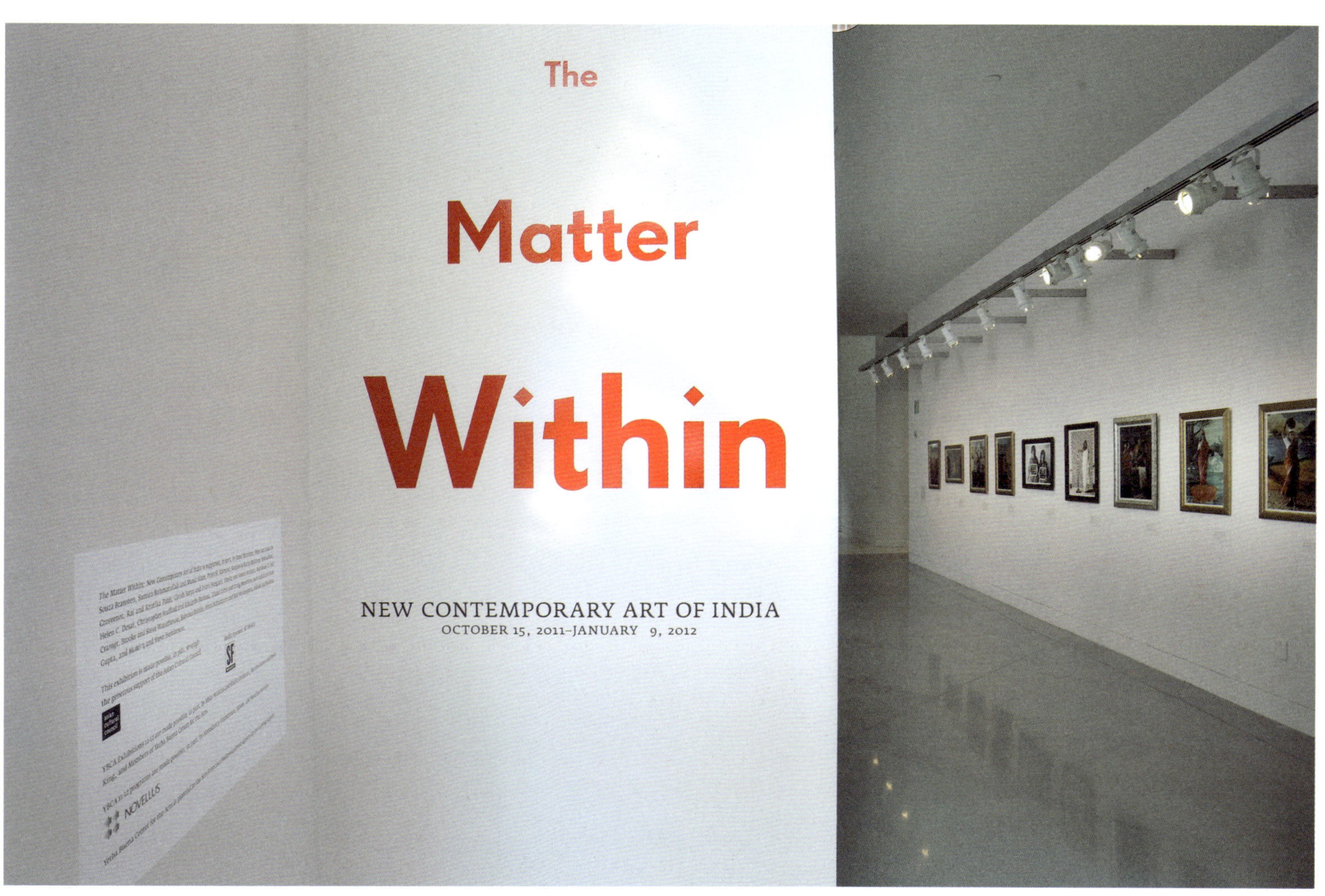

The Matter Within: New Contemporary Art of India is organized, in part, by Jane Brucker. Artists include Souza Bransten, Samira Rahimatullah and Manal Alam, [illegible]

This exhibition is made possible, in part, through the generous support of the Asian Cultural Council.

YBCA Exhibitions 11-12 are made possible, in part, by [illegible] King, and Members of Yerba Buena Center for the Arts.

YBCA 11-12 programs are made possible, in part, by [illegible]

Yerba Buena Center for the Arts is grateful to the [illegible]

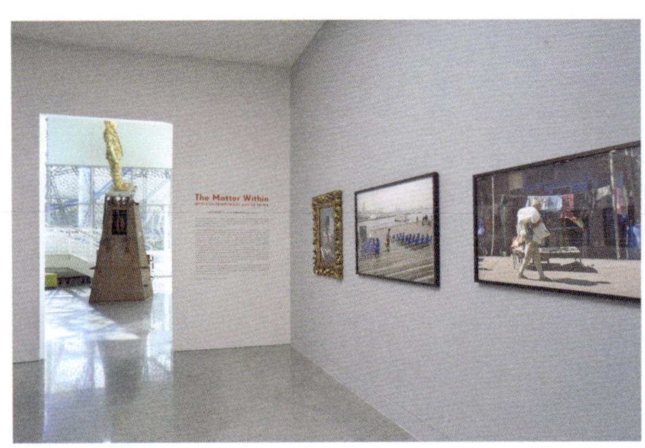

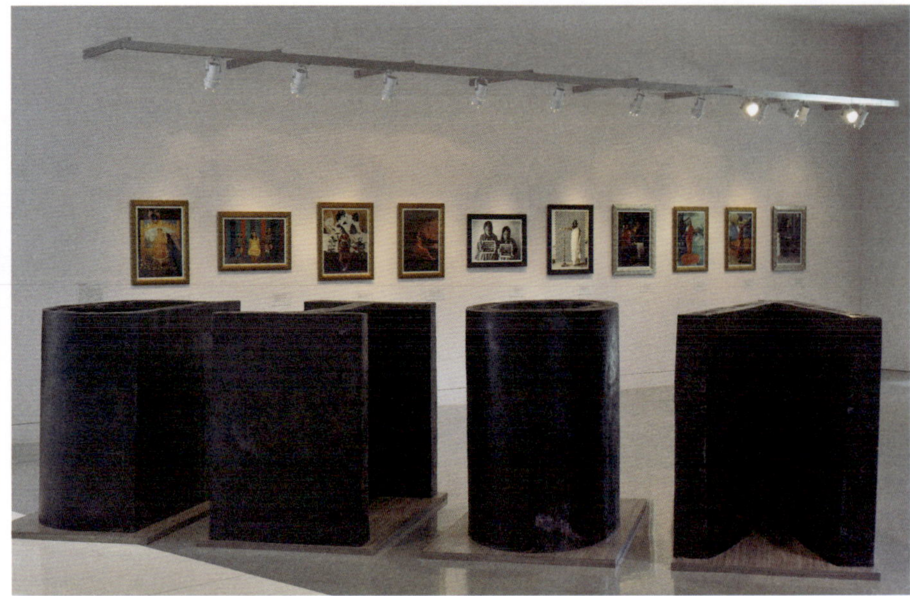

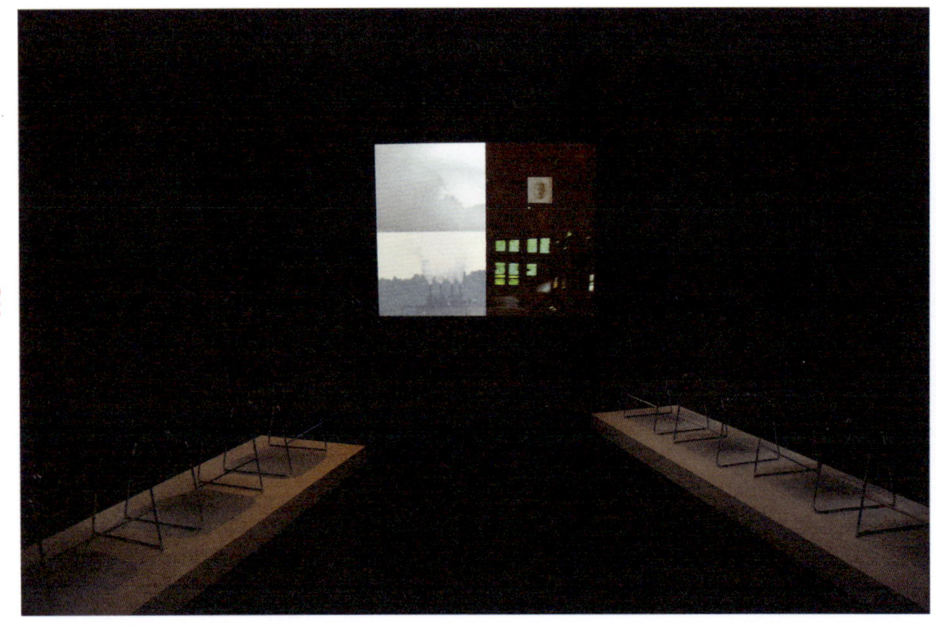

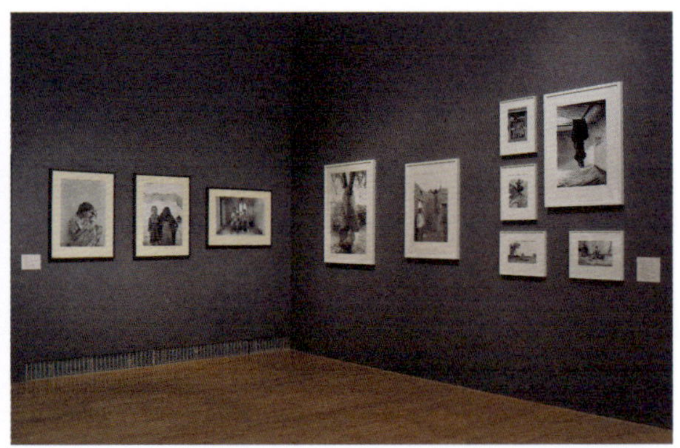

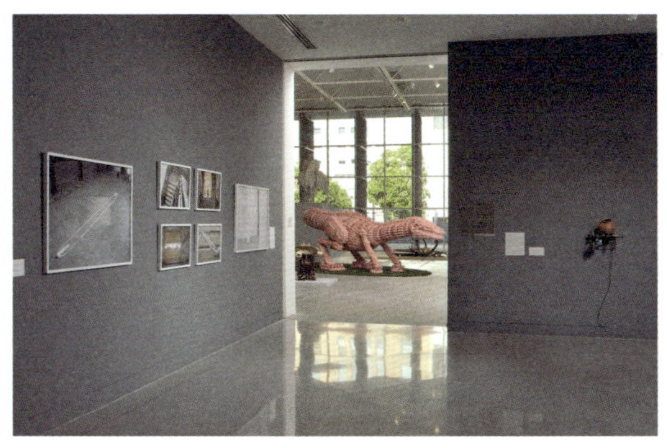

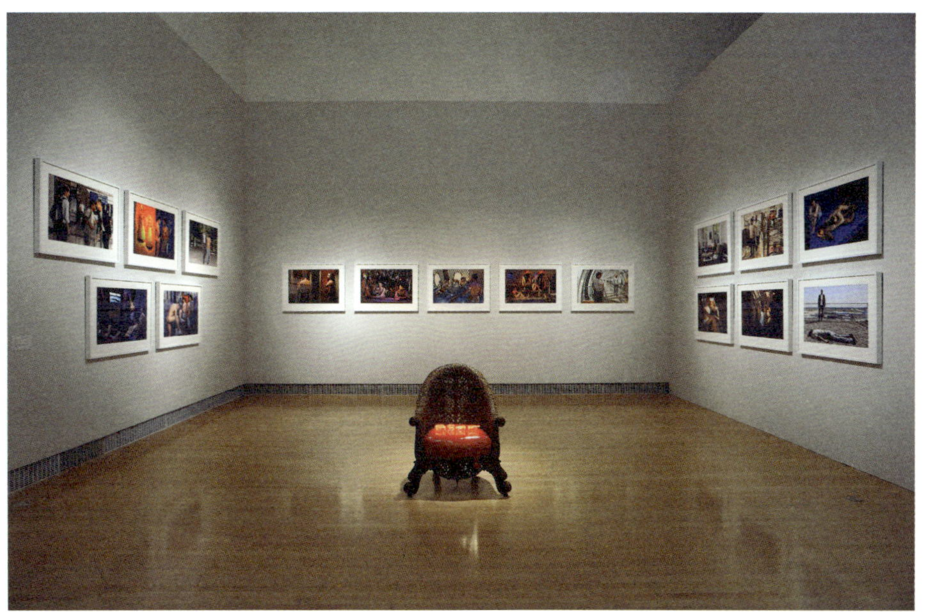

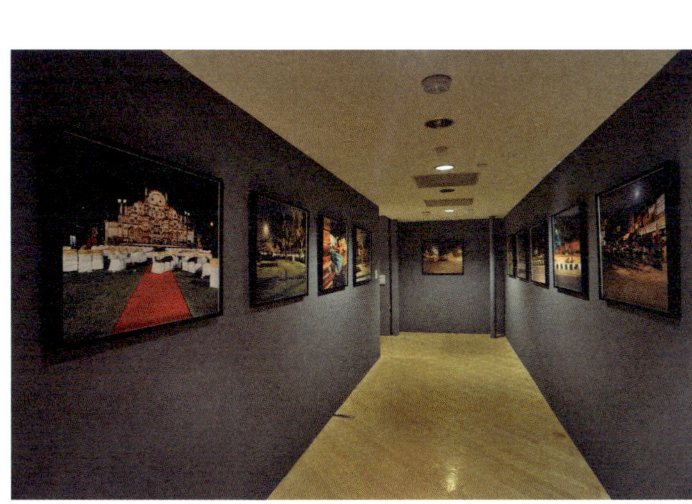

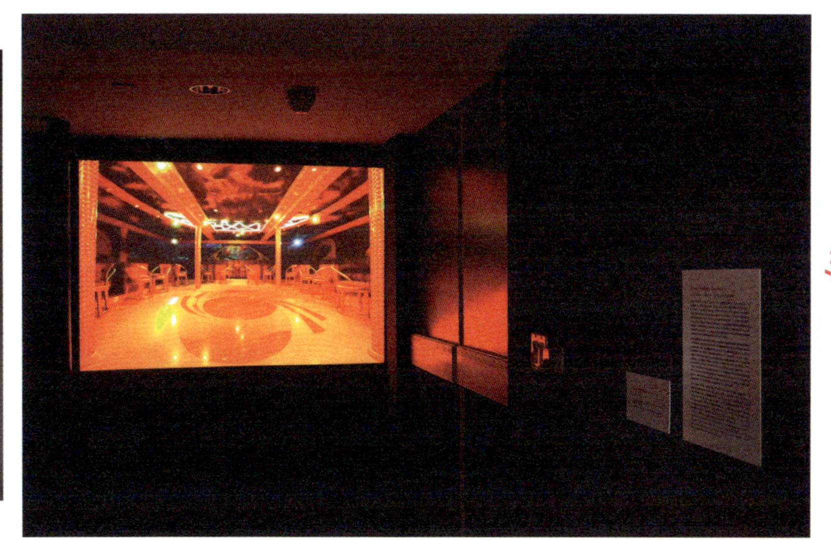

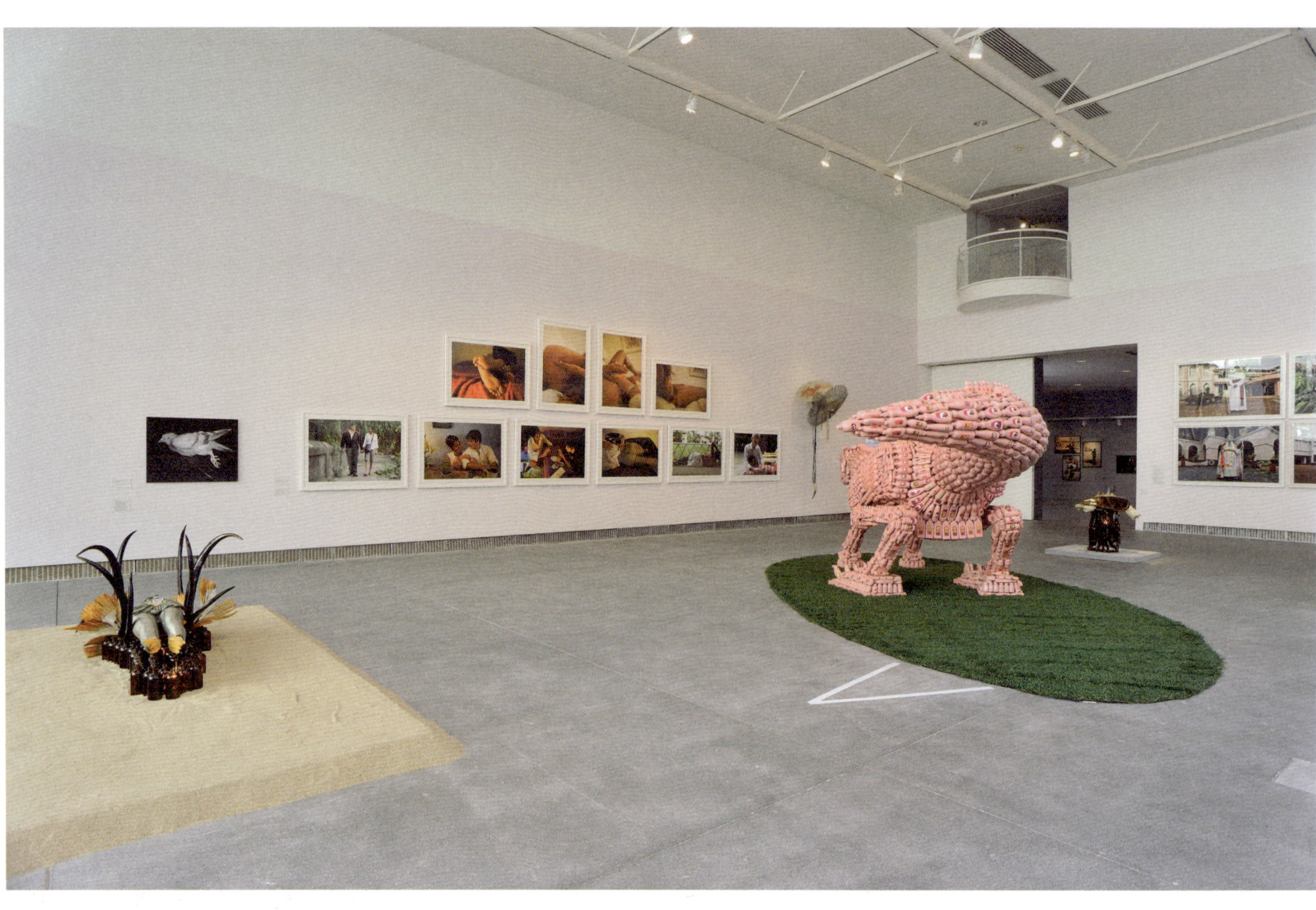

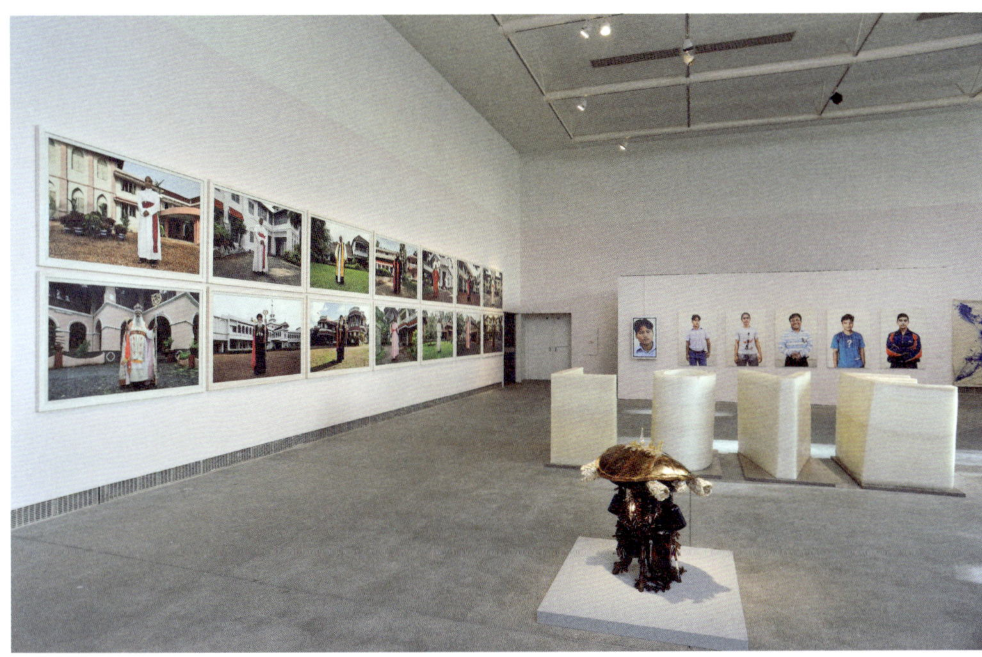

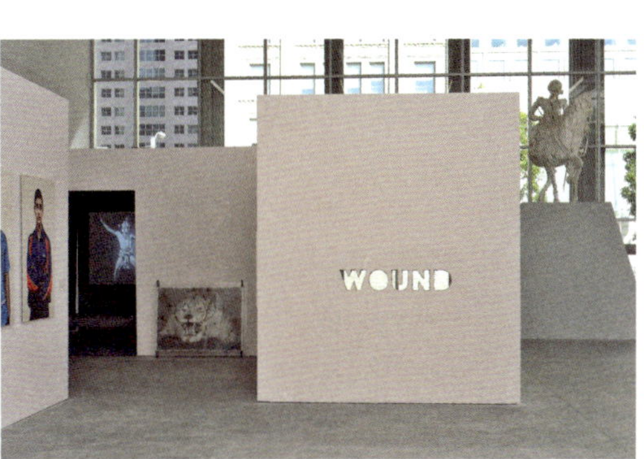
WOUND

EXHIBITION CHECKLIST

AYISHA ABRAHAM

I Saw a God Dance, 2011
Single-channel video with transferred Super-8 footage, color, sound, 20 min.; archival material courtesy Ashish Kokhar (The Mohan Kokhar Archive); music: Yashas Shetty; editing: Manasa Rao; dancers interviewed: Kumudini Lakhia, Mrinalini Sarabhai, Bhanumathi Rao, B. Saroja, and dance critic Sunil Kothari
Courtesy the artist; commissioned by Yerba Buena Center for the Arts

RINA BANERJEE

"a heart of two anchors take one bird and take one butcher, from ear to ear, its a familiar end she was with grin while meat and medicine poured, played yet with the poverty of country was a new friend so she withdrew her smile to clear one anchor that was not her faith the other was my mothers brother, enchanted china, giggled with Africa and strayed to stay in whips of lamb leather, feathers stained, shells that raised the last anchor human hate," 2011
Mosquito net, fish bone, umbrella, artificial horn, and pigeon feathers
Courtesy the artist and Haunch of Venison, New York

Lotions and potions like rivers where in quick motion, as well as essential oils and culture's notions, where these cultures would once be locked in harbor or empires court now took ride on the global, opened themselves up to mysterious and foreign incantations, 2011
300-year-old turtle shell, crystal, antique Victorian side table, amber glass bottles, and seashells
Edward Tyler Nahem Collection, New York

She drew a premature prick, in a fluster of transgressions, abject by birth she knew not what else to do with this untouchable reach, unknowable body as she was an ancient savage towed into his modern present, 2011
Female mannequin form (14-year-old tall girl), amber bottles, epoxy American buffalo horns, steel arm brace, Banarasi Indian wedding sari trim (silver, silk), Victorian replica doll head, Indian jewelry (22-karat-gold plated), glass magnifying dome, replica deer eye (glass), and Congo wooden elbow bangles (wood)
Courtesy the artist and Haunch of Venison, New York

Tender was her wound, pink and playful was her mood, 2011
Cowrie shells, silk cord, ostrich egg shell, wire, steel, glass, seashells, plastic, cotton thread, cultured and freshwater pearls, and feather fans
Courtesy the artist and Haunch of Venison, New York

CAMP

Al Jaar Qabla Al Daar (The Neighbor Before the House), 2009–11
Closed-circuit TV video, color, sound, 72 min.
Courtesy the artist

NIKHIL CHOPRA

Yog Raj Chitrakar: Memory Drawing IV, 2010
Digital photograph on archival paper; costumes: Tabasheer Zutshi; photography: Shivani Gupta
29 x 43 ½ in.
Courtesy the artist and Chatterjee & Lal, Mumbai

Yog Raj Chitrakar: Memory Drawing V (Part I), 2010
Video, color, sound, 9:28 min.; costumes: Tabasheer Zutshi; video: Lisa Cazzato-Vieyra, Serpentine Gallery, London
Courtesy the artist and Chatterjee & Lal, Mumbai

Yog Raj Chitrakar: Memory Drawing V (Part II), 2010
Digital photograph on archival paper; costumes: Tabasheer Zutshi; photography: Tina Lange
23 ½ x 35 ¼ in.
Courtesy the artist and Chatterjee & Lal, Mumbai

Yog Raj Chitrakar: Memory Drawing VI (16:00), 2010
Digital photograph on archival paper; costumes: Tabasheer Zutshi; photography: Shivani Gupta
37 x 28 x 3 in. (framed)
Courtesy the artist and Chatterjee & Lal, Mumbai

Yog Raj Chitrakar: Memory Drawing VI (17:30), 2010
Digital photograph on archival paper; costumes: Tabasheer Zutshi; photography: Shivani Gupta
43 ½ x 29 in.
Courtesy the artist and Chatterjee & Lal, Mumbai

Yog Raj Chitrakar: Memory Drawing VI (18:00), 2010
Digital photograph on archival paper; costumes: Tabasheer Zutshi; photography: Shivani Gupta
29 x 43 ½ in.
Courtesy the artist and Chatterjee & Lal, Mumbai

Yog Raj Chitrakar: Memory Drawing VIII (Day 18), 2010
Digital photograph on archival paper; costumes: Tabasheer Zutshi; photography: Tina Lange
23 ½ x 35 ¼ in.
Courtesy the artist and Chatterjee & Lal, Mumbai

Yog Raj Chitrakar: Memory Drawing IX (14:00), 2010
Digital photograph on archival paper; costumes: Loise Braganza; photography: Tina Lange
35 ¼ x 23 ½ in.
Courtesy the artist and Chatterjee & Lal, Mumbai

Yog Raj Chitrakar: Memory Drawing IX (17:00), 2010
Digital photograph on archival paper; costumes: Loise Braganza; photography: Tina Lange
35 ¼ x 23 ½ in.
Courtesy the artist and Chatterjee & Lal, Mumbai

Yog Raj Chitrakar: Memory Drawing X (Part I, 14:00), 2010
Digital photograph on archival paper; costumes: Loise Braganza; photography: Shivani Gupta
23 ½ x 35 ¼ in.
Courtesy the artist and Chatterjee & Lal, Mumbai

Yog Raj Chitrakar: Memory Drawing XI, 2010
Digital photograph on archival paper; costumes: Loise Braganza; photography: Nathan Keay, Museum of Contemporary Art, Chicago
35 ¼ x 23½ in.
Courtesy the artist and Chatterjee & Lal, Mumbai

ANITA DUBE

Wound, 2007
Drywall
Dimensions variable
Courtesy the artist and Bose Pacia, New York

Love, 2007–8
Wax candles
60 x 175 x 46 ½ in.
Courtesy the artist and Bose Pacia, New York

Void, 2007–8
Wax candles
60 x 175 x 46 ½ in.
Courtesy the artist and Bose Pacia, New York

GAURI GILL

Bacchu Khan at home, Barmer
14 x 11 in.

Bhana Nathji and Aancha Devi with Urma the year the camel died
11 x 14 in.

Bhana Nathji's home, Lunkaransar
14 x 11 in.

Boy bathing in Taalab, Baran
30 x 24 in.

Dai conference near Motasar
11 x 14 in.

Hanuman Nath with his daughter and Hem Nath, on Holi day, Lunkaransar
24 x 30 in.

Hurran, Barmer
14 x 11 in.

Ismat, Barmer
30 x 24 in.

Ismat's home, Barmer
30 x 24 in.

Jannat, Barmer
24 x 30 in.

Jogi home, Lunkaransar
30 x 40 in.

Jogi Panchayat near Dungargarh
11 x 14 in.

Jogiyon ka Dera, Lunkaransar
40 x 30 in.

Marwar ke Nath, Bikaner
11 x 14 in.

Mir Hasan with his grandfather Haji Saraj ud Din, oldest member of the community, in his last days, Barmer
14 x 11 in.

New homes after the flood, Lunkaransar
30 x 24 in.

Nimli and friend, Lunkaransar
30 x 24 in.

Sheila on her wedding day, Lunkaransar
40 x 30 in.

Sita Bhabhi on Holi, Lunkaransar
14 x 11 in.

Sushila with her family photographs, Osiyan
11 x 14 in.

Urma and Nimli, Lunkaransar
40 x 30 in.

All works from the series *Notes from the Desert*, 1999–2010
Gelatin silver prints
Courtesy the artist and Gallery Nature Morte, New Delhi

SHILPA GUPTA

Untitled (Sword), 2009
MS steel
93 ⅜ x 5 ¼ x 1 ⅙ in.
Kadist Art Foundation, San Francisco

SUNIL GUPTA

Untitled 1–10, from the series *Love, Undetectable*, 2009
Each 42 x 58 in. or 58 x 42 in. (framed)
Archival inkjet prints
Courtesy the artist and Vadehra Art Gallery, New Delhi

Untitled 1–16, from the series *Sun City*, 2010
Each 30 ⅛ x 40 ⅜ in. (framed)
Archival inkjet prints
Courtesy the artist and Vadehra Art Gallery, New Delhi

SIDDHARTHA KARARWAL

Hangover Man, 2011
Iron, cotton, wax
Sculpture: 120 x 36 x 84 in.; overall with base: 192 x 84 x 36 in.
Courtesy the artist

DHRUV MALHOTRA

Works from the series *Sleepers*, 2008–present
10 pigment prints
Each 23 ⅝ x 29 ½ in.
Courtesy the artist and Photoink, New Delhi

THE OTOLITH GROUP

Otolith III, 2009
High-definition video projection, color, sound, 48 min.
Courtesy the artists and LUX, London

SRESHTA RIT PREMNATH

Hide (01), 2010
Acrylic on canvas and screenprints on panel
Canvas: 89 x 60 in.; screenprints: each 29 ¹⁵⁄₁₆ x 29 ¹⁵⁄₁₆ in.
Courtesy the artist and GallerySKE, Bangalore

Hide (05), 2010
Acrylic on canvas and screenprints on panel
Canvas: 89 x 60 in.; screenprints: each 29 ¹⁵⁄₁₆ x 29 ¹⁵⁄₁₆ in.
Courtesy the artist and GallerySKE, Bangalore

Mask, 2011
Burnt photocopies on paper, Plexiglas, metal clamps
42 x 54 x 7 in.
Courtesy the artist and GallerySKE, Bangalore; commissioned by Yerba Buena Center for the Arts

PUSHPAMALA N. (WITH CLARE ARNI)

The Native Types—Circus (after a *Famous Circus* black-and-white photograph by Mary Ellen Mark), 2001
Chromogenic print on metallic paper
20 x 24 in.
Courtesy the artist and Bose Pacia, New York

The Native Types—Cracking the Whip (after a 1970s Tamil film still of Jayalalitha), 2001
Chromogenic print on metallic paper
24 x 20 in.
Courtesy the artist and Bose Pacia, New York

The Native Types—Criminals (after a police photograph, *Times of India*, Bangalore), 2001
Gelatin silver print
20 x 24 in.
Courtesy the artist and Bose Pacia, New York

The Native Types—Flirting (after a 1990s Kannada film still), 2001
Chromogenic print on metallic paper
24 x 20 in.
Courtesy the artist and Bose Pacia, New York

The Native Types—Lady in Moonlight (after a Raja Ravi Varma oil painting), 2001
Chromogenic print on metallic paper
24 x 20 in.
Courtesy the artist and Bose Pacia, New York

The Native Types—Lakshmi (after an oleograph from Ravi Varma Press, early 20th century), 2001
Chromogenic print on metallic paper
24 x 20 in.
Courtesy the artist and Bose Pacia, New York

The Native Types—Our Lady of Velankanni (after a contemporary votive image), 2001
Gelatin silver print
24 x 20 in.
Courtesy the artist and Bose Pacia, New York

The Native Types—Returning from the Tank (after an oil painting by Raja Ravi Varma), 2001
Chromogenic print on metallic paper
24 x 20 in.
Courtesy the artist and Bose Pacia, New York

The Native Types—Toda (after a late-19th-century British anthropometric photograph), 2001
Gelatin silver print
24 x 20 in.
Courtesy the artist and Bose Pacia, New York

The Native Types—Yogini (after a 16th-century Deccani painting), 2001
Chromogenic print on metallic paper
24 x 20 in.
Courtesy the artist and Bose Pacia, New York

RAQS MEDIA COLLECTIVE

The Surface of Each Day Is a Different Planet, 2009
Single-channel video projection, color, sound, 38 min.
Courtesy the artist and Frith Street Gallery, London

TEJAL SHAH

I AM, 2009
Digital slideshow
Courtesy the artist and Project 88, Mumbai

Women Like Us (1–5), 2010
Digital photographs on archival paper
Each 52 x 35 in.
Courtesy the artist and Project 88, Mumbai

TEJAL SHAH AND VARSHA NAIR

Encounter(s) I–VI, 2006
Each 16 x 24 in.
Digital photographs on archival paper
Courtesy the artist and Project 88, Mumbai

Encounter(s) VII, 2006
32 x 48 in.
Digital photograph on archival paper
Courtesy the artist and Project 88, Mumbai

SUDARSHAN SHETTY

Untitled from the series *Saving Skin*, 2008
Rotating matka (earthen pot) and motorized rotational mechanism
19 ¹⁄₁₆ x 9 ¹³⁄₁₆ x 11 ¹³⁄₁₆ in.
Courtesy the artist and GallerySKE, Bangalore

Untitled from the series *Stab*, 2010
Wooden chair, paint, fiberglass, neon
38 ⅜ x 34 ¹¹⁄₁₆ x 38 ⅜ in.
Courtesy the artist and GallerySKE, Bangalore

Untitled from the series *this too shall pass*, 2010
Gold leaf on fiberglass, milled steel, coin box, etched brass
Dimensions variable
Courtesy the artist and GallerySKE, Bangalore

BHARAT SIKKA

Broken Ash, 2010
Chromogenic print
31 ½ x 40 in.
Courtesy the artist and Nature Morte, New Delhi

Chintan, 2010
Chromogenic print
31 ½ x 40 in.
Courtesy the artist and Nature Morte, New Delhi

Flying Bird, 2010
Chromogenic print
40 x 50 in.
Courtesy the artist and Nature Morte, New Delhi

General, 2010
Chromogenic print
40 x 50 in.
Courtesy the artist and Nature Morte, New Delhi

Krishna, 2010
Chromogenic print
40 x 50 in.
Courtesy the artist and Nature Morte, New Delhi

Moth, 2010
Chromogenic print
40 x 50 in.
Courtesy the artist and Nature Morte, New Delhi

Opening Ceremony, 2010
Chromogenic print
31 ½ x 40 in.
Courtesy the artist and Nature Morte, New Delhi

Pigeon, 2010
Poster
31 ½ x 40 in.
Courtesy the artist and Nature Morte, New Delhi

Pigeon, 2010
Chromogenic print
31 ½ x 40 in.
Courtesy the artist and Nature Morte, New Delhi

Sculpture, 2010
Chromogenic print
18 ½ x 23 ⅛ in.
Courtesy the artist and Nature Morte, New Delhi

Septic Tank, 2010
Chromogenic print
31 ½ x 40 in.
Courtesy the artist and Nature
Morte, New Delhi

Sonam, 2010
Chromogenic print
31 ½ x 40 in.
Courtesy the artist and Nature
Morte, New Delhi

The Kite, 2010
Chromogenic print
31 ½ x 40 in.
Courtesy the artist and Nature
Morte, New Delhi

The Shepherd, 2010
Chromogenic print
18 ½ x 23 ⅛ in.
Courtesy the artist and Nature
Morte, New Delhi

Untitled, 2010
Poster
40 x 40 in.
Courtesy the artist and Nature
Morte, New Delhi

Untitled, 2010
Poster
40 x 50 in.
Courtesy the artist and Nature
Morte, New Delhi

Untitled, 2010
Poster
40 x 50 in.
Courtesy the artist and Nature
Morte, New Delhi

Untitled, 2010
Poster
40 x 50 in.
Courtesy the artist and Nature
Morte, New Delhi

Untitled (dusty street with lone figures),
2010
Chromogenic print
31 ½ x 40 in.
Courtesy the artist and Nature
Morte, New Delhi

Untitled (landscape with mountains), 2010
Chromogenic print
8 ⅜ x 10 ⅛ in.
Courtesy the artist and Nature
Morte, New Delhi

Untitled (the kiss), 2010
Chromogenic print
8 ⅜ x 10 ⅛ in.
Courtesy the artist and Nature
Morte, New Delhi

ANUP MATHEW THOMAS
Light Life, 2005
Single-channel digital slideshow of
90 images
Courtesy the artist and GallerySKE,
Bangalore

*His Beatitude Baselios Thomas I, Catholicose
of the East and Metropolitan Trustee,
Jacobite Syrian Christian Church*

*His Beatitude Cyril Baseliose Catholicos,
Major Arch Bishop, Malankara Catholic
Church*

*His Grace Dr. Mar Aprem Metropolitan,
Chaldean Syrian Church of the East*

*His Grace Mor Severios Kuriakose
Edavazhickal, Metropolitan of the Kananaya
Syrian Diocese, Kananaya Syrian Orthodox
Church*

*His Grace Most Rev. Dr. Philipose Mar
Chrysostam, Mar Thoma Metropolitan,
Malankara Mar Thoma Syrian Church*

*His Holiness Baselios Marthoma Didymus I,
Catholicose of the Apostolic Throne of
St. Thomas and Malankara Metropolitan,
Malankara Orthodox Syrian Church*

*Major Arch Bishop Mar Varkey Cardinal
Vithayathil, Syro Malabar Church*

*Mar Mathew Moolakkat, Archbishop
Kottayam Archdiocese, Kananaya Catholic
Church*

*Most Rev. Cyril Mar Baselius Metropolitan,
Supreme Head and Permanent Trustee,
Malabar Independent Syrian Church*

*Most Rev. Dr. Daniel Acharuparambil,
Metropolitan Archbishop, Latin Catholic
Church*

*Most Rev. Dr. K. P. Yohannan, Metropolitan
of Believers Church, Believers Church of India*

*Most Rev. Dr. Stephen Vattappara,
Metropolitan ACI, Anglican Church of India*

*Most Rev. Dr. T. C. Cherian, Presiding Bishop,
St. Thomas Evangelical Church of India*

*Rt. Rev. Thomas Samuel, Bishop Madhya
Kerala Diocese, Church of South India*

All works from the series *Metropolitan*,
2006
Archival inkjet prints
Each 43 ⅛ x 64 ⅛ in.
The Lekha & Anupam Poddar
Collection, New Delhi

THUKRAL & TAGRA
Artificial Strawberry Flavor—1, 2008
Corian cabinet, fiberglass bottles,
oil, acrylic
80 x 54 x 18 in.
Courtesy the artists, New York

Now in Your Neighborhood, 2008
Resin and decals on fiberglass bottles
with metal structure
88 x 84 x 360 in.
Harris C. Legome Collection,
Philadelphia

SELECTED BIBLIOGRAPHY

Anita Dube: Illegal. exh. cat., New York:
Bose Pacia Gallery, 2004.

*Ashok Sukumaran: Glow Positioning System
and Other Forms of Address*. exh. cat.,
New York: Thomas Erben Gallery,
2008.

Behr, Monique. *Raqs Media Collective:
The KD Vyas Correspondence: Vol. 1*.
exh. cat., Frankfurt: Museum für
Kommunikation, 2007.

*Being Singular Plural: Moving Images
from India*. exh. cat., New York:
Guggenheim Museum, 2010.

Chalo! India: A New Era of Indian Art. New
York: Prestel, 2009.

Daulet-Singh, Devika. "An Idea of
India." *OjodePez* no. 19, 2010.

Dehejia, Vidya, ed.. *Representing
the Body: Gender Issues in Indian Art*.
New Delhi: Kali for Women,
1997.

Edge of Desire: Recent Art in India. exh.
cat., London: Philip Wilson, 2005.

Gupta, Sunil. *CLICK! Contemporary
Photography in India*. New Delhi:
Vadehra Art Gallery, 2008.

Gupta, Sunil. *Disrupted Borders: An
Intervention in Definitions of Boundaries*.
London: Rivers Oram Press, 1994.

Gupta, Sunil. *Wish You Were Here:
Memories of a Gay Life*. New Delhi: Yoda
Press, 2008.

*Hanging Fire: Contemporary Art from
Pakistan*. exh. cat., New York: Asia
Society, 2009.

*Horn Please: Narratives in Contemporary
Indian Art*. exh. cat., Bern,
Switzerland: Kunstmuseum Bern,
2007.

Indian Highway. exh. cat., London:
Serpentine Gallery, 2010.

Indian Lady. exh. cat., New York: Bose
Pacia, 2004.

Kapur, Geeta. *When Was Modernism:
Essays on Contemporary Cultural
Practice in India*. New Delhi: Manohar,
2000.

Lee, Pamela. "How to Be a Collective
in the Age of the Consumer
Sovereign," *Artforum*, October 2009.

Narula, Monica, Shuddhabrata
Sengupta, Jeebesh Bagchi, and
Ravi Sundaram, eds. *Sarai Reader 07:
Frontiers*. Delhi: Centre for the Study
of Developing Societies, 2007.

*Native Women of South India: Manners
and Customs*. exh. cat., New Delhi:
Nature Morte; New York: Bose Pacia,
2006.

Nikhil Chopra: Yog Raj Chitrakar. exh. cat., Mumbai: Chatterjee & Lal, 2010.

Paris-Delhi-Bombay. exh. cat., Paris: Centre Georges Pompidou, 2011.

Pictures from Here: Sunil Gupta. London: Autograph/Chris Boot, 2003.

Pushpamala N.: Indian Lady. exh. cat., New York: Bose Pacia Gallery, 2004.

Raqib Shaw / Rina Banerjee. exh. cat., London: Thomas Gibson Fine Art Ltd., 2009.

Raqs Media Collective, ed. Double Take: Looking at the Documentary. New Delhi: PSBT in collaboration with Foundation for Universal Responsibility of H. H. the Dalai Lama, 1999.

Raqs Media Collective: Seepage. Berlin and New York: Sternberg Press, 2010.

Raqs Media Collective: The Impostor in the Waiting Room. exh. cat., New Delhi: Bose Pacia, 2004.

Sinha, Gayatri, and Paul Sternberger. India: Public Places Private Spaces: Contemporary Photography and Video Art. Newark, New Jersey: The Newark Museum, 2007.

Sood, Pooja, ed. The Khoj Book of Contemporary Indian Art: 1997–2007. Noida, India: HarperCollins, 2010.

Srivatsan, R. Conditions of Visibility: Writings on Photography in Contemporary India. Kolkata: STREE, 2000.

Sudarshan Shetty: this too shall pass. exh. cat., Mumbai: Dr. Bhau Daji Lad Museum, 2010.

Sunil Gupta: Queer. New York: Prestel, 2011.

Tejal Shah: What Are You? exh. cat., Mumbai: Galerie Mirchandani + Steinruecke, 2006.

The Audience and the Eavesdropper: New Art from India & Pakistan. auction cat., London: Phillips de Pury & Co., 2008.

The Self and the Other: Portraitures in Contemporary Indian Photography. exh. cat., Vitoria-Gasteiz, Spain: ARTIUM, 2009.

Where Three Dreams Cross: 150 Years of Photography from India, Pakistan, and Bangladesh. exh. cat., Göttingen, Germany: Steidl, 2010.

ARTIST BIOGRAPHIES

AYISHA ABRAHAM

Ayisha Abraham was born in 1963 in London and lives and works in Bangalore. She holds a BFA in painting from Maharaja Sayajirao University of Baroda, India (1987) and an MFA from Rutgers University (1995). In 1991 she participated in the Whitney Museum of American Art's Independent Study Program in New York. She has had several solo exhibitions in New York and India and has been exhibited in numerous group shows. In 2005 her film Straight 8 was screened at Ars Electronica, Linz, Austria, as part of the Srishti School of Art, Design, and Technology presentation. In 2005 she was an invited artist at the Khoj residency in Mumbai. Her short film One Way was screened at the Directors' Fortnight at the Cannes Film Festival in 2007. She is a member of the Bangalore artists' collective BAR1 and works as a visual arts consultant at Srishti School of Art, Design, and Technology in Bangalore.

RINA BANERJEE

Rina Banerjee is a multidisciplinary artist who was born in 1963 in Kolkata and is currently based in New York. Banerjee graduated from Case Western Reserve University in 1993 with a BS in polymer engineering, and in 1995 she completed an MFA at Yale University and won the Skowhegan-Yale Painting Scholarship. Banerjee's solo exhibitions have included Chimeras of India and the West at Musée Guimet, Paris (2011); Forever Foreign at Haunch of Venison, London (2010); and Look into my eyes and you will see a world unexplainable, out of place at Galerie Nathalie Obadia, Brussels (2009). Her group exhibitions have included What Is Sculpture at CRG Gallery, New York (2011); Wild Things at Kunsthallen Brandts, Odense, Denmark (2010); the 3rd Echigo-Tsumari Art Triennial, Japan (2006); and the Whitney Biennial at the Whitney Museum of American Art, New York (2000).

CAMP

CAMP was founded in 2007 by Shaina Anand and Ashok Sukumaran (with Sanjay Bhangar) as a collaborative project linking and discussing independent artistic and media projects across the city of Mumbai. Anand, born in 1975 in Mumbai, is a filmmaker and media artist who has been working independently in film and video since 1997. In 2001 she founded ChitraKarKhana, an independent project for experimental media. Anand has exhibited work at Khoj International Artists' Association, New Delhi; Ars Electronica, Linz; Frankfurter Kunstverein, Germany; the

Power Plant, Toronto; Serpentine Gallery, London; Gasworks, London; Cornerhouse, Manchester, England; and the biennales of Dakar, Senegal; Sharjah, United Arab Emirates; and Taipei, Taiwan. Sukumaran was born in Sapporo, Japan, in 1974. He studied architecture at the School of Planning and Architecture, New Delhi, in 1998, and then studied design at UCLA in 2003. His public projects, films, and installations have been shown widely and have received many awards, including the first prize of the UNESCO Digital Arts Award (2005), a Golden Nica at the Prix Ars Electronica (2007), and the Jury Prize at the 9th Sharjah Biennial (2009, as CAMP).

NIKHIL CHOPRA

Born in 1973 in Kolkata and now based in Mumbai, Nikhil Chopra works across theater, performance art, painting, photography, and sculpture. His fictional characters are influenced by India's colonial history as well as his own personal history. Chopra studied at Maharaja Sayajirao University of Baroda, India, from 1997 to 1999. He completed a BFA at the Maryland Institute College of Art in 2001, and an MFA in painting at Ohio State University in 2003. Chopra has presented his work in a number of solo exhibitions, including *Yog Raj Chitrakar: Memory Drawing X* at Chatterjee and Lal, Mumbai, and Dr. Bhau Daji Lad Museum, Mumbai (2010); *Yog Raj Chitrakar: Memory Drawing IX* at the New Museum, New York (2009); *Yog Raj Chitrakar: Memory Drawing V* at Serpentine Gallery, London (2008); *Yog Raj Chitrakar: Memory Drawing II* at Chatterjee and Lal, Mumbai (2007); *Sir Raja III* at the Fourth Floor, Kitab Mahal, Mumbai (2005); and *Sir Raja II* at Kinnear Warehouse, Columbus, Ohio (2003). Recent group shows include *Production Site: The Artist's Studio Inside-Out* at the Museum of Contemporary Art, Chicago (2010); *Marina Abramović Presents* at Whitworth Art Gallery, Manchester, England (2009); the 53rd Venice Biennale (2009); *Indian Highway* at Serpentine Gallery, London (2008); and *Time Crevasse* at the Yokohama International Triennial of Contemporary Art, Japan (2008).

ANITA DUBE

Anita Dube was born in 1958 in Lucknow, India, and lives and works in New Delhi. She graduated with honors with a BA in history from the University of New Delhi in 1979, and holds an MFA in art criticism from Maharaja Sayajirao University of Baroda, India. Dube has presented numerous solo exhibitions, including *Recent Works* at Bose Pacia, Brooklyn (2008); *Inside Out* at Bombay Art Gallery, Mumbai (2007); and *Phantoms of Liberty* at Almine Rech Gallery, Paris (2007). She has also participated in numerous group exhibitions, including

Paris-Delhi-Bombay at Centre Georges Pompidou, Paris (2011); *Conundrum* at Nature Morte, Berlin (2011); *Spiral Jetty* at Nature Morte, New Delhi (2010); *Beyond Globalization* at Beyond Art Space, Beijing (2009); and *Santhal Family Positions Around an Indian Sculpture* at Mukha Museum, Antwerp, the Netherlands (2008).

GAURI GILL

Gauri Gill was born in 1970 in Chandigarh, India, and currently lives and works in New Delhi. She holds BFAs from the New Delhi College of Art (1992) and Parsons The New School for Design (1994), and an MFA from Stanford University (2002). Gill's solo show *Notes from the Desert* was presented in 2010–11 at Nature Morte, New Delhi; Matthieu Foss Gallery, Mumbai; Focus Gallery, Chennai, India; and Urmul Setu, Lunkaransar, India. Her solo show *The Americans* was presented in 2008–11 at Nature Morte, New Delhi; Thomas Welton Art Gallery, Stanford University, Palo Alto, California; the Chicago Cultural Center; Bose Pacia, Kolkata and New York; and Mississauga Central Library, Ontario, Canada. In 2001 she presented the solo exhibition *What Remains* at Green Cardamom Gallery, London. She has had two-person shows with Tomoko Yoneda at Lucy Mackintosh Gallery, Lausanne, Switzerland (2009) and with Sunil Gupta at India International Center, New Delhi (2007). Her recent group exhibitions include *USA Today: After Katrina* at the Institut d'art Contemporain, Villeurbanne, France (2010); *Where Three Dreams Cross: 150 Years of Photography from India, Pakistan, and Bangladesh* at Whitechapel Gallery, London, and Fotomuseum Winterthur, Zurich (2010); *The Self and the Other: Portraiture in Contemporary Indian Photography* at Palau de la Virreina, Barcelona (2009); *Shifting Shapes: Unstable Signs* at Yale Art Gallery, New Haven, Connecticut (2009); and *Public Places, Private Spaces* at the Newark Museum, New Jersey (2007).

SHILPA GUPTA

Shilpa Gupta was born in 1976 in Mumbai, where she currently lives and works. She graduated from the Sir Jamsetjee Jeejeebhoy School of Art, Mumbai, in 1997. Gupta has received the Transmediale Award (2004), the Sanskriti Prathisthan Award (2004), and the South Asian Visual Artists Collective's International Artist of the Year award (2004), and she was a runner-up for the Leonardo Global Crossings Award (2005). Gupta's work has been shown in numerous solo exhibitions, including *Shilpa Gupta* at Fonderie Darling, Montreal (2011); *A Bit Closer* at the Contemporary Arts Center, Cincinnati (2010); *Half a Sky* at OK Offenes Kulturhaus OÖ, Linz, Austria (2010); and *While I Sleep* at Le Laboratoire, Paris (2009). Gupta has participated in the group

exhibitions *Last Ride in a Hot Air Balloon* at the 4th Auckland Triennial, New Zealand (2010); *Contemplating the Void: Interventions in the Guggenheim Rotunda* at the Solomon R. Guggenheim Museum, New York (2010); *Asia in Motion: Video Art and Beyond* at the Fukuoka Asian Art Museum, Japan (2010); *Younger Than Jesus* at the New Museum, New York (2009); *Everyday Miracles* at the 10th Biennale de Lyon, France (2009); the 3rd Yokohama International Triennial of Contemporary Art, Japan (2008); the 7th Gwangju Biennale, South Korea (2008); and *Indian Highway* at Serpentine Gallery, London (2008).

SUNIL GUPTA

Sunil Gupta was born in 1953 in New Delhi and lives and works in London and New Delhi. After attending college in Montreal, he moved to England to study photography at West Surrey College of Art & Design. He received an MFA from the Royal College of Art, London, in 1983. Gupta has presented numerous solo exhibitions, most recently *The New Pre-Raphaelites* at Grosvenor Gallery, London (2010); *Love, Undetectable* at Vadehra Art Gallery, New Delhi (2009); *Imagining Childhood* at Sepia, New York (2009); *Mr. Malhotra's Party* at Stephen Bulger Gallery, Toronto (2009); and *Homelands and Tales of a City* at Belfast Exposed, Ireland (2007). Gupta's work has been in the recent group exhibitions *Self and the Other* at Palau de la Virreina, Barcelona (2009); *En todas as partes (Everywhere)* at Centro Galego de Arte Contemporánea, Santiago de Compostela, Spain (2009); *Sh(OUT)* at the Gallery of Modern Art, Glasgow, Scotland (2009); *Make Art / Stop AIDS* at the Fowler Museum at the University of California, Los Angeles (2008); and *Street & Studio* at Tate Modern, London (2008).

SIDDHARTHA KARARWAL

Siddhartha Kararwal was born in 1984 in New Delhi and currently lives and works in Vadodra, India. He completed his BVA in 2006 and his MVA in 2009 at Maharaja Sayajirao University of Baroda. Kararwal received the Best Display award from Maharaja Sayajirao University in 2009, and he was a The Foundation for Indian Contemporary Art award runner-up in 2010. He completed a Bangalore Artist Residency, funded by India Foundation for the Arts, in 2010, and had a residency at Kashi Art Gallery in Kochi, India, in 2009. Kararwal has participated in the group exhibitions *Urban Testimonies and Size Matters . . . Or Does It?* at Latitude 28, New Delhi (2010); *Sakshi?* at Lalit Kala Akademi, New Delhi (2010); and *First Look* at Project 88, Mumbai (2009).

DHRUV MALHOTRA

Dhruv Malhotra was born in 1985 and grew up in Jaipur, India; he is currently based in New Delhi. He

graduated from Mumbai University in 2006. His work focuses on urban areas and engages with issues of progress, modernity, and the otherworldly. Malhotra's photographs were included in a group exhibition at the Festival International de Mode et de Photographie à Hyères, France, in 2010, where he was awarded a residency by the School of Visual Arts in New York. His first body of work, *Noida Soliloquy*, was exhibited at Photoink, New Delhi, in 2010. Photographs from his subsequent body of work, *Sleepers*, were included in the exhibition *New Ways of Looking* at the 2010 Brighton Photo Biennial in England.

THE OTOLITH GROUP

Founded in 2002 by Anjalika Sagar and Kodwo Eshun, the Otolith Group is a London-based, artist-led collective and organization that integrates film and video making, writing, workshops, exhibition curating, publishing, and the development of public platforms for close readings of the image in contemporary society. It has held events, presentations, and screenings at numerous international venues, in addition to curating and co-curating a number of exhibitions. Otolith has presented the solo exhibitions *A Lure a Part Allure Apart* at Bétonsalon, Paris (2011); *Thoughtform* at Museu d'Art Contemporani de Barcelona (MACBA) (2011); *In The Year 2103* at Experimenter, Kolkata, and Seven Arts, New Delhi (2010–11); and *A Long Time Between Suns* at Gasworks, London (2009). Otolith has participated in group exhibitions recently at the 11th Biennale de Lyon, France (2011); Alias Survey, Krakow, Poland (2011); and the Bucharest Biennale 4 in Romania (2010). They were among the shortlisted finalists for the Turner Prize in 2010 and participated in the Turner Prize exhibition that year at Tate Britain, London.

SRESHTA RIT PREMNATH

Born in 1979 in Bangalore and currently based in New York, Sreshta Rit Premnath is an interdisciplinary artist as well as the founder and editor of *Shifter* magazine. Premnath completed his BFA at the Cleveland Institute of Art in 2003 and his MFA at Bard College in 2006, and he attended the Whitney Independent Study Program in 2008. He has received the Art Matters Foundation Grant (2011), the Civitella Ranieri Foundation Fellowship (2011), and the Cleveland Institute of Art's Third Agnes Gund Award (2003). Premnath's work has been presented in the solo exhibitions *Storeys End* at Galerie Nordenhake, Berlin (2011); *Rhizome* at Wave Hill, New York (2011); LEO (*procedures in search of an original index*) at GallerySKE, Bangalore (2010); *Zero Knot* at Art Statements, Art|41|Basel (2010); and *Black Box* at GallerySKE, Bangalore (2008). He has participated in the recent group exhibitions *Before and After* at Galerie Balice Hertling, Paris (2010); *Spectral Evidence* at 1a Space, Hong Kong (2010); *Other Than Beauty* at Friedman Benda, New York (2010); *A Perfect Human* at Dorsch Gallery, Miami (2009); and *Moment as Monument* at Thomas Erben Gallery, New York (2009). Premnath curated *On Certainty* at Bose Pacia, New York (2009) and maintains *Project for an Archive of the Future Anterior*, an online archive of video interviews.

PUSHPAMALA N.
Born in Bangalore in 1956, Pushpamala N. is now based in Bangalore and New Delhi. She works in video, photography, and installation art, and is also a writer, theorist, and curator. She holds a BA in economics, English, and psychology from Bangalore University (1977) and an MFA in sculpture from Maharaja Sayajirao University of Baroda (1985). She has received several awards, including the Karnataka Shilpa Kala Akademi Award (1998), the Karnataka Lalit Kala Akademi Silver Jubilee Award (1988), and the Karnataka Rajyothsava Award (1986). Her work has been shown at numerous exhibitions, biennials, and festivals; recent venues have included Nature Morte, New Delhi (2008); Bose Pacia, New York (2008); Mori Art Museum, Tokyo (2008); Saatchi Gallery, London (2008); Tate Modern, London (2006); and École Nationale Supérieure des Beaux-Arts, Paris (2005). Her work is in several major collections, including those of the National Gallery of Modern Art, New Delhi; Centre Georges Pompidou, Paris; the National Gallery of Australia, Canberra; and Saatchi & Saatchi, London.

RAQS MEDIA COLLECTIVE
Raqs Media Collective (Jeebesh Bagchi, Monica Narula, and Shuddhabrata Sengupta), founded in 1992 and based in New Delhi, is a group of artists, media practitioners, curators, researchers, editors, and catalysts of cultural processes. Their work, which has been exhibited widely in major international spaces and events, may take the form of installations, online and offline media objects, performances, and encounters. Recent solo exhibitions include *Surjection* at Art Gallery of York University, Toronto (2011); *Reading Light* at Festival d'Automne, Paris (2011); *The Capital of Accumulation* at Project 88, Mumbai (2010); *The Things That Happen When Falling in Love* at BALTIC Centre for Contemporary Art, Gateshead, England (2010); *The Surface of Each Day Is a Different Planet* at Tate Britain, London (2009); *When the Scales Fall from Your Eyes* at Ikon, Birmingham, England (2009); *Escapement* at Frith Street Gallery, London (2009); and *Decomposition* at Asia Art Archive, Hong Kong (2009). They have been part of the recent group exhibitions *Paris-Delhi-Bombay* at Centre Georges Pompidou, Paris (2011); *The New Décor* at Hayward Gallery, London (2010); *Indian Highway* at Serpentine Gallery, London (2008); the 29th São Paulo Biennial (2010); and the 8th Shanghai Biennale (2010).

TEJAL SHAH
Tejal Shah was born in 1979 in Bhilai, India. She is now based in Mumbai and works with video, photography, and installation, focusing on feminist, queer, and political issues. Shah holds a BA in photography from the Royal Melbourne Institute of Technology (2000) and an MFA from Bard College (2008). She has exhibited widely in museums, galleries, and film festivals. Her solo exhibitions have included *What Are You?* at Thomas Erben Gallery, New York, and Galerie Mirchandani + Steinruecke, Mumbai (2006) and *The Tomb of Democracy* at Alexander Ochs Gallery, Berlin (2003). Her group exhibitions have included the Asia Triennial Manchester (2008); *New Delhi New Wave* at Primo Marella Gallery, Milan (2007); *Global Feminisms* at the Brooklyn Museum's Elizabeth Sackler Center for Feminist Art (2007); *Saturday Live* at Tate Modern, London (2006); *Sub-Contingent* at Fondazione Sandretto Re Rebaudengo, Turin, Italy (2006); and *Indian Summer* at École Nationale Supérieure des Beaux Arts, Paris (2005). Her works are in the collection of the Centre Georges Pompidou, Paris. In 2003 Shah cofounded, organized, and curated Larzish, India's first international film festival devoted to sexuality and gender pluralities.

SUDARSHAN SHETTY
Sudarshan Shetty was born in 1961 in Mangalore, India, and currently lives and works in Mumbai. He graduated from the Sir Jamsetjee Jeejeebhoy School of Art, Mumbai, in 1985. He was a resident at the Mattress Factory, Pittsburgh, in 2007, and a Ford Foundation Fellow at the New School for General Studies, New York, in 2006. Shetty's recent solo exhibitions include *Between the tea cup and a sinking constellation* at Galerie Daniel Templon, Paris (2011); *this too shall pass* at Dr. Bhau Daji Lad Museum, Mumbai (2010); *The more I die the lighter I get* at Tilton Gallery, New York (2010); *Six Drops* at GallerySKE, Bangalore (2009); and *Leaving Home* at Gallery Krinzinger, Vienna (2008). Shetty has also participated in numerous group exhibitions, including *Paris-Delhi-Bombay* at Centre Georges Pompidou, Paris (2011); *Indian Highway IV* at the Musée d'art contemporain de Lyon, France (2011); *Against All Odds* at Lalit Kala Akademi, New Delhi (2011); *Contemplating the Void* at the Solomon R. Guggenheim Museum, New York (2010); *Looking Glass: The Existence of Difference* at Religare Art, New Delhi

(2010); and *India Contemporary* at the Gemeentemuseum Den Haag, the Netherlands (2009).

BHARAT SIKKA
Bharat Sikka was born in 1973 in India and is currently based in New Delhi. He worked as a photographer in India before enrolling at the Parsons The New School for Design in New York, where he earned a BFA in photography in 2002. Sikka has shown his work in the solo exhibitions *Matter* at Nature Morte, Berlin (2011); *The Road to Salvador do Mundo* at Sunaparanta Goa Centre for the Arts, Panaji, India (2010); *Fashion Images* at Weiden + Kennedy, New Delhi (2009); *Indian Men* at Otto Zoo, Milan (2008); and *Space In Between* at the National Museum, New Delhi (2008) and Bose Pacia, Kolkata (2007). His group exhibitions have included *Concurrent India* at the Helsinki Art Museum, Finland, and Kulturhuset, Stockholm (2011); *Where Three Dreams Cross: 150 Years of Photography from India, Pakistan, and Bangladesh* at Whitechapel Gallery, London, and Fotomuseum Winterthur, Zurich (2010); *Il Giallo di Napoli* at Castel dell'Ovo, Naples, Italy (2009); *India Moderna* at Instituto Valenciano de Arte Moderno (IVAM), Valencia, Spain (2009); *India 3: New Delhi Republic of Illusions* at Krinzinger Projekte, Vienna (2009); *Tarn et Garonne: Landscapes and Portraits* at Place des Invalides, Paris (2008); and the Prague Biennial (2003). Sikka's photographs have appeared in many magazines and publications, including the *New Yorker*, *I.D.*, *Vogue*, *Vogue Hommes International*, and *Details*. *Time* magazine featured his work as among the Best Photographs of 2005.

ANUP MATHEW THOMAS
Born in 1977 in Kochi, India, Anup Mathew Thomas graduated from Srishti School of Art, Design, and Technology in Bangalore in 2003. He is currently based in Bangalore and Kottayam, India, where he works in photography to explore questions of institutionalization, identity, and representation. Thomas has participated in three international artist residencies: Khoj, Mumbai (2005); VASL, Lahore (2006); and Gasworks, London (2006). His recent solo shows include *Anup Mathew Thomas* at Contemporary Image Collective, Cairo (2010); *View from Conolly's Plot* at GallerySKE, Bangalore (2010); *Assembly* at GallerySKE, Bangalore, and Kashi Art Gallery, Cochin, India (2008); *Metropolitan* at Gasworks Gallery, London (2007); and *Recent Works* at GallerySKE, Bangalore (2007). He has been in the recent group shows *Notes on the (Dis)Appearance of Real* presented by Shrine Empire Gallery at Stainless Gallery, New Delhi (2010); *Docu Tour* at Gallery BMB, Mumbai (2010); *The Self and Other* at Centro Museo Vasco de Arte Contemporáneo (ARTIUM), Vitoria-Gasteiz, Spain (2009); *Lapdogs

of the Bourgeoisie* at Arnolfini, Bristol, England (2009); and *Reflections of Contemporary India* at La Casa Encendida, Madrid (2008).

THUKRAL & TAGRA
The New Delhi–based artists Jiten Thukral and Sumir Tagra work collaboratively as Thukral & Tagra in a wide variety of media, including painting, sculpture, installation, video, graphic design, product design, websites, music, and fashion. Thukral was born in 1976 in Jalandhar, India, and he holds a BFA from Chandigarh Art College (1998) and an MFA from New Delhi College of Art (2000). Tagra was born in 1979 in New Delhi; he attended Shankar's Academy of Arts, New Delhi, in 1999 and holds a BFA from New Delhi College of Art (2002) and a PG from the National Institute of Design, Ahmedabad, India (2006). Thukral & Tagra's solo exhibitions have included *Put It On, Again!* at Nature Morte, New Delhi (2011); *Thukral & Tagra Foundation* at Project Booth, Art Summit, New Delhi (2011); *Thukral & Tagra: Match Fixed* at Ullens Center for Contemporary Art, Beijing (2011); *Middle Class Dreams* at Arario Gallery, Seoul (2010); *Low-Tech Family Vacations* at Singapore Tyler Print Institute (2010); *Nouveau Riche* at Nature Morte, Berlin (2009); and *Thukral & Tagra* at Gallery Barry Keldoulis, Sydney (2009). They have also participated in the group exhibitions *Maximum India* at the Kennedy Center, Washington DC (2011); the 11th Biennale de Lyon (2011); *Concurrent India* at the Helsinki Art Museum, Finland (2011); and *Indian Highway IV* at the Musée d'art contemporain de Lyon, France (2011). Thukral & Tagra have received a number of awards, including "101 Emerging Designers of the World" in *Wallpaper* magazine's global edition (2006); the One Show Design award, New York (2004 and 2003); the *Graphis* International Award (2003); and the London International Award (2003).

CONTRIBUTOR BIOGRAPHIES

NANCY ADAJANIA

Nancy Adajania is a cultural theorist and independent curator. She is co-artistic director of the 9th Gwangju Biennale (2012). Adajania has written and lectured on transcultural art practices and on art and the public sphere at Documenta 11, Kassel, Germany; ZKM, Karlsruhe, Germany; Transmediale, Berlin; künstlerhaus, Vienna; and Gulbenkian Foundation, Lisbon; among other venues. From 2000 to 2002 she was editor-in-chief of *ART India*. She has proposed several new theoretical models, and her essays have appeared in numerous books and anthologies. Her publications include "Coomaraswamy to Ambedkar: Tracing the Vanished Horizons of the Vernacular in the Contemporary" in *Vernacular in the Contemporary: Part 2* (2011); "The Nth Field: The Horizon Reloaded" in *On Horizons: A Critical Reader in Contemporary Art* (2011); "New Media Overtures Before New Media Practice in India" in *Art and Visual Culture in India: 1857–2007* (2009); and "The Sand of the Coliseum, the Glare of the Television, and the Hope of Emancipation" in *Documenta Magazine No. 2 / Life!* (2007). Adajania was the editor of the monograph *Shilpa Gupta* (2010).

BETTI-SUE HERTZ

Since 2009 Betti-Sue Hertz has been director of visual arts at Yerba Buena Center for the Arts in San Francisco, where she has organized *The Matter Within: New Contemporary Art of India* (2011), *Song Dong: Dad and Mom, Don't Worry About Us, We Are All Well* (2011), *Audience as Subject* (2010 and 2012), *Renée Green: Endless Dreams and Time-Based Streams* (2010), and *Wallworks* (2009). From 2000 to 2008 she was curator of contemporary art at the San Diego Museum of Art, where she produced several major exhibitions and catalogues, including *Eleanor Antin: Historical Takes* (2008), *Animated Painting* (2007), *Transmission: The Art of Matta and Gordon Matta-Clark* (2006), *Past in Reverse: Contemporary Art of East Asia* (2004), for which she received the Emily Hall Tremaine Exhibition Award, and *Axis Mexico: Common Objects and Cosmopolitan Actions* (2002). Hertz has contributed to many periodicals, including *The Architect's Newspaper, Art Journal, Animation, Communication Arts, Flash Art, n.paradoxa*, and *Yishu*.

ZEHRA JUMABHOY

Zehra Jumabhoy is currently the Steven and Elena Heinz Scholar at the Courtauld Institute of Art. She is working on a PhD on subjects related to contemporary Indian art and postcolonial theory, supervised by professor Julian Stallabrass. She was assistant editor at *ART India* and continues to write for the magazine as its London correspondent. She also contributes regularly to *Artforum International*.

MAYA KÓVSKAYA

Texts on CAMP, Anita Dube, Sunil Gupta, Raqs Media Collective, Tejal Shah

Maya Kóvskaya is a New Delhi-based scholar, art critic, curator, and writer whose current research focuses on contemporary art and performative interventions in the public sphere in Asia. She has curated numerous international exhibitions, and her writings appear regularly in art magazines, academic journals, and books. She edited the book *China Under Construction: Contemporary Art from the People's Republic* (2007). She has taught at the university level in the United States and China; she worked and researched in China for fifteen years. She has received many academic honors and awards, including the inaugural *Yishu Award for Critical Writing on Contemporary Chinese Art* in 2010. Kóvskaya received her PhD from the University of California, Berkeley in 2009.

THIEN LAM

Texts on Gauri Gill, Shilpa Gupta, The Otolith Group, Anup Mathew Thomas

Thien Lam is the visual arts curatorial assistant at Yerba Buena Center for the Arts in San Francisco. She has also held positions at the San Jose Museum of Art and the San Francisco Arts Commission. For Yerba Buena Center for the Arts she has organized the exhibitions *John-Mark Ikeda: What Suits Us* (2012), *castaneda/reiman: Portrait of the Ground* (2011), and *Katya Bonnenfant: La Destitution de la jeune fille* (The Deposition of the Young Girl, 2010). For the San Jose Museum of Art she organized *Brice Marden: 12 Views for Caroline Tatyana* (2007) and *Kathy Aoki: The Cult of the Cute* (2006). She holds a master's degree from the Courtauld Institute of Art and a bachelor's degree from Williams College.

GEORGINA MADDOX

Texts on Siddhartha Kararwal, Dhruv Malhotra, Sreshta Rit Premnath, Sudarshan Shetty, Bharat Sikka

Georgina Maddox is interested in art practices that examine issues of gender, sexuality, marginalization, social hierarchy, and acts of agency and defiance. Her writings have appeared in *ART India, Take on Art, Art and Deal, Biblio*, and the *Indian Contemporary Art Journal*. She is currently working with the India Today Group as a senior assistant editor, and she has worked with the *Indian Express*, the *Times of India, Art India*, and *ARTnews*. She has made two independent short films, *Bombay Longing* (2001) and *No Fixed Address Too* (2004), and has curated several

MAYA KÓVSKAYA

exhibitions, including *Medium Movement and Metaphor* at NIV Art Center, Delhi (2011); *Super Power* at Gallery Threshold, New Delhi (2010); and *Pixel Power* at the Loft, Mumbai (2009). She has collaborated on video art projects with the artists Tejal Shah and Navjot Altaf, and on street art projects in Mumbai with the collectives Open Circle and Art Oxygen. She holds a degree in art history from Maharaja Sayajirao University of Baroda and a post diploma in mass communication from Sophia Polytechnic in Mumbai. She lived in Mumbai for ten years and currently lives and works in New Delhi.

PARUL DAVE MUKHERJI

Parul Dave Mukherji is a professor and dean of the School of Arts and Aesthetics, Jawaharlal Nehru University, New Delhi. She holds a PhD from Oxford University. She has lectured in India, Europe, the United States, Australia, China, and Japan. She coedited *Towards a New Art History: Studies in Indian Art* (2003); she guest-edited a special issue on visual culture for the *Journal of Contemporary Thought* (summer 2003); and she is a coeditor of Sage's forthcoming book *InFlux: Contemporary Art in Asia*. Her current research focuses on globalization and art theory, contemporary Asian art, and comparative aesthetics.

SAMIRA RAHMATULLAH

Texts on Ayisha Abraham, Rina Banerjee, Nikhil Chopra, Pushpamala N., Thukral & Tagra

Samira Rahmatullah is the founder of Alluvial Arts, an organization dedicated to promoting Bangladeshi contemporary art in the San Francisco Bay Area. Previously she was a consultant at FSG, a strategy consulting firm for the social sector, where she conducted program strategy development and performance evaluations for foundations and corporations. Before that Rahmatullah was an investment banker in JP Morgan's Tax-Exempt Capital Markets group, where she helped develop debt and derivative-based financing solutions for the capital projects of government authorities and nonprofit organizations. She is on the board of directors of Yerba Buena Center for the Arts and is also on the board of directors of Refugee Transitions, a nonprofit organization that helps refugees resettled in the Bay Area develop English language, life, and job skills necessary to become self-sufficient. She holds an MBA from Stanford's Graduate School of Business and a bachelor's degree from Barnard College, Columbia University.

The Matter Within: New Contemporary Art of India
October 15, 2011–January 29, 2012

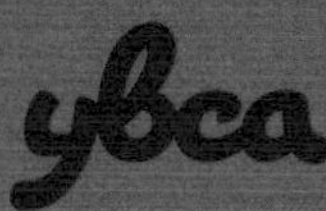

Yerba Buena Center for the Arts
701 Mission Street
San Francisco, CA 94103-3138
415-978-ARTS
www.ybca.org

The Matter Within: New Contemporary Art of India is supported, in part, by Rena Bransten, Peter and Leela De Souza Bransten, Samira Rahmatullah and Munir Alam, Priya H. Kamani, Sanjeev & Kathy Malaney, Rekha Patel; Grosvenor, Raj and Krutika Patel, Girish Satya and Purvi Sangani, Sheila and Ketan Kothari, Rajnikant T. and Helen C. Desai, Christopher Stafford and Eduardo Barbosa, Diana Cohn and Craig Merrilees, Berit Ashla and Aron Cramer, Brooke and Steve Waterhouse, Sabrina Riddle, Petra Schumann and Rob Wullenjohn, Ashish and Namrata Gupta, and Monica and Steve Henderson.

This exhibition is made possible, in part, through the generous support of the Asian Cultural Council.

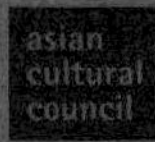

Media sponsor: *SF Weekly*

YBCA Exhibitions 11-12 are made possible, in part, by Mike Wilkins and Sheila Duignan, Meridee Moore and Kevin King, and Members of Yerba Buena Center for the Arts.

YBCA 11-12 programs are made possible, in part, by Abundance Foundation, Adobe, Hewlett-Packard, Koret Foundation, and Novellus Systems.

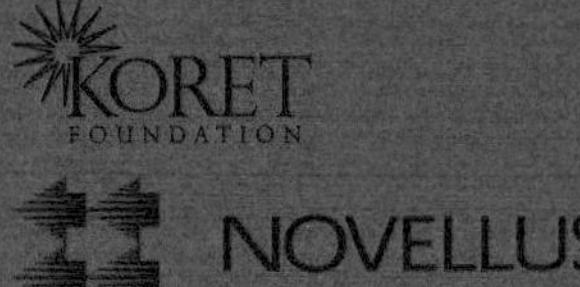

Yerba Buena Center for the Arts is grateful to the San Francisco Redevelopment Agency for its ongoing support.

ABOUT YERBA BUENA CENTER FOR THE ARTS

Founded in 1993 out of an expressed need for an accessible, high profile arts center devoted to contemporary art of all genres, YBCA presents contemporary art from the Bay Area and around the world that reflects the profound issues and ideas of our time, expands the boundaries of artistic practice, and celebrates the diversity of human experience and expression. YBCA is an integrated site for creative endeavor; a unique fusion of art, innovation, and ideas in a social environment. It serves as a curated platform for the dynamic convergence of artists, inventors, thinkers, producers, and the community, working together to sustain multiple levels of participation, propel short- and long-term social change, and ensure that contemporary arts and living artists are vital to our society. YBCA's artistic offerings include a year-round exhibition program, two annual performance series, a celebrated year-round art film program, a community rentals program making YBCA performance spaces available to Bay Area performing arts organizations at affordable rates, and award-winning community engagement programming. Distinguished by its widespread support of local, national, and international artists in the performing, visual, and media arts, YBCA is also recognized for its innovative approach to audience-centered programs and for its partnerships with other arts and community organizations. YBCA selects Big Ideas around which to organize its wide-ranging programs. The current Big Ideas include: ENCOUNTER: Engaging the social context, SOAR: The search for meaning; REFLECT: Considering the personal; and DARE: Innovations in art, action, audience. These ideas, which encompass art from all disciplines, are designed to focus investigations of contemporary art and its relationship to the larger world. Using the Big Ideas as portals, YBCA has established a framework of thought that invites exploration and risk taking, quiet reflection, and active engagement.

IMAGE CREDITS

pp. 29–30 (top): Courtesy Rina Banerjee and Haunch of Venison, New York

p. 30 (bottom): Courtesy Rina Banerjee and Edward Tyler Nahem Collection, New York

pp. 33–35, 37, 39, 41–43, 45–47, 49–51, 115–119: Phocasso/J.W. White

pp. 61–63, front cover: Courtesy Nikhil Chopra and Chatterjee & Lal, Mumbai

pp. 65–67: Courtesy Gauri Gill and Gallery Nature Morte, New Delhi

pp. 69–71: Courtesy Sunil Gupta and Vadehra Art Gallery, New Delhi

pp. 73–75: Courtesy Dhruv Malhotra and PHOTOINK, New Delhi

pp. 77–79: Courtesy Pushpamala N. and Bose Pacia, NY

p. 81: Courtesy Tejal Shah and Project 88, Mumbai

pp. 82–83: Courtesy Tejal Shah and Varsha Nair and Project 88, Mumbai

pp. 85–87 , back cover: Courtesy Bharat Sikka and Gallery Nature Morte, New Delhi

pp. 89–90: Courtesy Anup Mathew Thomas and the Lekha & Anupam Poddar Collection

p. 91: Courtesy Anup Mathew Thomas and GallerySKE, Bangalore

pp. 103–5: Courtesy Ayisha Abraham

pp. 107–9: Courtesy CAMP

p. 111: Courtesy The Otolith Group

pp. 113–15: Courtesy Raqs Media Collective

Designed by
Stripe SF / Jon Sueda
with Megan Lynch

Copyedited by
Lindsey Westbrook

Printed by
Overseas Printing, Printed in China

ISBN
978-0-9826789-4-7

Library of Congress Control Number
2012935177

Available through
D.A.P. / Distributed Art Publishers, Inc.
155 Sixth Avenue, 2nd Floor
New York, NY 10013
Tel: (212) 627-1999
Fax: (212) 627-9484
www.artbook.com

Front cover image:
Nikhil Chopra
Yog Raj Chitrakar: Memory Drawing IV,
2010

Back cover image:
Bharat Sikka
Untitled (dusty street with lone figures),
2010